For Ray and Martha

To those whose paths I have not crossed, I am nobody.

To some, I am strong.

To most, I am ordinary.

Yet my life has been anything but ...

Ray of Sunshine

By mid-morning it was already a scorcher—the type of heat that shade can't fix. Still, I had taken the side streets through older neighborhoods where mature trees might provide relief from the sun. My ten-speed Schwinn protested with a clicking noise as I shifted into low gear, preparing for the hill up ahead. When I finally reached the home I worked out of, I tossed my bike on the front lawn and ran to the bathroom to throw up.

It was the summer of 1988, and the Midwest was in the worst drought since the "Dust Bowl" years in the mid-1930s. Minnesota seemed to be at the drought epicenter, its driest summer on record. The daily weather report was always the same: high humidity, record-breaking temps, and no relief in sight.

I should not have been out in the heat that day, much less on a bike, but my husband had been in an accident, totaling his pick-up truck. He had taken my car to work and wasn't home yet. Rather than risk being late, I had decided to bike the two miles to my job. Pregnant. In the heat. Cursing my husband the entire way. *We can't even coordinate our commute to work,* I thought. *How are we going to take care of a baby?*

For the past four months I had been trying to come to terms with my unexpected pregnancy. Rusty and I had only been married a short time, and we hadn't even talked about starting a family. To be honest, I wasn't even sure I liked children. What if mothers who said that you love your own more than anything had been lying this whole time?

Rusty had been patrolling the streets of St. Paul the day I found out I was pregnant. I had waited until after his shift to give him the news in person, but I rushed to tell my grandma.

1

She was dying of lung cancer. Much of her day was spent lying on the couch, oxygen running through a tube in her nose. I walked up to my grandparents' cedar shake rambler, a small corner house on the East Side of St. Paul. Grandpa greeted me with a hug. Grandma pushed herself up to a seated position on the couch, and with thin, frail arms, she reached for me. I took her hand in mine and shared the news. Tears streamed down her cheeks, and in a weakened voice she said, "I hope I'm still here."

"You will be." I smiled.

After my visit, Grandpa walked me out to my car. "You just gave Grandma a gift—a reason to keep going," he said. And with that, I felt less unsure about becoming a mother.

In the months that followed, the little life inside me grew, but Grandma's life was reaching its end. Each time I visited her, she would tell me, "I'm hanging on to see that little guy." Grandma was the only one who knew I was having a boy. At the very least, I wanted her to know a great-grandson was on the way, just in case.

On December 30, 1988, nearly seventeen hours after being induced, I finally went into labor. At one point, my doctor said, "The baby's starting to crown, and it's really dark."

Rusty shot me a look and said, "What do you mean the baby's *dark?*"

To be clear, I am a blonde Scandinavian and Rusty is a fair-skinned Irishman. My doctor quickly clarified. "The *hair*. The baby has dark *hair*." If I wasn't in so much pain, I might have laughed.

The second our adorable baby boy, with a full head of black hair, was placed in my arms, I instantly fell in love with him. I had no idea I could love someone so much. I'd never experienced that level of happiness before. I guess it is true: you love your own more than anything.

Later that evening my parents came to the hospital to see their first-born grandchild. My father, whom everyone called Buzz, myself included, couldn't get over his grandson's long hair. "This little guy already needs a haircut. It's over his ears."

"Don't you remember, Buzz?" Mom asked. "Darla had hair just like that."

Rusty sat at my bedside reading the newspaper while Mom held our baby. When he said he was looking through the obituaries to find a good name for our son, we all busted out laughing. "Well, they're dead now." Rusty shrugged. "They're not using the name anymore."

After my parents left, I asked Rusty to set the newspaper down. "Listen, I was thinking about something my grandma said when I told her I was pregnant. She said that she hoped she would still be here to see our baby. What do you think of the name Ray? You know, like a ray of hope."

"You might be on to something."

"Would we give him a formal name like Raymond? Call him Ray for short?"

"No, just Ray. If he's not real bright," Rusty joked, "he will only have three letters to learn to write his name."

"You're insane." I laughed. "What about a middle name?"

"How about Lewis? Same as mine?" Rusty asked.

"Ray Lewis. Ray Lewis Garvey." I tried it out. "I like it."

A few days after leaving the hospital I brought Ray to my grandparents' house for his debut. Grandma's eyes lit up as I placed Ray in her arms. "I've been waiting to meet you," she said to her great-grandson.

I sat close by on the couch, spotting Grandma in case she was too weak to hold Ray for very long. When I pulled his hat off, Grandma marveled at Ray's dark hair. "He looks just like you when you were a baby." She smiled. Then she began to sob. "I won't be here to watch him grow up." It was true, and

I had no words. We both cried, holding Ray between us. It was the most bittersweet moment I could imagine.

In all my years I cannot recall a single time when my grandpa called me. We saw each other often enough so he never had the need to call. But that year when his wife was dying, he called me every week. "Can you bring that little Ray of sunshine over?" he would ask. "He's the only thing that perks Grandma up."

Grandma hung on for six more months before she passed away. I continued to bring Ray to see Grandpa as often as I could. They developed a special bond, grinning from ear to ear as soon as they saw each other. Grandpa died of a heart attack when Ray was a year old—just six months after losing his wife, the love of his life. I think he died of a broken heart, but not before dubbing his great-grandson Ray of Sunshine.

Ruling Out the Worst

I think there are show-offs in this world and there are entertainers. There's a big difference. Show-offs like to get attention for themselves, while entertainers perform to make other people happy. Ray was an entertainer.

He seemed to study people, honing in on the smallest of nuances. It was as if he were looking for material for his act and crafting comedic timing—as a *toddler*. Scarcely able to string together two words, nonetheless Ray began doing impersonations. Some nights he took his final bottle snuggled next to me on the couch. Usually I had the TV on, watching Johnny Carson. I didn't think Ray paid attention to the show, but one night he surprised me. I should preface by saying that my father, whom Ray referred to as Ba-pa, resembled Johnny Carson. One night, just as Ed McMahon, the *Tonight Show* announcer, made his legendary introduction ("Heeeere's Johnny!"), Ray pulled a bottle out of his mouth and said, "Heeeere's Ba-pa!" Sometimes he introduced his grandpa that way when he entered a room. It never got old.

It wasn't long before he was impersonating other late-night talk show hosts. One day Ray crawled up on a kitchen chair and grabbed a grocery list from the table. He held it up to his face as if he were reading a card and said, "Num-ba ten!" When I realized he was imitating David Letterman doing his top ten list, I busted out laughing. Then Ray took a pencil and tapped it on the table a few times before tossing it over his shoulder. With a huge grin, he made the sound effect of breaking glass—something Letterman did when one of his jokes bombed. It was pretty impressive considering Ray's age. He probably should have been learning nursery rhymes, not doing late-night talk show bits, but this was far more entertaining than "Mary Had a Little Lamb."

So, life was good. I had a wonderful husband and a comical little boy whom I adored. But something started to gnaw at me. People began making comments about Ray's size, and not in a polite way. Somewhere along the way, "Oh, he's so adorable," turned into, "He sure is a little guy." Or, "How old did you say he was?" Or, "My neighbor's kid is about the same age, but he's way bigger." The kind of stuff new parents love to hear.

Any mention of Ray's size around my parents and they were quick to brush it off. "Look at you. You're practically a giant," Buzz teased, "and you were our smallest baby." I'm a little shy of 5'8", hardly a giant. But Buzz was roughly my height. In heels, I towered over him.

On the other hand, Rusty is over six feet tall with an athletic build. He claims to have been a scrawny little kid, and he reasoned that Ray would eventually shoot up and fill out, too. But I sensed something was off. Ray had a lot of energy and was totally engaged in the world around him. He certainly didn't look or act sick, but we were constantly changing diapers. Everything seemed to go straight through him. And he didn't just fuss a little bit when he was hungry. He frantically pulled at his hair—screaming and crying in desperation—as if he were starving.

At first we didn't make much of it. After all, he was happy and content between feedings. We just thought he had a big appetite and was a little demanding. But for all he ate, he wasn't growing very fast. Whenever I expressed concern about Ray's slow weight gain despite his huge appetite—not to mention how often we changed Ray's diapers—his pediatrician downplayed it.

"Switch his formula," he told me. "Maybe he'll tolerate a different brand better." Or, "Ray's teething. Sometimes that causes loose stools. Give him time," he assured me. "Some kids start out small. He'll grow."

But in my heart I knew something was wrong. Multiple times a day, Ray had massive stools that smelled strongly of whatever he'd last eaten. It just didn't seem normal to me.

Not until Ray was nearly a year and a half, and at the bottom fifth percentile on the growth chart, did his pediatrician address the issue. "He seems to have a malabsorption problem," he said at a regular check-up. "I think we should perform a sweat test to see if he has cystic fibrosis."

"What is cystic fibrosis?" I asked. "I don't think I've heard of that."

"Well, let's just start with the sweat test so we can rule out the worst. Then we can go from there." He scribbled something down on a form. "Here, bring this to the front desk. They'll help you schedule an appointment for the test." Before I could ask any questions, he scurried out of the room. I was left sitting there with my son, thinking, *Rule out the worst? How bad is cystic fibrosis if it's the worst? And what the hell is a sweat test?*

When I handed the receptionist the doctor's form, her cheery smile faded.

"What?" I snapped, still irritated with Dr. Elusive.

She stood up and motioned for me to follow her. With Ray on my hip, she led me into a small storage closet, then whispered, "Do you know what cystic fibrosis is?"

"No. The doctor didn't explain it. He just said Ray needs to have this test done so we can rule out the worst."

"Well, let's hope so. Cystic fibrosis isn't good."

This was crazy, hiding in a small room with her whispering. "Just tell me what it is," I demanded.

Darla Garvey

"It's a genetic disease that affects the lungs and digestive system. The life expectancy is late teens, early twenties at best." And just like that, she led me back to the front counter, opened her appointment book, and threw out a couple of dates. It was as if the storage closet conversation, just two seconds earlier, had never happened. Unable to speak, I nodded at the mention of the first date available. She handed me an appointment card and I left, holding Ray close to my chest. Through tears I searched the parking lot for my car, fumbling for keys in my bag. I buckled Ray in his car seat and slipped behind the wheel with the words *life expectancy, late teens,* and *early twenties* swirling around in my head. I felt myself floating, thinking, *This can't be real.*

I don't know how I managed to drive, but somehow I ended up at our neighborhood library. It was 1990. Pre-internet. I pulled a medical journal off the shelf and began reading about cystic fibrosis. The article said that cystic fibrosis, or CF, is a hereditary disease. "A defective gene causes a thick buildup of mucus in the lungs, pancreas and other organs. In the lungs, the mucus clogs the airways and traps bacteria, leading to infections, extensive lung damage and eventually, respiratory failure."

Oh my God, this is a cruel disease, I thought, *but thankfully, Ray doesn't fit the bill.* The article talked about a variety of symptoms, including persistent coughing (at times with phlegm), pneumonia, bronchitis, wheezing, and shortness of breath. Ray never showed any signs of respiratory problems. One ear infection, but he hadn't so much as had a single cold. I was so relieved. Clearly his pediatrician was off base.

Then I read on. "In the pancreas, the mucus prevents the release of digestive enzymes that allow the body to break down food and absorb vital nutrients, resulting in malnutrition and poor growth. Symptoms include frequent greasy, bulky stools." While Ray did not exhibit any of the respiratory symptoms described in the medical journal, they might just as well have put his picture in the digestive system section.

The article summarized that people with cystic fibrosis have a shortened life expectancy due to a *failure to thrive*. Feeling dizzy, I laid my head on the table. The room was spinning, and I thought I was going to throw up. I remembered now seeing those very words written on the top of the doctor's form—the reason he'd provided for ordering the sweat test. *Failure to thrive*.

Sickened, I pushed the medical journal aside and wiped away tears. My son was perfectly content at my side, playing on the floor with a toy truck. I looked down at his healthy pink cheeks. His beautiful thick hair that had turned from black to sandy blonde. Ray looked up at me and smiled. He was beautiful. He was perfect. He was healthy. This was bullshit!

When we walked through the front door of our apartment, Ray ran to his dad, who scooped him up in his arms. "Hey, buddy." To me he said, "How did the appointment go?"

Speechless, I shook my head.

"What happened?"

Rusty quickly set Ray down near his toy box at the far end of the living room, then came back to me. "Why are you crying? What the hell's going on?"

Burying my face in Rusty's chest, I cried harder, eventually calming down long enough to tell him everything. Falling off the growth chart. The sweat test. Ruling out the worst. The blunt receptionist in the storage closet. Shortened life expectancy. Late teens. Early twenties.

Rusty looked sick to his stomach. He needed time to process, but I didn't afford him that. I had to tell him everything before the details slipped away. I told him what I had read at the library. Hereditary, defective gene, thick sticky mucus that clogs the airways, infections, malnourishment, bulky stools, poor growth, and failure to thrive.

"What if he has this disease, Rusty?" I sobbed. "There's no cure."

He stood silent for a long time, then uttered, "Ray doesn't have it. His doctor's an idiot. Why didn't he explain anything about this disease while you were there?"

"I don't know. It was weird. I didn't even know what to ask. He didn't give me a chance, though. He just dropped the bomb and left the room."

"That's the point. You had to find out at the library. He's an idiot. So is his receptionist. He's followed Ray since he was a baby. He's never suspected anything was wrong with him, and now he throws this at us?"

"I know. I know. Shhhh." I gestured toward Ray, still occupied with his toys. "I think something *is* wrong with Ray, though," I whispered. "He's fallen off the growth chart now, and all we do is feed him."

"Stop it. You can't assume he has a disease just because he's small. Look at my dad. Look at your dad. They're both little guys. It's not a big deal."

"I don't know, Rusty. You keep saying that, but ..."

With his jaw set, Rusty ran both hands through his hair, then dared to say, "So you found one line in a medical book about frequent, bulky stools that you think describes Ray, and all of a sudden he has a death sentence?"

"Don't say that!" I gasped.

Rusty paced the floor now. I took a seat on the couch and rubbed my temples. "Look," I said. "I don't know what to think. All I know is I love that boy, and I don't want anything to be wrong with him."

"We'll bring him to that sweat test thing, whatever it is, and you'll see. He's doesn't have cystic fibrosis."

"But ..."

"No more buts. Please, just stop."

Emotionally drained, I understood. I needed it to stop, too. Rusty took a seat next to me on the couch. Silently we watched our son from across the room. We were both scared, and too scared to admit it.

"It's going to be okay. When's the test?" Rusty patted my knee.

"Two weeks."

"Enjoy the next two weeks with Ray and try not to think about it. I don't want to talk about this anymore."

Sweating It Out

Over the next two weeks, we lived as if we didn't have a care in the world. We brought Ray to our outdoor pool for daily swims, watching him splash in delight. We made frequent walks to the ice cream shop just three blocks away. Ray saw every animal at Como Park Zoo and even walked out of the park holding balloons, just because. Favorite foods were served, hugs were given more frequently, and horseplay was widely encouraged. There were even more bubbles in the tub at bath time. But somewhere during this two-week fantasy world we created, I made my way back to the library. I wanted so badly to read something that would put my mind at ease before the sweat test. Something that would prove Ray didn't stand even a remote chance of having CF. Something blatant like *It's entirely unheard of for blonde-haired boys to have cystic fibrosis.*

Instead, because life isn't the fantasy we create, I learned that "In people who have cystic fibrosis, the salt travels to the skin's surface with the water and is not reabsorbed. Because of this, the skin of a child who has cystic fibrosis is abnormally salty. Parents may notice salty-tasting skin when they kiss the child." The article ended with a startling old Irish saying: "If your child tastes of salt, he is not long for this world."

I went home that day and made a career out of kissing, even licking Ray, to determine if his skin tasted of salt. One minute, I was absolutely certain he was made from nothing but salt. The next, I wasn't sure his skin tasted any saltier than my own.

Soon enough, my library research and salt licking days came to an end as I drove to the pediatric clinic with my son.

Rusty was called into work and didn't accompany me, which was fine. After all, this was just the test itself. I was told the results wouldn't come back until the following day. The day we would learn Ray's fate, *together.*

A lab tech brought us back to a room, where I sat Ray on a bed while the tech explained what the test looks for. "Normally, the skin's surface contains very little sodium, but people with cystic fibrosis have two to five times the normal amount," he said. "The sweat test will measure the amount of sodium chloride in your son's sweat."

The test was pretty straightforward. In a nutshell, it consisted of strapping two metal electrodes to Ray's forearm. A gel disc containing pilocarpine, a drug that stimulates sweating, was placed under the electrodes. For five minutes, a tiny electric current was applied to help carry pilocarpine to the sweat glands. After the lab tech removed the electrodes, he taped a dry piece of filter paper to the area. He called the paper a sweat patch. Ray was encouraged to move around and play for the next thirty minutes to work up a sweat. When the tech came back to the room, he removed everything from Ray's arm. He examined the sweat patch for a moment before placing it in a sealed container.

"Why does the patch have a circle on it?" I asked.

"It's just the margins used to measure the amount of sweat."

"Is there something wrong?"

"I was just checking that we've collected enough sweat," he said. "I'll take this to the lab."

"Okay. So that's it? We can leave? We'll get the results tomorrow, right?"

"Why don't you stay put? The doctor will want to talk to you."

I changed Ray's diaper and fed him a snack. We waited for an uneasy amount of time, a sick feeling festering inside me. Suddenly, Ray's pediatrician entered the room. With arms folded across his chest, he leaned against the far wall. His body language told a silent story I didn't like. Finally, he said, "I took a look at the lab work. It doesn't look good, Darla. I'm sorry."

Choking back tears, I covered my mouth to muffle a scream. "I didn't know I was getting test results today," I managed to say. "My husband isn't even here. What are you saying, exactly? Ray has cystic fibrosis?"

"It would appear so. But sometimes, at a clinic like this, the labs can show a false positive."

And with those words there was hope. "A false positive? That can happen? Then what?"

"Yes, sometimes the reliability of the test is operator-dependent. To ensure the most accurate results, I'm going to send you to the University of Minnesota CF clinic to repeat the test. Their sweat tests are analyzed by a CF-certified lab."

"Well, why didn't we just start there if they're the CF experts?" I wiped my eyes and blew my nose. "You're putting us through a lot, you know?" I added, wishing Rusty was at my side.

"I know. This is tough. I already called the U of M. They have a date open next week to repeat the sweat test." He handed me a card with the appointment information. "They also set up a meeting with Dr. Warwick after the test, just in case. He's the best in the field."

I left the clinic with Ray, holding on to a small glimmer of hope. I wasn't particularly impressed with Ray's pediatric care. If it took his doctor a year and a half to prescribe a sweat test, I prayed his lab tech was also ten steps behind. Never before had I hoped someone in the medical field was entirely incompetent at his job.

Rusty and I spent yet another week hoping for the best and preparing for the worst. I say that now, and it sounds ridiculously trite because it is. It's a pointless cliché people use even when they know full well there's little they can do to prepare. Hope, I understand. Preparing for the worst? Well, we weren't sure what that entailed, so how could we prepare for it? We were terrified and had a million unanswered questions. *How will we care for our son if he has a life-threatening illness? How will we give him the life he deserves in spite of CF? What will the future hold for him? For us? Will we helplessly watch our son's health decline? Will we lose our Ray of sunshine? Or is there some hope? A medical advancement, perhaps?*

At the University of Minnesota, the sweat test was repeated in the same fashion. Ray ran up and down the hallways at the clinic, working up a sweat. He looked so joyful. It broke my heart to think this little boy might have a life-threatening disease and here he was, clueless. Just running around, giggling while kicking a soccer ball in the hallway.

At one point, I peeled back the plastic wrap on Ray's arm and peeked at the sweat patch. It looked exactly how I remembered it at the pediatric clinic, sweat pooling beyond the margins. My mouth dropped.

"What?" Rusty asked.

"He flunked."

"What are you talking about? How do you know?"

"It looks the same. He flunked the test, Rusty." I burst into tears.

Some time later, the lab results were in and we learned what we weren't prepared for—the worst. We were ushered to a family lounge area and waited to meet Dr. Warwick. Judging by the tear factor and solemn mood in the room, Ray seemed to sense that it was time to sit still. He crawled up in my lap and nestled his head against my chest. I rubbed his back with one hand, reaching for a tissue with the other.

Dr. Warwick walked in and introduced himself. He looked like an absent-minded professor, thick glasses and thin gray hair sticking up like onion sprouts. To tell the truth, I don't remember everything Dr. Warwick said, but I do know his message was grim. He explained more of what I had already researched. Essentially, the genetic cause and devastating effects of cystic fibrosis. When asked what we were to do from this point on, he described the care our son required. Daily respiratory treatments to help him cough up mucus from his lungs, supplementary enzymes to help absorb food, and antibiotics to ward off lung infections. He informed us that Ray needed to be admitted into the hospital as soon as possible for further testing and to begin respiratory treatment. At the same time, Rusty and I would take classes at the hospital to learn more about CF and how to administer the treatments at home. Dr. Warwick referred to the respiratory procedure as bronchial drainage, or BD, a manual method that helps move mucus from the airways.

Some of what Dr. Warwick said registered with me. Other times, he made about as much sense as Charlie Brown's teacher: *Wah wah, wah wah wah wah.* He certainly didn't sugar coat anything. When Rusty asked about life expectancy, he simply said, "Some kids are luckier than others."

We drove home from the hospital in silence. I imagine Rusty was wrestling with the same thoughts I was. As parents, you want the best for your children. You want them to experience joy and success. I felt like every hope and dream I had for Ray had been crushed by a stupid sweat patch.

The overwhelming devastation I felt that day was equally as powerful as the intense feeling of love I had felt when Ray entered the world. I couldn't bear the thought of him suffering or leaving the world at a young age.

The week-long hospital stay that followed was overwhelming to say the least. Ray was put through a battery of tests and treatments, often times while we were in educational meetings. I hated that he was left in the care of strangers. I could hardly focus on what they were trying to teach us, longing to be with our son instead.

The bronchial drainage procedure was more challenging than we'd imagined. In theory, it sounded like a piece of cake. After breathing in nebulized medication that thins the mucus and opens the airways, the CF patient simply lies down on a flat surface while a therapist cups her hands and raps on the patient's torso. Every couple of minutes, the patient shifts to a new position so the therapist can concentrate on each lobe of his lungs. The patient is encouraged to cough during the half-hour process.

But in reality, the procedure was a nightmare for our toddler, who had no idea why the hell someone was holding him in place, rapping her hands against his little body.

Rusty and I watched from the sidelines while Ray received BDs several times a day. We were told to observe for the first couple of days. Then it was our turn to administer the treatment. It was heartbreaking to stand by watching Ray fight, scream, and squirm while someone pounded on him. Reaching his arms out, Ray cried and pleaded for us to stop the madness.

As a parent, your natural instinct is to protect your child from distress or harm. I wanted so badly to yank Ray from the therapist's arms and run straight out of the hospital. Instead, we encouraged Ray to lie still.

During one of Ray's treatments, I decided I could not watch. I simply couldn't deal with it. It was Rusty's turn to take a break, probably off getting coffee or something to eat. I walked out of the therapy room and left Ray to struggle on his own—basically, I abandoned my son. Slumping to the floor in the hallway, I broke down, listening to Ray wail. Suddenly, my parents were standing over me. Mom asked, "What's going on? Why are you on the floor?"

Pointing to the door, I said, "I can't take it."

"He needs you, Darla," Buzz insisted, listening to Ray cry out, "Mama!"

"You have to go back in," Mom added.

"This is God awful. I can't do this."

"I'll go in with you," Buzz offered. Mom opted to wait in the hallway.

When we entered the therapy room, Ray reached for his grandpa, crying "Ba-pa! Ba-pa."

When Buzz took Ray's hand, the therapist threw him a dirty look, as this caused Ray to squirm and kick in an attempt to break free. "It's okay, buddy. Hang in there," Buzz encouraged. Choked up, he eventually pleaded with the therapist to stop. "That's enough now."

"He has to learn to lie still through the whole treatment," the therapist said firmly. "It takes half an hour. He has five minutes to go."

Buzz and I stood helpless, watching Ray struggle. Five minutes felt like a lifetime. When the therapist finished, Buzz quickly scooped Ray off the table and into his arms, wiping sweaty hair from his grandson's forehead.

We found Mom standing in the hallway, tears streaming down her cheeks. She had been listening outside the door. Later, Buzz admitted how disturbing it had been to witness Ray's treatment. He said he felt sorry for Ray and sorry for what we were going to have to do to our son each day. "Stay strong," Buzz said.

Each night, the nurses encouraged us to go home and get a good night's sleep, as our days were long and draining. We waited until Ray was sound asleep before tiptoeing out of his room. It killed me to leave him overnight, especially in a crib that had a mesh-like tent over it to protect him from climbing out. He looked like a caged animal. Each morning, we scurried back to the hospital in hopes of arriving to Ray's room before he awoke.

Before long, we were sent home to care for Ray as we had been taught. The atmosphere in our home shifted the moment we unpacked several bags of medication and a box of supplies. It was now evident a child with an illness resided here. In an attempt to remedy this, I immediately cleaned out a kitchen cupboard, tucking away prescription bottles, tubing, and nebulizer cups. I hid an air compressor behind a chair, out of sight, and pretended our lives were still normal. The three of us were about to discover that nothing could be further from the truth.

Breaking a Horse

I was already exhausted just thinking what the next forty-five minutes would bring. Unlike his mom and dad, Ray had clearly put his unpleasant hospital stay behind him. As far as he could see, there wasn't a respiratory therapist in his home trying to hold him down on a padded table to pound the mucus from his lungs. No one was here forcing him to breathe in nebulized medication through a mask. Ray had said goodbye to all the nurses, doctors, and respiratory therapists in the hospital. The bad guys were gone. He was home now, and he was safe. Or so he thought.

I was about to start the third and final bronchial drainage procedure of the day. The first two hadn't gone so well. In fact, the experience was downright disturbing. Ray recognized the neb cup in my hand and knew what was about to take place. A playful expression turned to one of terror. His little body momentarily froze before he threw down his toy, crying out, "No, Mama! No!"

Speaking in a calm voice, I said, "It's okay, Ray. Come sit on my lap and I'll tell you a story. You'll be okay, honey. Come on."

Attempting to escape from the apartment, he ran to the front door and tried unsuccessfully to turn the handle. Tears rolled down his cheeks as he pressed his back firmly against the door, perhaps wishing he could disappear right through it. Like a traffic cop, with straightened arms extended, he ordered me to halt. His face turned red with anger, his eyes wild. I scooped him up in one arm, holding the neb cup in my other hand. Taking a swing, he tried to knock the cup from my hand, still screaming, "No, Mama, no!"

I shushed him and bounced him gently as we made our way across the room to the rocking chair, an air compressor already placed at its side.

"Just sit in Mama's lap and we'll get this over with," I said, failing to persuade.

Ray wriggled and squirmed while I tried to position him on my lap to place the mask over his face. I tightened my hold as he attempted to tear off the mask. Crying hard, his eyes met mine. A look of betrayal seemed to say, *Oh no, Mom. Not again.*

I felt terrible springing this on him for the third time today. But there would never be a perfect time to do his treatment. It would always be an unwelcome disruption to his day. Maybe it would be easier if he were older and I could talk to him about cystic fibrosis. Explain to him how these treatments kept his lungs clear. But he was only seventeen months old. He didn't even know what lungs were. There was no way to explain it. It wasn't like I could call a family meeting and give him the breakdown.

Here's your new schedule, Ray. You're going to wake up in the morning and call for me from your crib, excited to start the day. Your bedhead hair, sticking up in a hundred different directions, will make your first appearance of the day an adorable one. Clearly anxious to be lifted from the crib, you will rattle the rail like a tiger in a cage. You'll reach for me and smile, thinking today will be fun and carefree like all your other days —but it won't.

I'm going to scoop you out of your crib and change another unbelievably messy diaper because most of the food you ate the night before traveled straight through you. The sticky mucus in your body is blocking enzyme secretions from your pancreas, messing up your digestive system.

Next I'm going to feed you breakfast. But first I'm going to break up some pills and slip them into applesauce. They're pancreatic enzymes. Judging by what's in your diaper, I'll wonder why the enzymes haven't done the trick yet. Maybe your body has to get used to them, I'll reason. Bringing a spoon of enzyme-filled applesauce to your mouth, I'll make a funny face or a silly noise so as to distract you. You'll never see the pills coming.

After breakfast we'll play at the park or take a dip in the pool. You'll be free to be a normal little boy, and I'll try not to show you how sad I am. I'm faking it, too consumed with what's looming over us. But you'll never really know, will you?

When we come back inside, I'll let you play with your toys for a short time before I trudge into the kitchen. I'll put some medication into a sterile nebulizer cup. The liquid medicine will turn into a fine mist once the neb cup is attached to an air compressor. You will breathe the mist into your lungs, but placing the mask over your face is going to throw you into a panic. You're going to feel trapped. But you have to buck up. We're all trapped now.

I will rock you and try to comfort you while you fight to remove the mask. I'll have to get tough, restraining your arms firmly against your sides. You will squirm to break loose so I'll tighten my grip, only making you fight harder to get away. You'll throw your head from side to side like a wild dog trying to break out of a muzzle. I will notice tears running out from under the mask and choke back my own. I'll try to explain why you have to hold still and keep the mask on, but you won't listen or care. My words hold no meaning. How can they? You're only a toddler, after all.

After fifteen minutes, when I finally lift the mask from your tear-stained cheeks, you'll think the worst is over, but it's not. Things are going to get ugly. I'm going to pound the snot out of you—literally. I'm going to try to move the mucus from your lungs by pounding my cupped hands against your upper back while you're still seated on my lap, the first of several positions. In turn, you're going to try to hop off my lap and make a run for it. But I'm not going to let that happen. Instead I'm going to wrap one arm across your chest, holding you tightly in place while I rap on your back with my free hand. I'll question why any of this is necessary since you never cough up any mucus. The doctors told us we have to do this treatment three times a day, regardless. They said bronchial drainage is preventative. They made it sound so simple, telling us it's like brushing your teeth. You don't wait until you have a cavity to start brushing. We're not supposed to wait until mucus builds up in your lungs, potentially clogging your airways, before doing BDs.

So I'll diligently rap on your back just like they showed us in the hospital. The pounding—or percussion, as they say—won't physically hurt you. It's the restraining part you find more troubling. You will feel restricted, and you're going to fight me. In fact, you're going to kick and scream and cry hard. But crying is good, they told us. It opens your airways more, so we're supposed to let you cry and not stop pounding—not even to hug you. The respiratory therapists got upset when I did that in the hospital. They told me it made you think you were done with your treatment, making it twice as hard to get started again. I figured you were going to give me hell no matter what and I could not stand to let you cry so long. So I sneaked in a hug to comfort you from time to time.

At some point we'll end up on the floor, because I'll find it impossible to balance your flailing body in my lap. I will drape one leg over your hips to hold your lower body still, freeing up both hands to pound on your chest. This will really tick you off, and you're going to twist your wiry body like a wrestler who doesn't want to get pinned by his opponent. Occasionally I'll look away because the pleading look in your eyes breaks my heart. It's going to make me sick to my stomach to pin you to the floor. I will feel like an abuser—a monster—beating on her helpless child. The doctors preached about the importance of BDs—the best way to keep your lungs healthy—so I've convinced myself I have no choice.

I hate that we've taken to the floor, but it is safer here. You kicked yourself right off my lap in the hospital. It was scary, but I caught you before you landed on the tile floor. The doctors told us pounding with your body on a firm surface, like a carpeted floor, will dislodge the mucus better. A soft lap absorbs the pounding and is less effective. So I guess it's better that I have you on the floor, but it feels so wrong.

By this time, your face will have turned an angry purple, and you'll have worked up a sweat. I'll marvel at your strength and wonder where it came from. How did my easy-going little boy get this fire inside him? I'll try to distract you. Maybe tell you a story or sing you a song, but it will be pointless. You're too worked up to be remotely entertained. I can't outsmart you, kid. You're a bright one—and a tough one.

One of the therapists in the hospital told us getting you to sit still and tolerate your therapies will be like breaking a horse. He said he never saw a CF patient so young fight so hard. He also told us this will be to your advantage. You're a fighter, and you're going to need that determination to deal with cystic fibrosis.

After half an hour, I'll stop pounding on you, but not until exactly one half of an hour. The pulmonary specialists at the University of Minnesota have me terrified that if I cheat you out of even thirty seconds, something horrible will happen. So I'll watch the clock. Every two minutes I'll switch you to a different position and begin pounding again.

Some positions are harder than others. You particularly hate lying face down on your tummy while I pound on your back, so I'm going to save that for last—hoping you'll be too tired to keep up the fight. But as soon as I roll you on your stomach, you're going to try to spring up off the floor like you're doing a push-up. Your determination will amaze me. I'll hate doing it, but I'll squash your efforts and press my forearm against your shoulders, forcing you back down to the floor. Somehow you'll muster up the strength to lift your head—the only part of your body that isn't pinned down. You'll struggle to crane your neck and look over your shoulder at me. The desperation in your eyes is going to kill me. I'm going to tell you it's okay, but we both know it's not. I will avoid eye contact, opting to watch the clock instead. This will make me feel incredibly insensitive, and I will loathe myself as much as the procedure.

Towards the end of the BD, you're going to get tired of holding your head up, so you'll let it drop. Thumping your forehead on the carpet, you'll sob in defeat. I will cry as well. It's emotional for both of us.

Once we're done, I'll scoop you up in my arms and rock you. I'll tell you I love you and that it's over. Your exhausted little body will collapse into mine and you'll rest your head on my shoulder and hug me, and I'll wonder how you still can. I'll wonder if there will be a day when you'll stop hugging me because now I am the bad guy. Three times a day I will disrupt whatever you're doing, hold you down, and pound on each lobe of your lungs for exactly one half of an hour. This will be your daily schedule, Ray, forever.

I'm hoping for an easier time down the road. A day when you will comply with your treatments without a struggle. There's no sign of it now, but maybe someday you will break like a horse.

In or Out

Three days passed after returning home from the hospital without a word from Rusty. He left for work with hardly a goodbye. Returning late at night, he crawled in bed, turned his back and pretended to sleep. We sat across the dinner table, eating in silence. He only interacted with Ray, and then without the usual enthusiasm. Finally, after three days of his bullshit, I called him out at dinner. "Are you sticking around, Rusty? Or am I doing this on my own?"

He lowered his fork to the plate and stared at me.

"I need to know," I said, "are you in or out?"

He was slow to respond.

I waited.

"I'm not going anywhere."

"Good. You better start helping with Ray's treatments too. I'm going to need a break once in a while. It's too much for one person."

Rusty nodded in agreement, but in reality, much of Ray's hands-on care continued to fall on me. Most times because of Rusty's work schedule. Other times because he couldn't bring himself to do it, even on his days off. After Ray was diagnosed, I cut back my hours at work. At the very least, I trusted Rusty to take care of things while I was working. However, over time, I learned he rarely did a full half hour of pounding. Sometimes he only administered the nebulized meds, skipping the dreadful bronchial drainage procedure altogether. Ray revealed this to me during his treatment one day.

"Stop, Mama!" he cried while I rapped on his chest.

"No, Ray. I'm sorry, but we have to do this."

"Dad doesn't."

This inconsistency became a source of contention in our marriage. I was strict with treatments, insisting if anything were to happen to Ray, like a lung infection, it wouldn't be for lack of effort—at least on my part. Of course, Rusty didn't want our son to get sick either, but he believed Ray could move mucus from his lungs by simply being physically active. It would take several years for me to lighten up and occasionally substitute aerobic play for bronchial drainage.

For the most part, we had the same approach to parenting, which basically went like this: *Ray comes first*. Still, marriage and parenting, under the best of circumstances, take effort. Now throw in a chronic illness and let the stressful games begin.

Three months after Ray's diagnosis, at a CF check-up, I told Dr. Warwick how dreadful things were at home. That every single treatment turned into a physical and emotional battle. I broke down and said, "I'm not cut out for this. I cannot plead, coax, bribe, read, or sing my way through one more respiratory treatment."

Dr. Warwick told me what I already knew: Quitting was not an option. Then he assured me, with time, BDs would get easier. I wanted to ask him if he had ever met Ray. Instead, I said, "Our family dynamics have shifted. I hate the tension in our home, and I'm exhausted trying to manage Ray's behavior during BDs. I feel like CF is slowly taking my son, chiseling away at his wonderful personality."

He listened to me intently before suggesting that we teach family members how to do a bronchial drainage procedure, adding that family support can make a big difference to CF patients and their parents. I informed Dr. Warwick that my family wasn't ready to step up to the plate. They couldn't even be in the same room if I administered BDs in their presence, much less offer assistance.

As a second option, Dr. Warwick suggested we hire a respiratory therapist to take the pressure off of us. I wondered why we hadn't thought of this ourselves. But the plan quickly backfired. If we thought Ray was difficult for us, he was twice as difficult for the therapist. He was unable to handle Ray on his own, so I had to hold my son's legs down while he tried to pound on him. It felt more barbaric than doing it myself. To make matters worse, the therapist grew short and impatient with Ray as he kicked and swung at him every chance he could get. Worse still, Ray looked at me like I was some sort of conspirator. His eyes seemed to say, "Seriously, Mom. You're going to help this big jerk pound on me?"

We let the therapist go after three days.

At Ray's next CF appointment, I told Dr. Warwick about our disastrous experience with the therapist and complained that his treatments were still a next-to-impossible task. He decided that, given Ray's healthy-looking chest x-rays, and the fact that his lungs sounded clear, we could cut back to just two treatments a day. This was a game changer. Ray still put up a good fight, but having the entire day between morning and evening BDs freed up time to do fun, normal activities. Now there was a hint of what life had once been—carefree and enjoyable. Cystic fibrosis didn't steal our entire day.

Ferndale Street

Before we married, I had lived on the second floor of a Victorian home on Mounds Boulevard in St. Paul. It was a charming place with all the character you'd expect from an older home, complete with a fireplace and bay windows from floor to ceiling, providing a fantastic view of the Mississippi River and city skyline. After we married, Rusty and I moved to an apartment in Roseville, a suburb of St Paul, where we were the youngest couple in the building. I wanted to stay in St. Paul —maybe rent out a floor in a mansion in the historic Summit Avenue area. Anything but the Rose Mall Apartments. But, working late and sleeping in, Rusty reasoned that the elderly tenants wouldn't throw loud parties and wake him. Somehow he won that argument.

On one side of our apartment was a nursing home, and on the other, a funeral home. I told Rusty when these old people move out, they either go to the left or to the right. While he slept peacefully during the day, I was bombarded the second I stepped outside the door with Ray. He was the only child in the building, so all the residents clamored to get their hands on my baby. As intrusive as it felt sometimes, it was actually kind of sweet. Often times, we found a stuffed animal or a small gift for Ray placed outside our door. Francine was my favorite neighbor. She always asked to hold Raymond. When I corrected her and said, "It's just Ray," she responded, "I know. But I like to call him Raymond for short."

I hate to credit cystic fibrosis for much of anything, but it's undeniable that it changed our perspective on life. It made a huge impact on how we lived and how we parented. We felt a sense of urgency to squeeze in everything we could. We focused on the present and pushed aside any fear of the future, always hopeful medical advancements would change our circumstances. In the meantime, we vowed to give Ray the life he deserved, starting with a solid foundation. We purchased a lot on Ferndale Street in South Maplewood, breaking ground in a neighborhood where Ray could play and explore with other children. In December of 1990, we left the Rose Mall Apartments, saying goodbye to Francine and the others.

We received an unexpected gift from Buzz. Not only did he lay our block foundation, he bricked up the entire first level. Rusty became Buzz's trusted laborer, recruiting several of his friends to help as well.

At the time, Buzz was a foreman with Knudson Construction Company. He would stop at our building site on his way home from work and lay brick until the sun set, at which time he would announce, "Losing daylight. I'm outta here." Then he would remind us, "I don't do cleanup. That's your deal."

Our original house plans included a wood-burning fireplace, but after Ray's diagnosis, we scrapped the idea. Any trace of smoke in our home would be unhealthy for our son. But I'll never forget how Buzz objected when I dared to suggest he build a brick accent wall where the fireplace would have been. He firmly articulated, "Jesus Christ! How much brick do you think I'm going to lay?"

"All of it." I smiled.

He shook his head. Then threw me a look that indicated just maybe he'd think about it. I'm happy to say that with the help of his cousin, Corky Denisson (also a bricklayer), we have a lovely brick wall with track lighting in our living room. Our home was as much a source of pride for my dad as it was for us. Buzz often said he was happy he could help provide a solid place to raise his grandson.

That first summer in our home, Ray was just two and a half years old and anxious to meet anything that moved, saying hello to every child, adult, or dog who came within two feet of our yard. It wasn't long before he became friends with Jim Holm, a boy who lived across the street and was just a year older than Ray. Jim was big for his age and Ray small for his. Ray was a rule breaker and Jim the voice of reason. They were polar opposites in so many ways, like Mutt and Jeff, yet somehow their friendship worked.

One day, while gazing out our front window, Ray asked, "Where's Jimmy?"

I said, "I don't know. He must be inside right now."

"Ahhh … doing therapy," Ray reasoned.

I realized then that Ray thought every child did respiratory treatments. All kids eat, nap, play, and do BDs. We knew there'd be a day when Ray would discover not every child has cystic fibrosis, but we didn't know how that would evolve or what it would mean to him.

Assuming Ray might face challenges regarding socialization and acceptance, we encouraged him to participate in anything he was interested in. This generally meant buying sporting equipment and hanging practice and game schedules on the fridge. While he may not have been the star athlete in every sport, he was decent and gave it his all, his coaches marveling at his dedication and effort. Best of all, he got to be part of a team like every other kid.

Over the years, Ray played baseball, basketball, hockey, football, was a wrestler, learned to ski, took swimming lessons every summer at Carver Beach, and earned a black belt in karate by the time he was ten years old. Turns out, he didn't need a push from us at all. He grew strong and confident, playing sports, drawing people in with his humor, and refusing to be identified by an illness. I learned quickly that I was far from being the mother of a delicate boy with cystic fibrosis, worried how her son would fit in. Maybe there were restrictions inside our home, a healthcare routine to adhere to, but outside, he was never on the sidelines waiting to be accepted. *He* accepted everyone else, masterminding all the games and encouraging everyone to join in. If ever there was a more incorrect label to describe Ray, it was *failure to thrive*. Not only did he thrive in his new environment, he became the ringleader on Ferndale Street.

There are sixteen houses on our block, eight on each side of the street. Over the years families have moved from the neighborhood, but at its peak there were thirty-six children on our block alone. It didn't take long before every one of them knew the Garvey kid. Ray established relationships with all the children and their parents. He figured out who belonged to whom long before we did. If he heard one of us say something like, "I wonder which house that guy lives in?" Ray was quick to answer, "Oh, that's Patrick's dad. He lives in the white house."

So friendships grew quickly, and most often the action on Ferndale Street took place at our house, the doorbell constantly ringing for Ray. I think children gravitated toward Ray because he liked people so much. He didn't discriminate either. You didn't have to be the coolest, the fastest, the smartest, or the best at anything to hang out with Ray. You just had to be willing to join in his games. Besides being a good friend, at least two other factors solidified Ray's popularity in the neighborhood: Halloween and K9 Boone.

Halloween

The most frightening thing about Ray's first Halloween on Ferndale Street didn't come in the form of ghoulish costumes or scary decorations. It came in the form of weather. A snowstorm arrived just hours before the trick-or-treaters should have been making their rounds, dumping nearly three feet of snow in the Twin Cities. The 1991 Halloween blizzard still holds the record for highest snowfall total of any storm in Minnesota history.

That was the year Ray dressed as a St. Paul police officer. I don't know how I did it, but I managed to alter my husband's extra-large uniform shirt, scaling it down considerably to fit our little boy. He wore a police hat, blue pants, and a thick belt to hold a flashlight in place, and a ridiculous-looking mustache. And he played the part, too, resting the flashlight on top of his shoulder, shouting orders to imaginary bad guys. "Freeze! Put your hands up!"

Unfortunately, he wasn't able to show off his costume that year, nor his acting skills. With snow up to my knees, I only managed to trudge across the street to one house, the Rick family, hauling a pint-size police officer on my back. Other than Officer Ray Garvey and me, there wasn't a single trick-or-treater out that night. But for giant drifts of snow, the street was deserted. Ray didn't get a true sense of what happens on Halloween night until the following year, when he covered more ground as Batman.

With an eye for detail, Ray decided the costumes in the store did not portray Batman the way he saw Batman. He insisted, "The real Batman wears his underwear on the outside

... they have to be gray." So I dyed a pair of his underpants gray and slipped them up over his costume, making his rendition of Batman almost comical. Laughter erupted each time a neighbor opened their door and took note of Batman's underpants. That year, Ray was a trick-or-treat hit, but not nearly the hit he was the following year. The year Elvis came to town.

When Ray was four years old, he caught his first glimpse of Elvis Presley on TV. It was the anniversary of Elvis's death, and they were running a marathon of his old movies. Ray immediately became a fan. Not only did he learn lyrics to a number of Elvis songs, he mastered his dance moves too, the Jail House Rock rubber leg and gyrating pelvis included. It's one of the only times I remember him trading in his friends and staying indoors to watch his new idol on TV.

That summer, Ray spotted a sewing pattern for an Elvis costume in a store. The infamous Vegas white jump suit and cape. Pointing to the picture of Elvis on the front of the pattern, he said, "Mom, *this* is what I want to be for Halloween."

Examining the pattern, I said to him, "Oh, Ray, this looks way too hard to sew. You'll have to come up with something else."

"Can you at least *try* to make it?" he pleaded.

"I don't know. This thing has a zipper in it."

"So?"

"So zippers are tricky."

"But I really want to be Elvis." I had to laugh, as he had already moved on to specifics, adding, "I need to comb my hair up in the front like cool Elvis. Not fat Elvis."

Ray's enthusiasm was so earnest, I bought the pattern and soon began sewing. I even managed to put the zipper in. I bedazzled the jump suit and matching wide belt with colorful jewels, adding yellow metallic gimp braiding to the high collar and to the cuffs and the bell bottoms. With gold fabric paint,

34

I wrote ELVIS across a cape of shiny white satin. It turned out much better than I had anticipated, but my Mr. Particular complained his costume just wasn't quite right. "Elvis doesn't wear tennis shoes. I need white boots." So I bought my little boy white boots—in the girls' department.

From August to October of that year, Ray grew out his hair so he could style it the way Elvis had. Whenever my parents saw him, they said, "Tell your dad to take you to the barber." Deciding to keep his costume a secret, Ray never told his grandparents why he was growing out his hair, much less tell them we were going to color it black with temporary hair dye.

He kept his costume secret from his friends too, coming up with all sorts of stories. He told his friend Jim, and Jim's sister Pam, that he was probably going to be a Teenage Mutant Ninja Turtle. Same as Jim. Those ninja turtle costumes were all the rage back then and could be found in almost any store. So my neighbor Linda, Jim and Pam's mom, wasn't convinced when Ray told her I was *sewing* his costume—in August no less.

Several years later Linda told me how she had pried the truth out of Ray just days before Halloween. She confessed it didn't take much because Ray could not contain himself any longer, finally admitting that his real costume was the late, great Elvis Presley. She also remembers how Ray pleaded with her, "Don't tell my grandma. It's still a secret."

"We didn't really believe Ray's outrageous idea of being Elvis." Linda laughed. "I had no idea he was such a fan at the tender age of four. My children didn't even know who Elvis was, so they couldn't wait to see what Ray's costume was going to look like."

"It was an unexpected choice," I told her. "It's not like Rusty and I are big Elvis fans, but Ray saw him on TV and that was it. He was going as Elvis."

Linda went on. "I remember my children and I sat on our front porch, the three of us just waiting for Ray to step out your front door. When we finally saw him crossing the street, I couldn't believe it. The little boy with all the big stories really did come out to celebrate the night dressed as Elvis."

I asked her, "Do you remember how he would flip open his cape to strike his Elvis pose on every doorstep? Then he curled up his lip and called out, 'Trick-or-treat, Baby!' in his best Elvis voice."

"I remember that," Linda said. "He stayed in character the whole night, and everyone was smiling from ear to ear. Each time he collected candy, he'd say, 'Thank you. Thank you very much.' Linda chuckled. "What a hound dog."

Though the adults on the block got a kick out of Ray, the children on Ferndale were totally confused by his get-up. My husband stayed home in order to pass out candy that year. When Ray finally came home from trick-or-treating, Rusty asked if his friends even knew who he was supposed to be. Ray said, "No ... but they liked my cape." And to think I went to all the trouble sewing that damn costume. Turns out all a kid really needs on Halloween is a cape.

Once in a while I catch myself thinking back to that night. The excitement. The laughter. Ray's big secret. I can still see the neighbors asking mini-Elvis to wait at their doorstep so they could grab their cameras and photograph him—bulbs flashing in the night like *paparazzi*. Even if his friends didn't know who the King of Rock-n-Roll was, they seemed to recognize there was something special about the little boy in the flashy white jump suit. They bounced along at Ray's side, happy to be part of the magic he created.

K9 Boone

In 1991, Officer Russ Garvey joined the St. Paul K9 Unit. Believe me, the last thing I wanted living with our little boy was a ferocious police dog. But soon enough a German shepherd named Johnny 5 was housed in a kennel in our backyard. He was small and unimpressive, hardly exhibiting the drive needed to work the streets. In fact, two more experienced K9 handlers had already passed on him, choosing to partner up with better-suited dogs. The K9 trainers told Rusty not to get too attached to the scrawny mutt, as the dog was merely a spare until they could find a replacement.

Johnny 5 was the name of a robot character in the 1986 film *Short Circuit*. Rather than stick with a moniker that suggested malfunction or failure, Rusty changed Johnny 5's name to Boone. Boone was the small town in Iowa where his dad hailed from.

Ray wanted so badly to play with Boone, but Rusty insisted he keep his distance until he could trust Boone's temperament. So, while Rusty worked on obedience training in the backyard, Ray watched from the window. When Ray was finally allowed to pet Boone, it was obvious we had nothing to worry about. Boone was incredibly gentle, even tolerating Ray's excessive horseplay. Boone's friendly demeanor was so trustworthy and consistent, we let him roam freely in our yard. I can only remember one time when Boone wandered off. Even then he just crossed the street and jumped in the back seat of our neighbor's car.

At home, Boone didn't seem like much of a police dog. He was more like the neighborhood mascot, drawing kids in as much as Ray did. Everybody loved Boone. But the neighborhood mascot had another side to him. Ray and I discovered this at Rusty's first regional dog trial, competing in apprehension bite work. We could not believe Boone was the same animal that lay on our front porch like a lazy old farm dog. Sitting in the bleachers, we watched Boone take off down the football field after Mark Slettner, a K9 officer and Rusty's decoy. Boone bit down and latched onto Mark's arm, padded by a sleeve, and didn't let go until Rusty commanded him to do so. In that moment, our sweet, lovable dog looked mean and aggressive. In disbelief, Ray said, "That's Boone?"

Rusty, Mark, and Boone made bite work look effortless, their timing so precise it appeared choreographed. Rusty and our dog Boone became an exceptional team. Over the years, they won dozens of medals and trophies in regional and national dog trials throughout the United States—one year earning top billing, first place overall in the nation.

With all of their success, Rusty and Boone gave Ray some bragging rights. Ray was proud of his dad and enjoyed watching him receive applause at K9 award banquets. At one such dog trial, Rusty placed high in several events. One by one the trophies accumulated on the table in front of him. Ray, maybe four years old at the time, kept count. To confirm Rusty was in the lead, Ray asked a little boy at the next table, "Hey, how many trophies did your dad win?"

Rusty immediately felt silly when he overheard Ray. He handed me the keys to his squad car and asked that I quickly stick his trophies in the trunk.

He was also a little embarrassed, yet amused, when Ray answered the phone one day. It was Jim Decowski calling, another K9 officer. Ray called out, "Hey, Dad. The K9 cop who combs his hair like Elvis and never wins a trophy is on the phone."

In first grade, Ray's big mouth got him in trouble. As the story goes, Ray was in the bathroom when he noticed a couple of kindergarten boys pushing each other around. Ray told them to knock it off, adding, "My dad's a cop and he has a police dog. He can arrest you and take you to jail."

The boys went back to class and told their teacher about the older boy who had threatened them in the bathroom. The next thing he knew, the two boys and their teacher appeared in Ray's classroom, looking for the culprit. She asked all the boys to stand up so her students could pick out the aggressor. Ray was quickly identified. He had hardly made it off the school bus when his teacher called to inform me of his inappropriate behavior. I assured her our son had meant no harm. After all, he was the one trying to tell the younger boys how to behave, but we would be sure to have a word with Ray. Later, Rusty laughed that our seven-year-old son had already been in a police line-up.

Ray missed Boone and his dad in the evenings, often asking Rusty why it took him so long to catch the bad guys and come home. In second grade, he wrote a poem titled "Russell," taking a stereotypical pot shot at cops and a solution to his dad's long hours. Never mind his redundant stylings.

RUSSELL
I am a police cop and I like donuts and soda.
I need pop to live and soda to move.
I am a very good cop.
I saw a bad guy when I was once on duty, so I called 911.

With Boone as his partner, I didn't worry too much about Rusty working the streets, until one summer day when he was called in on his day off to assist in the search and capture of a cop killer. That morning, I had a headache. After making breakfast for Ray, I lay down on the couch and asked that he wake me when his cartoon show was over, allowing me a good half hour to sleep off a migraine. But, engrossed in cartoons, Ray never woke me. When I finally got up, I noticed Rusty was gone, his squad car missing from the driveway.

"Ray, where's your dad?" I asked.

"Some guy called and said Dad had to go to work and look for a bad guy."

A short time later, my friend Lori Swanson called, asking if Rusty was working.

"Yeah, he got called into work. I'm not sure what's going on."

"Turn the TV on. It's all over the news," Lori said.

Finding something else for Ray to do, I flipped the channel and watched the terrifying events unfolding. A suspect had murdered Officer Ron Ryan, Jr. after he had responded to a routine "slumper" call—a man sleeping in his car in the parking lot of Sacred Heart Church on St. Paul's East Side. We later learned that after obtaining the subject's license, Officer Ryan had headed to his squad car to check out the man's identification when the assailant shot him five times. Rusty and Boone were among the K9 officers called in to help search for the suspect. My heart raced as I followed the story on the news. That cop killer was still out there. So was my husband. So was Boone.

I brought Ray to the neighbor's house and asked that they keep him away from the TV. Then I scurried back home. The search for the suspect continued, minute-to-minute coverage on every local news station. From both ground and helicopter, live video footage showed the intense manhunt as it progressed throughout the day. K9 units, state and county officers, and SWAT teams were all there, zeroing in on one East Side neighborhood. Residents were asked to stay indoors while law enforcement searched yard to yard, house to house.

Glued to the TV, I paced the floor and prayed the cop killer would soon be apprehended. Instead reporters announced that a second officer had been shot—this time a K9 handler, as well as his dog. I frantically searched the TV screen, hoping to get a glimpse of Rusty and Boone, but I couldn't find them anywhere in the chaos. I half expected to hear a knock at my door, an officer delivering bad news.

My phone began to ring off the hook. It seemed everyone I knew was calling to see if Rusty and Boone were safe. I was home alone, freaking out, until my mom came over and sat with me. Both of us anxiously awaited more details on the officer shooting.

Some time later, it was revealed that the K9 officer had been pronounced dead at the hospital, yet his name would not be released until family members were contacted. The phone calls picked up, and I answered each one with overwhelming worry. Was I the family member they were trying to contact?

Then I received a call from Brad Schlesinger, a neighbor and a Ramsey County sheriff's deputy.

"Darla. It's Brad. Has anyone contacted you yet?"

"No." I felt light-headed and leaned against the kitchen counter for support.

"I'm working security at the hospital." It seemed like an eternity before he added, "It wasn't Rusty."

Immediately I thought how my relief would be someone else's sorrow. And someone I most likely knew, as the K9 families were close. "Brad ... who was it?"

"Tim Jones."

"Oh no," I gasped. "He's Rusty's friend. He was just here last night."

And with that, I cried for Tim's wife, Roxy, and their two young children, whose lives would never be the same. My heart ached for the loss of Ron Ryan, Jr., as well. My thoughts were with his parents, who would soon have to bury their son. I could never have foreseen it then, but there was a day coming when I would understand their pain much more fully.

After Brad's phone call, the nightmare continued. The suspect was still on the loose. And all those searching for him were still in danger, my husband included.

Eventually, reports came in that Tim Jones's dog, K9 Laser, had also died from gunshot wounds. Suddenly, having Boone at Rusty's side was of little comfort.

We didn't have cell phones back then. But even if we had, I know Rusty would not have stopped long enough to call me that day. He was focused on doing his job. It was not until the suspect was in custody that he walked to a pay phone to let me know he was okay. I'll never forget that dejected look of anguish in his eyes when he finally walked through our front door.

Ron Ryan, Jr., the young son of a well-respected St. Paul police officer, and Tim Jones, the leader of the K9 unit, were honored by the close-knit community of St. Paul and the entire state of Minnesota. The outpouring of love and respect for their ultimate sacrifice was overwhelming.

Officer Garvey and K9 Boone were an effective team for over a decade. Boone, once predicted to wash out in training, became one of the most decorated and most stalwart canines in the country.

They were an effective team at home, too, assisting in Ray's respiratory treatments. After Ray breathed in the nebulized meds, Rusty took Ray outside or down to our unfinished basement, where he tossed a ball to Ray, then gave Boone the command to "Fetch 'em up!" Ray would catch the ball and take off running around in circles, Boone hot on his tail. Around and around they'd go, Ray laughing and working up a sweat. It was a two-fold exercise, great fun and a respiratory workout.

To Boone, chasing Ray was a game. To Ray, Boone was everything.

They say a dog is a man's best friend. Given their tight bond, perhaps Boone was Ray's best friend—but only for a couple of years. Two months before Ray turned five, his *real* best friend came to join us.

A Strong Name

I wasn't sewing an Elvis costume in August because I'm one of those over-achieving moms who plans everything in advance. No, I was sewing so our son would have the costume he wanted before our second child was born. I was due at the end of October and wanted Ray set to go on Halloween in case I was in the hospital.

Ray had mixed feelings when we told him I was pregnant. Sometimes he was excited about being a big brother. Other times he seemed worried that a newborn would dethrone the king. He made that very clear one day, when we asked if there was a name he liked for his baby brother or sister.

"Yeah, call it Butthead."

"Ray. That's not very nice," I said.

"Well I like it. When you call us to eat, you can say 'Ray, Butthead, dinner's ready.'"

This time around, we didn't know the gender of our baby. Throughout my pregnancy, I was sure I was having another boy, until the night before I went into labor. I sat in a rocking chair in the new baby's room, recently painted and decorated. Looking at the soft colors, I took note of the glass knobs I had added to the drawers of an antique dresser that would double as a changing table. I thought, *This looks like a girl's room*. It didn't seem likely that crystal glass hardware could determine such a thing, but I remember looking at those knobs, thinking, *I'm definitely having a girl*. And, truth be told, that scared me. I knew how to be a mom to a boy, but I was nervous just thinking about a girl. What if she turned out to be a girlie girl? Growing up, I was a tomboy. I didn't even play with dolls, and I don't particularly like the color pink. *What if we do have a girl and all she wants to wear are pink dresses?*

Boys are easy. Sweat pants, t-shirt, a quick comb across the head and you're out the door. Doesn't even matter if his socks match. A girl? That probably meant going shopping, which I hate. Plus pony tails, dance lessons, and painting her fingernails. *She's probably going to insist that her socks match too.*

But gender wasn't really a concern. I would embrace whatever came our way, boy or girl. What I mostly worried about was another diagnosis of cystic fibrosis.

Rusty and I are among the ten million Americans who are symptom-free carriers of the defective CF gene. A child must inherit two recessive CF genes, one from each parent, to have cystic fibrosis. With each pregnancy, there is a one in four chance that both parents will pass on the CF gene, resulting in a child born with the illness. The odds were in our favor, a 75% chance our baby would be okay, and at the time, there was more hope than ever for a cure.

In 1989, researchers discovered the Cystic Fibrosis Transmembrane Regulator (CFTR) gene and learned that a mutation in this single gene causes CF. Genetic researchers began exploring gene therapy to correct the faulty CFTR gene, ever hopeful that their research would lead to new drugs to treat or ultimately cure cystic fibrosis. There was hope and excitement in the CF community, of which we had become a part. So much so, that when one of the pulmonary specialists at the U of M learned we were expecting, he told us not to worry. "There will be a day soon when we will tell parents, the bad news is your child has cystic fibrosis, and the good news is your child has cystic fibrosis. It just won't matter one way or the other. Everything is going to be okay," he assured us.

So there was hope as we welcomed our second child— yes, a baby girl. We hardly got a glimpse of her before she was whisked away to the intensive care unit. Part way into the delivery, there were signs of meconium and a risk for meconium aspiration syndrome, which could potentially block our baby's airways. The medical staff quickly suctioned our daughter's airways and successfully avoided any respiratory distress.

When our little six-pound daughter was finally placed in my arms, I looked down at a small, fragile-looking child. I held her as she cried, her little lips pursed. She reminded me of a baby bird chirping in its nest. Her skin was wrinkled and saggy, like a worn-out teddy bear missing its stuffing. She had a male balding pattern—a rim of brown hair around the sides and bald on the top. Her soft, gooey ears stuck to her head like cookie dough. "I think she came out too soon," I told Rusty. "She's not done baking." She looked adorable and comical at the same time, and we absolutely loved her.

Rusty picked Ray up from my parents' house and brought him to the hospital to meet his little sister. Ray crawled in bed with me while Rusty placed our newborn in his arms. When I took her pink beanie off to show Ray her hair, he started to laugh. "She looks like an old man," he stated, then planted a kiss on his sister's cheek.

That night, I wrote out a list of girls' names. I could not settle on anything, but I knew Butthead was out of the question. The next morning, Rusty came to the hospital with a list of names he was considering. He asked that I read from my list first, then proceeded to ruin every name I suggested.

"How about Lila? Lila Garvey is a pretty name."

"We can't name her Lila. That's Jon's wife's name."

"Jon is our friend, not family. It's not like there'd be two Lilas in the room at Christmastime," I reasoned.

I glanced at the second name on my list. "How about Emma?"

"No. That sounds too much like enema."

"Seriously? Enema? You're ridiculous. What's on your list?"

"My grandma's sister was Goldie."

"Goldie Garvey? Yeah, that's not happening."

He went down his list until he came to Martha, my maternal grandmother's name. Ironically, I had had Martha on my list too, but crossed it off, deciding it was too big of a name for a tiny baby. But Rusty kept going back to it. "Martha Garvey. Why don't you like it?"

"All these names are too old-fashioned, including Martha. Especially Martha. Keep thinking."

"Look, there's a chance she might have CF. She's going to need a strong name, and I don't know anyone stronger than your grandma."

It was true. My grandma was amazing. She lived on a farm with my grandpa in Atwater, Minnesota. She had eleven children, was physically and mentally strong, and had a wonderful sense of humor. She was hard working, kind and thoughtful, a selfless woman who put her family first. Everyone loved my grandma—Martha Hovey. Still, I wasn't sure it was the right name for our daughter. However, Rusty caught me at a weak moment, his sentiment toward my grandma so sweet. So Martha it was.

I suspected Martha had cystic fibrosis the moment I changed her diaper in the hospital. It was the same distinct smell I remembered when I'd changed Ray's diapers. My heart sank, and I prayed I was wrong. Maybe I was just looking too hard.

A few weeks after she was born, Martha's pediatrician called. She started with the words that usually mean bad news will follow. "Are you sitting down?" A buzzing sound rang in my ears as I listened to what came next. "I'm sorry. Your daughter tested positive for cystic fibrosis."

Martha was too small to do a sweat test—that would come later to confirm. Her initial diagnosis was the result of a blood test. I would have questioned the validity of the blood work, like I had the result of Ray's sweat test, but I was holding a salty-skin baby in my arms, one in desperate need of enzymes. This much I knew.

Rusty stood at my side while I spoke to the doctor, tears rolling down my face. I hung up and, without a word, passed Martha off to him. I ran to our bedroom and slammed the door. Flopping onto the bed, I sobbed into my pillow. Angry with God, I cried out. *I begged you. I prayed for a healthy baby. Why didn't you hear me?*

A short time later, Rusty came up to the bedroom to check on me. Devastated himself, he offered no words. Instead he quietly shook his head while I ranted. Finally, he suggested I leave the house. "Darla, just go somewhere," he pleaded. "Ray doesn't need to see you upset. I've got the kids." The both of us falling apart in front of each other was too much, so we parted ways.

I drove around aimlessly, eventually ending up at Sue Anderson's place. Sue was a childhood friend. I burst into tears the second she opened the door. I collapsed on her couch and told her the news. She handed me a beer. Sue and I had grown up across the street from each other and had a tight bond— like sisters. Our childhoods had been simple and carefree, but now, as adults, we found ourselves faced with difficult challenges. Sue was going through a divorce at the time, and while a divorce is sad, it isn't the end of the world. It's a choice. You can heal from it and move on. No one chooses a disease. I didn't know how I would stay strong and move forward, raising two kids, both with a life-threatening illness. I felt like I was sinking into a dark hole, and I felt guilty and responsible for Martha's illness. Ray's diagnosis had been a complete shock. It felt different with Martha. I kept asking myself, "What did we do to her?"

Eventually, I left Sue's and drove to my parents' home, thinking about my children's future. Cystic fibrosis is an individualized disease. Like Dr. Warwick had told us, some kids are luckier than others. Would my children be among the lucky ones? What if one did well and the other did not? How would either of them cope with their illness? How would Rusty and I smooth the way for them?

Ray was already asking questions about CF. I'll never forget driving home from his first day of Sunday school. When I asked Ray what he had learned, he said, "I learned that God loves everyone, he watches over us, and he helps us. Is that true, Mom?"

"Yeah, I guess it is."

"Well, I don't believe it."

I knew I had a strong-willed child, not always an easy sell, but even I was surprised that he was questioning religion on day one, at the tender age of three.

"What makes you think that, Ray?"

"If God watches over me, why does he let me fall off my bike? And if he helps everyone, why doesn't he help me up?"

I glanced at my little philosopher, sitting in his car seat, and chuckled.

"I don't think God loves me," he continued.

"Of course he does," I said, completely stunned.

"No, he doesn't."

"Why would you say that?"

"If God loves me, why did he give me CF?"

"Well, I don't think he *gave* you CF."

"Yes he did. If he made me, he gave it to me."

At the time, I couldn't make any more sense of religion than my three-year-old could. Life is too complex to think there's a simple answer from above. Rusty and I aren't faithful church-goers by any means, but we had decided to introduce religion to Ray and let him make of it what he wanted. His questions came early and often as he tried to make sense of his world. Now I wondered about Martha. How would she feel about CF? God? Life? I felt so inadequate in that moment, certain I would fall short on emotional support for my children, because, really, how do you bend reality?

We would eventually discover that Ray's and Martha's strength would come from each other far more often than from their parents. A bond would form like none other. But I couldn't possibly know that then. My heart hurt, and I was afraid of what lay ahead.

I pulled into my parents' driveway, dreading what I was about to tell them. They knew this was the day we were to receive test results. My visit turned into a three-way cry fest. Buzz and Mom were devastated but promised they would be there for us. And they were, for the most part. They were loving grandparents, developing close relationships with Ray and Martha. In turn, our children loved going to Grandma and Grandpa's house. But doing respiratory treatment would never be their thing. Their support came in the form of love, not in the form of hands-on respite care. With two CF children, administering four treatments a day—sometimes six or eight if one or both were sick—we would have appreciated a break from assembly-line BDs. But over the years, I came to terms with my family's limitations and stopped looking for what they could not provide.

A Common Denominator

Over the next several months, as much as I fought it, I slipped into a depression. I adored my children and did everything I could to care for them, but almost in a zombie-like state. With the extensive care our children needed, someone had to pay the bills and someone had to provide their hands-on care. Rusty and I slipped into our respective roles. I left my job as a typesetter at American Financial Printing and became a stay-at-home mom while Rusty worked the streets. This meant we had to tighten up our budget and make do without a second income.

Each day I administered Ray and Martha's daily treatments, using a padded table—also called a BD table—recently added to our collection of medical equipment. Ray seemed to accept BDs a little better with his sister receiving the same treatment. It was a welcome change, as I had little energy to argue with him about completing his treatments.

I went through the motions of the day, preparing fattening food to help maintain Ray's weight and sneaking a small enzyme pill on the end of Martha's tongue before quickly popping a bottle of formula in her mouth. Miraculously, she swallowed her pills without choking and gained weight at a steady pace.

Two days a week, I brought Ray to preschool and spent a couple of hours alone with my daughter. Usually she napped. Usually I did too. Being depressed is tiring.

Each night, I rocked Martha to sleep, whispering in her ear, "I will love you. I will hold you. And I will rock you. I'm sorry, it's all I can do right now, but wait for me. I'll get there soon, I promise."

In my funk, I had hardly noticed what was taking place right under my nose, until one day when I placed Martha on a blanket in the living room and asked Ray to keep an eye on her while I started dinner. Suddenly, Ray ran into the kitchen. Alarmed by the sound of his quick footsteps, I thought something had happened to Martha. Before I could ask, Ray blurted, "Isn't Martha beautiful?" Then he ran back in the living room to play with his sister. I stood at the stove for a moment and took in Ray's announcement. *He only sees the beauty in this wonderful little girl, not an illness. What the hell is wrong with me?*

I turned the burner off and joined my children in the living room. Ray pulled his little sister to a seated position on the blanket and said, "Watch this, Mom." Then he smiled at Martha and said, "Where's your nose?" Martha immediately pointed to her nose. I was shocked. She seemed far too young to identify body parts.

"Oh my gosh, Ray. You taught her that?"

"Yeah, she knows a lot of stuff. Watch this. Where's your ears?" Ray asked, and Martha pointed to her ears. I plopped down on the couch and watched the two interact as a wave of guilt washed over me. *My God, what else have I missed out on?*

I know it probably sounds corny, but I physically felt something lift in that very moment. An awakening of sorts. I had spent so much time in a fog, feeling sorry for my kids for having CF. So much time looking at them and thinking, *Oh dear, you two have no idea how serious this is.* I had wasted time feeling sorry for myself in a way, too, I suppose. But that day, my five-year-old son changed everything with three simple words. *"Isn't Martha beautiful?"*

I began to watch more closely, taking in all the good. I loved seeing how happy Ray and Martha made each other. Whenever Martha woke up from a nap, she bounced on the crib mattress, reaching her arms out, not for me, but for her brother. Their bond started immediately and grew stronger over the years. They were remarkable individuals, even more remarkable together. The destructive feelings of guilt and fear I had been carting around turned into feelings of joy for what I had. Two beautiful children.

There weren't more than a few weeks in her life when Martha didn't do respiratory therapy. With an early start to her routine, she was generally more compliant than Ray. Of course, there were certainly days when she fussed and squirmed during her treatments, but nowhere near the fight Ray had put up as a toddler. Regardless of compliancy, administering treatment to both kids was time consuming and exhausting, to say the least. But when Ray was six years old, medical advancements in CF made our lives a little easier. Around that time, Dr. Warwick co-invented a chest wall oscillation device called the Vest Airway Clearance System, or simply "the vest." Essentially, the vest is a mechanical way of clearing mucus from the lungs. Two hoses extend from the vest and attach to the airway clearance machine. The machine fills the vest with air like a blood pressure cuff, creating compressions to the chest, helping to loosen and move mucus from the lungs. In addition to compressions, the machine shoots bursts of air through the hoses, taking the place of percussion by hand.

Ray buckled into the vest, much like he would wear a life jacket. Every five minutes, we increased the speed and frequency of air pressure from the machine, building up to an almost intolerable, intense squeezing and shaking of his body. Once Ray reached that final setting for five minutes, he immediately unbuckled the vest and tossed it onto the floor. Like a little bull busting out of a pen, he left his CF world behind, running off to do better things.

While the new procedure was physically easier on Rusty and me, the noise level of the airway clearance machine was ridiculous. And if Ray wanted to watch a movie during his treatment, the TV had to be at full volume. It drove me crazy.

Over the years, the machines have gotten a lot smaller and less noisy. But back then it was a cumbersome piece of equipment, weighing over a hundred pounds. Even though it was on wheels, it was difficult to transport if we even entertained the idea of traveling. But worst of all, it was nearly impossible for Ray to communicate during treatments. The vibration of the vest created a staccato voice, making it sound as if he were riding in a car on an extremely bumpy road. Additionally, we administered his nebs at the same time, his voice muffled behind a mask.

Martha wasn't big enough to do the vest yet, so I still used the padded table for her BDs. I felt disconnected from Ray as he sat tethered to a machine across the room. I never thought I'd say this, but some days I asked if I could pound on Ray rather than fire up that damn loud machine. I missed having physical contact with my son. The BD table was more intimate. We could carry on a conversation and laugh and joke with one another—that is, on days when Ray didn't squawk about doing his treatment. The first time I asked Ray if I could pound on him instead of doing the vest, he said, "Really, Mom?" and willingly hopped on the padded table with a huge smile on his face. He obviously missed that personal connection with his mom, too.

But the most profound connection Ray had was with his sister. Ray didn't know anyone else with cystic fibrosis except Martha. They were in this together, and often times in cahoots. I can't count how many times I had to drag them out from under a bed or coax them out of the storage area under the basement stairwell as they hid to avoid their treatments. I can't count how many times they refused to come inside when it was time for therapies, often taking refuge inside a friend's home.

Ray continued to ask questions about his illness. Some were simple and relatively easy to answer. For example, one night when Ray was about six years old, while I tucked him into bed, he asked, "Who makes me sick all the time? God?" He was fighting a cold then, fed up with doing four treatments a day.

Again with the God questions. I steered clear of that and said, "You know how I remind you to wash your hands all the time?"

"Yeah," he responded between coughs.

"Well, there's something called germs that can make you sick if you don't wash."

"Yuk! Then I hate germs," Ray stated before drifting off to sleep.

It was only a matter of time before Martha began asking questions of her own. Both her and Ray's inquiries centered on the same central theme: *Why? Why do we have CF?*

I tended to get choked up, searching for the right words. In my head, in those moments, all I thought was, *You guys have CF because of your parents' crappy genes.*

But Rusty was quick to respond in positive ways, turning their attention to all the things they could do in spite of CF. His can-do attitude was profoundly apparent at a CF fundraiser we attended when Ray was in first grade and Martha just two years old. We raised money and participated in the Minneapolis Great Strides Walk to cure cystic fibrosis. I co-chaired the event that year with a gentleman whose granddaughter had CF. In order to spread CF awareness, he decided to set up a canopy tent at the start/finish line, under which he placed a padded table where he and his granddaughter would demonstrate what bronchial drainage entails.

While he performed his granddaughter's BD to the crowd of walkers, Ray was busy putting on a different sort of demonstration. Rusty had asked Klint Klaas, Ray's karate instructor, if he would bring a few of his students to the fundraiser to perform karate moves. Klint didn't hesitate to say yes. That day, before walkers took to the event route along Lake Calhoun, Ray proudly led his class in a number of *katas*, or series of choreographed patterns of karate movements. Klint did a fine job speaking on behalf of his students, featuring Ray front and center—not as the poor kid with cystic fibrosis, but rather the focused and accomplished young karate student who just happened to have CF.

Ray and Martha received plenty of encouragement from us, but no one championed for them better than they did for each other. Cystic fibrosis was a common denominator, bringing a brother and sister especially close. If one of them was having a difficult time, the other came to the rescue.

For example, when Martha was three years old and Ray eight, I took them to a park one summer day for a picnic. We spent the afternoon playing outdoors until the sun was about to set. A protest developed when I announced it was time to go home. My children sensed what would inevitably follow. Going home meant they had to do treatments.

Ray pleaded for five more minutes on the playground. I was about to cave in to his request when Martha burst into tears and took off running. I ran after her, scooped her up in my arms and carried her to the car. Disappointed by our quick departure from the park, Ray sadly trailed along at my side. He opened the back door of the car, making way for his screaming sister. With her back arching and little legs kicking, I struggled to buckle Martha in her car seat.

"Why do we have to have CF?" she screamed, tears rolling down her hot little cheeks. Unable to muster up a good answer, I slid behind the wheel. In the rearview mirror, I watched as Ray wrapped one arm around his sister's sweaty neck before stating, "Martha, you want to know why we have CF? I'll tell you why. It's because God doesn't give CF to weak people. He only gives it to tough people, and we're tough, Martha. We can do it."

I readjusted the rearview mirror to hide my tears. Ray, the little guy who constantly questioned religion, was now using it to console his sister.

As the years passed, Ray and Martha's bond grew stronger. Separating them was nearly impossible. One early evening while doing the dishes, I watched the neighborhood activity from the kitchen window. Rusty was on the porch having a Popsicle with the kids. Ray's buddies were playing football across the street. When Seth, Justin, Jim and Tyler spotted Ray, they called out, "Hey, Ray! Can you play?"

"I'll be right over." Ray finished tying the laces on his high tops.

Martha quickly finished her Popsicle, rushing to join her brother. Before she could get a running start, however, Rusty pulled her onto his lap.

"You stay here, Martha. We'll find something else for you to do." Rusty worried Martha would get hurt playing rough with the older boys. Plus he didn't think Ray should be responsible for his little sister all the time. But I don't think Ray ever thought of Martha as a responsibility.

Martha began to cry, reaching her arms out to her brother. "Raaay! Wait for me," she called out.

Halfway down the front lawn, Ray stopped in his tracks and hollered, "Dad, just let her come with me."

Rusty waved him on. "She'll be fine, Ray. You go ahead."

Squirming to get down, Martha cried out again, "Ray!"

Still standing in the yard, Ray yelled, "Dad, it's okay. Let her come with me. She's good." He added, "We pass the ball to her."

Rusty let go of Martha, and I watched as she practically stumbled down the front lawn to catch up to Ray. He took her hand in his before crossing Ferndale Street. When they got to the other side, I heard Ray call out to his friends. "Hey, you guys! My sister's going to play, too. Take it easy on her."

Not only was Ray protective of Martha, he never sold her out—never told her to get lost. In turn, Martha rarely had to seek out friends on her own. She was built into Ray's crew. When I looked for either kid, I found them both.

Until the Sun Sets

To the south of our home, the large scaffold structure of Carver ski jump stood high above the tree line. On winter nights the ski jump glowed brightly. We could see the jumpers ski halfway down the ramp, but because the trees blocked our view, we missed their flight, never knowing if they stuck their landings.

During ski-jumping tournaments, cheers from spectators reached our front porch. Many times the excitement drew us to the ski jump. Bundled up, I would walk Ray and Martha down Ferndale Street to watch those brave souls glide through the air. But it was during the summer months when the ski jump really called to us. Actually, it was just the landing hill we were most interested in.

I come from a long line of ski jumpers, Buzz included. I grew up near Battle Creek ski jump, and as a young girl I watched my father, my Great Uncle Pete Denisson, and his sons, Tim and Corky, compete on the St. Paul Ski Club. Battle Creek ski jump was also a summer hangout for me and my friends. After hearing stories of my childhood pastime, one afternoon I found Ray in the garage trying to slice up a cardboard box with a large knife.

"What are you doing, Ray?"

"Cutting a couple pieces of cardboard for me and Martha. Can I take her to the landing hill to slide? You used to do it when you were my age."

"Sure. Cut off a piece large enough for me, too."

"Are you serious, Mom?"

"Yeah, that's the best part of being your mom. I get to cash in on being a kid again." I added, "Do you know how stupid I'd look, at my age, sliding down the hill by myself?"

"Yes I do," Ray answered too quickly.

With cardboard squares tucked under our arms, we steered our bikes one-handed down to the jump, cutting through the park on its blacktopped trails. We ditched our bikes in the tall grass, ignored the "No Trespassing" sign, and squeezed our way through an opening in the chain-link fence. Wispy purple and golden-yellow wildflowers were sprinkled across acres of wooded land surrounding the ski jump. Mature trees filtered the sun's light as we stopped to watch four deer amble through a clearing in the distance.

With long skis balanced over their shoulders, hundreds of ski jumpers have trudged up the old wooden stairs alongside the landing hill. We climbed the same steps, carrying cardboard rather than skis, our anticipation nonetheless exciting. Over and over we sailed down the bumpy hill screaming and laughing, often ejected from our makeshift sleds.

That summer day at the ski jump—the first of many—is ingrained in my mind forever, and I know now that I am one of the lucky ones. I had the innate sense to pay attention to even the simplest of pleasures. I took in the life around me and didn't find out when it was too late that I should have watched more closely.

Our front porch, partially shaded by a large red burning bush, was one of my favorite places to watch Ray and Martha play. Countless evenings, from a faded rattan rocker, I looked on as my children soaked up the last drops of summer sunshine. Rusty and I had loosened up the rules and allowed Ray and Martha to close up shop on Ferndale Street. It was hard to call it a day when they were feeling well. And so they played until the sun set.

For the most part Ray and Martha were old souls, unimpressed with material things. What they *did* seemed far more important than what they *had*. I often joked that I could hand either of them a stick and they'd find a way to entertain themselves.

In his signature black high-top Converse sneakers, Ray tore around the neighborhood on a thirty-year-old banana seat bike. Other boys his age were not interested in riding a retro bike without hand brakes and multiple gears, but Ray loved to slam his weight back on his pedals and come to a skidding stop in the driveway.

Martha quickly outgrew her little pink bike with training wheels and rode Ray's old bike. At some point the foot pedals went missing. Remarkably, Martha rode that wreck of a two-wheeler when she was just three years old, barefoot. She curled her little monkey toes over the metal pegs, anxious to go wherever her big brother was leading.

Ray's favorite place to drag Martha, and anyone else willing to risk their parents' reprimand, was the junkyard. It wasn't really a junkyard, you know, with barbed wire fencing or a guard dog. It was actually an elderly man's back yard—a large piece of property, deeply wooded and scattered with discarded objects. I don't remember how the kids first stumbled upon it, but once he'd discovered it, Ray was drawn to the place, always hoping to find some small treasure.

One spring afternoon, I gave my spaghetti sauce another stir and wondered what was keeping Ray so long. He often lost track of time and never stayed in one friend's yard long enough for me to find him. Rather than make a dozen phone calls, I had learned to get his attention with an ear-piercing, four-fingered whistle. If he didn't hear me himself, one of his friends was sure to call out, "Ray. Your mom wants you." From any given direction, I might faintly hear Ray call back, "I'm commming!"

That afternoon, I whistled for him several times from the front porch, and again from the back patio, with no response. Frustrated, I went inside.

"Martha, where do you think your brother went?"

She looked up from a cartoon show. "I don't know ... maybe the junkyard?"

"I'm going to set the table. Will you go out front and watch for Ray?"

With Rusty at work, I had pulled just three plates from the cupboard when suddenly I heard Martha's little footsteps thump across the kitchen floor. She screamed, "Mom. Ray caught a rabbit! Come see it."

I followed her outside to find Ray standing in the front yard with his friends, a large gray-and-white rabbit cradled in his arms.

"Where in the world did you get that rabbit?" I asked.

"I was down at the junkyard with Patrick and I just caught him."

"No one catches a rabbit, Ray."

"Well, I did," he said.

"It must be injured or something," I insisted.

"No, he looks fine to me." He snuggled the rabbit closer to his chest.

"How could you possibly catch that rabbit?"

"He was just sitting there," Ray began to explain.

"And you just grabbed him before he had a chance to run?" I interrupted.

"Yeah, I walked up to him real nice and slow and grabbed him. It wasn't that hard, Mom. He was just sitting in his cage."

I burst out laughing and then insisted the boys return the junkyard man's pet rabbit to its hutch. But not before I snapped a picture of Ray and Patrick with their "catch."

Carver ski jump, the junkyard, and a neighborhood playground a few blocks away were about as far as any kid on Ferndale Street was allowed to explore. And even then, they were instructed to travel in groups or have an adult accompany them. Sadly, Martha and Ray would never experience the far-reaching freedom that both Rusty and I had enjoyed in the 1960s and '70s, largely in part because the 1990s brought with it a heightened sense of fear for our children's safety.

In 1989, a horrific event in Minnesota had caused a drastic change in the way mothers and fathers parented. That year, an eleven-year-old boy named Jacob Wetterling was abducted in the small town of St. Joseph, Minnesota, about an hour northwest of the Twin Cities. Jacob, his older brother, and a friend were biking home from a Tom Thumb convenience store when a masked man came out of nowhere and ordered the boys to toss their bikes into a ditch and lie face down on the ground. The man let Jacob's brother and the friend go, but Jacob wasn't so lucky. His abduction would remain a mystery for twenty-seven years. His body wasn't found until 2016.

There was a collective nationwide heartbreak for the Wetterling family, but Minnesota folks were especially affected. If something so monstrous could happen in the innocent little town of St. Joseph, we feared it could happen anywhere. And so the reins were pulled in and children were supervised more closely. Consequently, Ferndale Street became a close-knit neighborhood where parents looked out for the well-being of *every* child—not just their own. The African proverb "It takes a village" accurately describes the way of life on our block back then. This, in my opinion, was both good and bad: good that our children were monitored, but bad that they could not get away with anything or solve their own problems without an adult intervening.

Nevertheless, we loved that Ferndale was a lively street that turned into an instant playground the second any child stepped outside. Justin and Tyler Rick lived directly across the street. They were close in age to Ray and Martha, and the four of them were inseparable. Then there was Jim, who lived next door to the Ricks. He was academically gifted and had more interest in computer games and books than he did in outdoor sports. Yet Ray made a career out of coaxing him outside to play. Linda often told us how Ray would march into their house and call out to her son, "Jim! Get your lazy butt off the computer. I set up the nets. You're playing street hockey." And if Ray could flirt with Pam while he waited for Jim, that was a bonus.

Pam, Laura and Jessie were the oldest girls in the neighborhood and the nurturing caretakers of the younger girls on the block: Martha, Brooke, Katelyn, and Sidnee—the funny little girl who was known for knocking on our door to ask, "You got any snacks, Darla?" She wasn't the only kid to cash in on the treats I regularly doled out to help my little ones maintain their weight.

There were five brothers who lived at the end of the road. They wore rain boots every day, no matter the weather. No one ever called them by their first names. The five brothers were lumped together as one entity. They were the Peade boys.

Patrick lived on the corner and was notorious for wandering into people's garages and helping himself to anything that caught his fancy. When neighbors saw Patrick coming down the street, one by one, every opened garage door immediately went down.

Garett, a little freckle-faced boy, lived across the street from Patrick. He was a few years younger than Ray, yet he tore around with the older boys and rarely wore a t-shirt. All summer long, adults on the block rubbed sunscreen on Garett's little sunburned shoulders.

And then there was Seth, the little guy who lived on the other side of the Ricks. Most kids found Rusty's size and police presence a bit intimidating, but not Seth. He wasn't afraid of anyone, including Rusty. He actually bossed him around, saying things like, "Hey, Rusty, you better move your squad car so it doesn't get dented. We're going to shoot pucks." Rusty got a kick out of Seth, impressed with his directness, and usually did what he was told.

There was no doubt that Ray was the ringleader, the Ferndale conductor, rounding everyone up to play, but I'd be lying if I said it was all good-natured. Ray and Seth were a lot alike and became best buds—and sometimes holy terrors. They were confident boys who were far too brave for their own good, often venturing off beyond our comfort zone. They were also huge pranksters. By no means were either of them mean-spirited, but sometimes they took it a step too far. Seth's dad, Stu, had been in the military. His idea of punishment for both his son and ours came in the form of push-ups. If he saw they were up to no good, Stu ordered the boys to drop and give him twenty. Many times over the years, I watched the two little guys pumping out push-ups in Seth's driveway. I think they almost liked getting in trouble so they could impress Stu with their perfect push-up form.

On most days, the Ferndale Street gang hung out at our house, partly because I encouraged it so I could keep an eye on our little Dennis the Menace and his friend Seth, and partly because the children knew I allowed a fair amount of chaos in our yard. I didn't care if the kids covered every inch of our driveway with sidewalk chalk, or dragged out the garden hose to fill up squirt guns and water balloons, carrying out a water war on a hot summer's day. I didn't bat an eye when the boys built wooden bike jumps in the street just outside our home. Except for the time Ray had Martha and her friend, Audra, lie down next to the bike jump, insisting that he could jump clear over the both of them. Which he did—more than once—before I had a chance to pull the plug on his Evel Knievel daredevil move.

Winter brought its own flair of chaos. Friendly-fire snowball fights, building snowmen and snow forts, and sledding in our backyard were regular affairs.

Rusty wasn't quite as welcoming of such disorder, and everyone knew it. When he came home, the neighborhood kids tried to scurry away before he could yell at them to clean up whatever disaster was left behind from that day's shenanigans. Things were put back in order, but the next day the circus started all over again.

Of all the neighborhood games, Ray and Martha were most famous for organizing flashlight tag. The weekly summer ritual began and ended on our front porch. Before the games could begin, Ray made the exact same announcement. Holding up Rusty's sturdy police flashlight for everyone to see, he said, "This is my dad's flashlight. Don't drop it. It cost a hundred bucks."

As word got out about flashlight tag, kids from a three-block radius joined in. Every Friday night was met with excitement. However, I remember one week when the turnout was unusually low, and Ray was worried that flashlight tag would have to be canceled. He asked if he could run down a few blocks to get the booger boys. "Who are the booger boys?" I asked.

"You'll see." A few minutes later, two young boys trailed behind Ray, both with snot-encrusted noses. Ray gestured toward the boys and whispered, "See. I told you, Mom."

Still short on players, Ray went to the Holms' to get Pam and Jim. Pam was on the phone with a girlfriend. When her friend overheard Ray at the door, she asked, "Is that Ray? Is he getting flashlight tag going? I'll be right over." Pretty soon, a car full of high school kids pulled up in front of the Holms' house.

And so, from our front porch, I watched a familiar sight —the glow of a flashlight lighting up the dark summer sky as the tagger searched for someone to tag. I witnessed high schoolers assisting the preschoolers as they darted through the lawns along Ferndale Street. I heard the sound of quiet laughter paired with the whispers of friends instructing each other on where to hide. And, on that legendary night of flashlight tag, I saw my son and daughter running hand and hand—ducking behind a hedge, or army crawling under someone's porch—together.

"When you have exhausted all possibilities, remember this: you haven't."

~ Thomas Edison

This Day Came Too Fast

Though he had once been round faced, a recent drop in weight was now noticeable even in Ray's smile, his teeth seemingly too large for his face. He was ten years old and falling off the growth chart—again. Oddly, Ray didn't seem the least bit affected by his slight build. Even at his lowest weight, he walked with confidence and maintained a unique style. You'd never know that under a baggy pair of cargo pants or a vintage sweatshirt, there was hardly enough meat to cover his bones.

While Ray struggled with each and every ounce, Martha looked the picture of health. On a warm spring afternoon, Rusty and I worked in the yard while the kids rode their bikes up and down the street. I looked at Ray's thin legs sticking out from his shorts and took note of how easily Martha kept up with her older brother, light brown hair blowing off her shoulders as she pedaled fast.

Resting against a rake, I pointed out the obvious. "Ray's getting so thin. I'm worried."

"He just started drinking those weight gain shakes. Give him a chance," Rusty said. "He'll fill out. He's fine." Once again, he reminded me that he had been a skinny kid too.

"It's not the same. You don't have CF. If he gets sick, he has nothing to work with."

"Look how happy they are on their bikes. Stop worrying. Today's good."

I tucked those two words in the back of my mind, revisiting them many times over the years. Sometimes, all you get is one day. One day when, if you're smart enough to stay in the moment, you realize that *today's good*.

The University of Minnesota CF clinic was busy and understaffed when our children were young. Ray and Martha's pulmonary function tests and physical exams lasted half the day because their schedule was always backed up. I got ready for CF checkups the same way I got ready for a picnic, packing a small cooler for lunch. We eventually moved Ray and Martha's care to Minneapolis Children's Respiratory and Critical Care. Dr. McNamara, a pulmonary specialist, was now following the two. With fewer patients, appointments took a fraction of the time, and we felt confident that Dr. McNamara was up to date on the latest CF research and patient care.

However, by the end of the fourth grade, Ray was heading downhill. At a checkup, Dr. McNamara noted that Ray had not gained a single pound from his previous visit. He said it was time for us to discuss the next step: a gastrointestinal tube, or G-tube, for supplemental feedings. Dr. McNamara had hinted at this once before, but I'd quickly shrugged it off, asking what else we could do. That was when he'd prescribed high-caloric weight gain shakes specifically designed for CF patients. This time, he was more firm about the G-tube.

As much as Ray respected Dr. McNamara, he did not appreciate what his doctor was now presenting. He only listened to the G-tube spiel for a minute before he interrupted, "No way. I'm not getting a tube." Then he looked past Dr. McNamara and glared at me, as if to ask, *Are you in on this stupid idea, Mom?*

Teary-eyed and unable to speak, I failed to put Ray at ease. Dr. McNamara broke through the tension between us and told Ray that a lot of his CF patients benefitted from tube feedings. He asked his nurse to bring a G-tube in to show us. Ray stared at the contraption in the nurse's hand while Dr. McNamara described how the tube was surgically placed in the stomach, pointing out that just a portion of it would show on the outside of his tummy. He compared this part of the tube to that of a valve on a beach ball, referring to it as a button, which somehow made it sound cute. He insisted no one would even notice it under Ray's clothes.

Tears welled as Ray examined the device. I can't remember the entire conversation between the two. Only one of Ray's questions stands out now. "Can I get it wet?"

"Sure, you can shower with it," Dr. McNamara said.

"No, I mean could I still swim?"

Dr. McNamara insisted the tube wouldn't change anything about Ray's daily life, not even swimming. At night, a bag of formula would slowly drip through the tube via a pump. During the day, the valve on the cute little button would remain closed, and Ray could eat regular meals and go about his business as usual. But, at the end of their discussion, Ray firmly reiterated, "I don't like it. I'm not getting one." He tried to sound brave, but his lower lip was quivering.

Martha sat in my lap, listening. She was only five years old, yet she looked concerned for Ray. Maybe worried about herself, too. Would she have to get a feeding tube someday?

Dr. McNamara looked to me for support. Instead I said, "There must be something else we can try."

He shrugged and said we were stuck between a rock and a hard place. He pointed out that Ray's love of sports was a Catch-22. It was good for his lungs, but competitive sports burned more calories than he could afford to lose.

About to start spring league hockey, Ray blurted, "I'm not getting a tube, and I'm not quitting hockey."

Dr. McNamara told Ray that a feeding tube would not interfere with hockey and that gaining weight meant gaining strength, which in turn would help Ray perform better on the ice.

"I'm already good on the ice," Ray said. "I'll drink more weight gain shakes, I promise."

In the end, Dr. McNamara cut Ray a deal. He asked to see him back in one month. If Ray had gained at least three pounds by then, he'd drop the subject of a feeding tube—for now.

"Deal," Ray said, and quickly hopped off the table and skipped out of the clinic.

While Ray celebrated his victory, inside I wanted to die. He would be hard pressed to put on three pounds in four months, much less four weeks, because Ray hated the shakes. To make things more manageable, rather than drinking a full glass all at once, we poured the shakes into shot glasses, making Ray take "shake shots" throughout the day. Rusty was good at catching Ray on the go. It was more likely he would slug back a shot without a fuss if it meant he could continue out the front door to join his friends.

Over the next four weeks, tensions in our home rose to an all-time high. Determined to help Ray avoid surgery, I added fattening ingredients to food in every creative way I could think of. Rusty went into coaching mode, encouraging Ray to push himself to eat like he would push himself in wrestling. But this was not a fun sport. Ray's opponent was his own stubborn body, one he couldn't quite overtake. Once filled with joyful conversations and laughter, mealtime turned into a stand-off of sorts between father and son. Ray insisted he was finished eating even when his plate wasn't clean. Rusty impatiently pleaded for him to eat more, down to counting bites. "Eat two more bites of everything on your plate, and then you can go play."

I supported Rusty and encouraged Ray, but watching our son's determination slowly fade was heartbreaking. His weigh-in was getting closer, and we were getting more desperate.

One night Ray fussed about finishing dinner, pushing food around his plate with a fork. Exasperated, Rusty informed him that he couldn't hang out with his buddies unless he first drank a shake. With tears in his eyes, Ray watched his dad pour a full glass, not a shot glass. Ray sat at the kitchen counter, unwilling to even lift the glass to his mouth. "I can't do it, Dad."

"Yes, you can."

Ray sat quietly, staring at the glass.

Growing impatient, Rusty asked, "Do you want to get a tube?"

"No, I don't, Dad. But I'm full."

"Damn it, just do it, Ray."

"Listen," I interrupted. "He just ate. Let's try the shake later."

"Stay out of this, Darla."

"No. I'm not staying out of this. He's my son, too, and anyone can see this isn't manageable right now. He can drink it later. What's the difference?"

In an attempt to keep the peace, Ray took a gulp, then proceeded to gag. Rusty accused him of faking it. So Ray forced another sip, gagged, and threw up all over the counter.

"I'll take care of this, Ray. You go play." I nearly cried as I waved him on.

"Why did you let him go? Why didn't you just stay out of it?"

While wiping the mess off the counter, I laid into Rusty. "I know you're frustrated and you want to fix this. I know you think I'm undermining you and that I'm too easy on Ray. But, goddamn it, Rusty. That was ridiculous."

"He has to fight for this, Darla."

"I get it, but the kid was full. You're putting too much pressure on him, and it backfired. He threw up and wasted every single calorie, so what did that accomplish?"

That night when I tucked Ray in bed, he said, "Mom, I'm trying."

"I know you are, Ray." I took a seat at the end of his bed. "Remember Dr. McNamara said the feeding bag holds four cans of formula? It's kind of like your shakes, only even more calories. It would pump into a tube while you're asleep. You wouldn't even know it was happening. And you'd never have to drink another shake again."

Ray stared at the ceiling, and I could almost see his wheels spinning.

"I know it sounds awful to have something inserted into your tummy," I continued. "But maybe it's not as bad as you think."

"I really don't want the tube, Mom."

"Let me ask you something, Ray. Do you think you could drink four cans of formula every day *and* eat your meals and snacks? If you could, you wouldn't have to get the tube."

"I don't think I can do four. It's really hard." Ray wiped his eyes dry. "Dad's mad at me. He wants me to be tough, but sometimes it's hard to be tough."

"Trust me, Ray. It might seem that way, but your dad's not mad at *you*. He's mad at the *situation*. He wishes this wasn't happening to his little guy. He loves you." Before I turned out his light, I added, "By the way, Ray. You're the toughest kid I know."

During the days leading up to Ray's weigh-in, I hid the scale, claiming it was broken. Unaware of Ray's current weight, we drove to the CF clinic praying he had packed on at least three pounds. We collectively held our breath as Ray stepped on to the doctor's scale. Staring at the number, Ray immediately broke down.

Dr. McNamara referred us back to the University of Minnesota to discuss surgery with their medical team. We were introduced to Dr. Carlos Milla, who spoke about the benefits of tube feedings and the low risk of the procedure. All the while, Ray wiped away tears. Patting our son on the back, Rusty said, "How about you give the tube a try for a while? If you gain a bunch of weight, we'll have it removed."

"It can come out?" Ray looked surprised. That hadn't occurred to him, and to be honest, it hadn't occurred to me either.

Dr. Milla looked like he was about to intervene but thought better of it.

"Yeah. You don't have to have it forever," Rusty said.

"How long then?" Ray asked.

"I don't know. Maybe a year?"

"So, I can get it out when I start middle school?" There was some hope in Ray's voice until Dr. Milla stepped in, explaining that when teenage boys go through puberty, they need to eat like crazy in order to grow. Teenagers with cystic fibrosis have to eat even more. "The feeding tube will help so you don't miss a big growth spurt," he said.

"Well, maybe you just use the tube until you start high school, then," Rusty suggested.

Ray sat quietly for a moment, then asked, "If I decide to do this, when do I have to have surgery?"

Before Dr. Milla said anything about a surgery date, Rusty firmly stated, "You can enjoy the whole summer, Ray. We'll wait until August."

"I guess." Ray reluctantly agreed, wiping tears from his eyes. I imagine he hoped that somehow we'd all forget about this nonsense come August.

That shirtless summer, Ray tore around the neighborhood with his buddies and spent many afternoons swimming at Carver Beach. He looked as if he didn't have a care in the world, but I often wonder if the thought of surgery loomed over his head like it did ours.

Darla Garvey

We took an RV trip that summer to visit our friends Lori and Tim McIntosh in Evansville, Indiana, camping at Jelly Stone Park in Wisconsin along the way. Ray and Martha had a wonderful time sleeping in the RV with the McIntosh kids and taking refuge from southern humidity at a nearby pool. But soon enough, August rolled around.

Ray was admitted into the hospital a couple of days prior to the surgery. He received four vest treatments a day to tune up his lungs before being put under anesthesia. He had been playing football with his buddies in Tyler and Justin Rick's back yard right up to the last second before heading to the hospital. In fact, I literally pulled out of the driveway and called for him from the car window. I watched as Ray grudgingly set a football down on the lawn, said goodbye to his friends, and sauntered across the street. Opening the back door, he slid in and said, "This day came too fast."

A nurse escorted us to Ray's hospital room on the fifth floor of Minneapolis Fairview Hospital. Before she even opened the door, however, Ray was gone. He had spotted a playroom on our way in, threw me a quick smile, and took a detour to check it out.

Just then, a little boy on a big wheel bike zoomed down the hallway. Ray stopped the kid and asked where he'd gotten the bike. "They store bikes in a closet down there somewhere." The little boy pointed.

Later that afternoon, Rusty and Martha came to the hospital. Martha entered her brother's room with apprehensiveness written all over her face. Immediately putting her at ease, Ray hopped out of bed and led Martha down the hallway in search of the bike closet. Moments later, we heard their laughter as they raced each other up and down the hallway.

The night before his surgery, we were told Ray's surgeon couldn't stop by and talk to us as promised. I insisted that I at least speak with him over the phone. Late in the evening, I took his call, standing at the nurse's station. He assured me that meeting Ray wasn't necessary, that he was already familiar with Ray's case and that the surgery was a simple, straightforward procedure. He already rubbed me the wrong way, his tone so smug.

He ran down the steps to a gastrostomy; then he told me he would also perform another procedure, something called a Nissen.

"Excuse me, what is a Nissen?" I asked.

He explained how it was a necessary step to avoid potential reflux and subsequent aspiration issues during tube feedings. That sounded reasonable to me until he described how he was going to wrap the top part of Ray's stomach around the outside of his esophagus. Then the "wrap" would be stitched in place.

"Hold up. We're talking about my son here. This sounds pretty involved."

With an impatient exhale, he said, "What more do you want to know about the procedure?"

"For starters, why wasn't it mentioned before now?"

"I don't know, but a Nissen is part of the surgical plan in the morning."

"Whose plan?" My voice was shaking now. "This is the first I'm hearing about it."

After a few more frank exchanges, the surgeon went on to say, "Just so you know, a Nissen is irreversible. Once the stomach and esophagus are attached, it's permanent."

"What does that mean for Ray?"

"It means your son won't be able to throw up."

"What are you talking about? What happens if he gets sick?"

"Nothing can move up from the stomach to the esophagus after a Nissen, so he'll have to open the valve and expel stomach contents from the G-tube."

"You've got to be kidding me." Time seemed to stand still as a disturbing image flashed before me. One of Ray at school. He's sitting at his desk, feeling nauseous. In a panic, he reaches under his shirt and, in front of the entire class, opens the valve on the button. Vomit spews from the tube and splashes onto the floor. Humiliated, Ray runs out of the classroom.

"So what happens when we remove the tube?" I asked the surgeon.

"I don't understand. Why would you remove the tube?"

"Because that's what we promised our son."

"If you remove the tube, he'd have no way to throw up. The Nissen cannot be undone."

"So what's he supposed to do when he's sick and nauseous?"

"Therein lies the problem. If you remove the feeding tube … well, I don't know … I guess he could put a tube down his nose and let it come up that way."

"Good God. You mean to tell me, if my son feels like he has to throw up, we have to rush him to the hospital and have a tube shoved down his nose?"

"Look, I'm just telling you. That's his only option if you remove the tube. I just don't understand why you'd want to remove it," he repeated.

"You don't have to understand. He's not your son. Look, this changes everything. I'm sorry, but the deal is off. Cancel the surgery." I slammed the phone down, briefly taking note of two nurses standing at the station with their mouths gaping open, before making a second call to Rusty. He had taken Martha home to do her breathing treatment and tuck her in bed.

"You seriously canceled the surgery?"

"Yeah. What was I supposed to do, Rusty? He sprung this on us at the last minute."

"You did the right thing. Did you tell Ray there is no surgery tomorrow?"

"No. He's sleeping in his room. I'm at the nurse's station." I went on, "What if I hadn't insisted on talking to the surgeon tonight and he just went ahead with the Nissen without our knowledge? Ray would be stuck with the tube forever." Then I asked, "What do we do now?"

"Let's get ahold of Milla. We need to sit down with him. Maybe there's something else we can do to prevent reflux problems. I don't know."

"Okay. I'll talk to someone here. Set something up for tomorrow."

"Hey, Darla."

"Yeah?"

"Calm down, okay? We'll figure this out."

The next morning we met with Dr. Milla. After I detailed my conversation with the surgeon, Rusty added, "Look, our son is down the hall lying in a hospital bed. He's trusting us to make decisions for him. We're trusting you to give us all the information we need so we can make the *right* decision."

In the end, Dr. Milla suggested that we take baby steps, prescribing an antacid for Ray to take at night before tube feedings. "We can save the Nissen as a last resort, if needed," he said.

Surgery was back on for the following morning. It was a success, but the sight of the tube was a bit jarring. Rather than a cute little button, like a beach ball valve, a long, thick tube extended from Ray's stomach. It was over a foot long, coiled up and secured in place with a mesh-like girdle. When they changed the dressing, and Ray saw it for the first time, he burst into tears. "What the heck is this? It doesn't look like what they showed us, Mom."

The nurse quickly explained that Ray would only have the large tube until the opening in his stomach healed. Then it would be replaced with the button. She compared it to how people have to wear thick stud earrings when they first get their ears pierced. Then, once the hole heals, they can swap out the studs for wire earrings. I wondered why someone hadn't explained this to us *before* the surgery, but I decided it was probably for the best. We would have been hard pressed to get Ray on board if he had seen the large, unsightly tube.

When we came home from the hospital, I unpacked cases of cans of formula, dozens of feeding bags and tubing, and quickly shoved them in an armoire in the kitchen. I brought the pump and pole, from which the feeding bags would hang, up to Ray's room. Funny how these two simple items immediately turned my son's bedroom into a hospital room.

That night, after Ray took his antacid pill, I hooked him up to his first at-home tube feeding. Lying on the bottom bunk, Ray lifted his pajama top and carefully uncoiled the long tube while I tried to pretend it was completely normal. Martha peered over the railing, watching closely from the top bunk. Ray looked at the tube and said, "I don't like this thing. I look like an alien. If I knew it was going to look like this, I never would have signed up for it. But, if someone has to have it, I'm glad it's me and not Martha."

With tears rolling down my cheeks, I connected the tubing and turned on the pump.

"Mom, why are you crying?" Ray noticed.

"Because that was the most beautiful thing you could have said. I don't think you even know how exceptional you are." I wiped my eyes. "You've got a pretty nice brother, Martha."

Sometimes I wondered where this kid had come from. He had more grace and kindness than Rusty and I put together—and a heck of a lot more courage. I know for a fact, if I had

had a feeding tube when I was ten years old, my first thought would have been, "Why couldn't my sister get this stupid thing instead of me?"

Behind the Laughter

As brave as Ray was, I worried the G-tube would be the CF tipping point. From the outside, no one really sees cystic fibrosis, but a feeding tube can be detected. Would this be the thing that put Ray over the edge? The thought of him being slow to smile was a real concern, but within the first month after using the feeding tube, Ray put on ten pounds. He was already a confident kid, but he seemed even more self-assured as he continued to gain weight in the months that followed. He looked strong and healthy, his cheeks chubby now. He even felt different when I hugged him. No longer bony, but meaty. Best of all, that wonderful grin of his never faded. His positive attitude didn't change, either. Nor did his love of sports. Finding clever ways to protect the tube site, he wore his karate sparring belt under his breezers for extra padding and continued to play hockey. Dr. McNamara was right—more weight plus more muscle equaled better performance on the ice. Ray Garvey, #9, came out onto the ice like gangbusters.

He kept wrestling, too, a tight singlet and Ace bandage securing his G-tube in place. And he still played basketball, making one simple request of his coach. At practice he pulled his coach aside, discreetly showed him the G-tube, and said, "From now on, I have to play shirts, not skins, okay?"

Staying fully clothed in sports uniforms was one thing, but the following summer I wondered if Ray would still want to take swimming lessons at Carver Lake. When I asked, he shrugged and said, "I do, but I don't know. What about this thing?" He pointed to his stomach.

"Well, you could just keep a muscle shirt on. I've seen other boys do that at the beach."

"Yeah, me too, and they look stupid, Mom."

"Okay." I thought for a second. "How about we put a bandage over the area?"

"What?" He rolled his eyes.

"Yeah, then you can come up with a good war story of how you got injured."

"Do it, Ray. You have to take lessons with me," Martha pleaded.

"I am not wearing a stupid t-shirt or a bandage."

"You know, the tube is nothing to be ashamed of, Ray. You don't have to cover it up. If anyone asks, just tell them what it is. Who cares?"

Ray thought for a minute, then said, "I got it. I want a wet suit."

I smiled at his flamboyant choice, then set off in search of a wet suit.

On the first day of swim lessons, Ray and Martha gathered with their class at the lifeguard tower, waiting for their instructors. It was a sunny morning, yet a cool breeze blew off the water, a chill in the air. All but Ray stood shivering, colorful beach towels wrapped tightly around every swimmer's shoulders. Ray was warm and comfortable in his wet suit, yet he stood out like a sore thumb. Just as I'd expected, kids began to ask questions.

"What the heck are you wearing?" I overheard one boy ask.

"It's a wet suit," Ray nonchalantly responded.

"Why are you wearing that weird thing?" A little girl wrinkled her nose.

Before Ray could answer, his swimming instructor suddenly appeared and said, "Good idea, Ray. That wet suit's gonna keep you nice and warm."

When their swimming lessons were over, the children ran out of the water, quickly reaching for their beach towels for warmth. Martha grabbed her towel, too, then found her brother leaning against the lifeguard stand like a cool surfer dude. He smiled while the other kids shivered, some asking their parents, "Can I get a wet suit like Ray's?"

On the way home, Ray said, "Don't tell my instructor, Mom, but the wet suit helps me swim better. I float in it. Hardly have to kick."

I loved how Ray and Martha came to solve their problems, often depending on humor to get them through. Their playful antics were a constant source of entertainment for us, too. It seemed like one or the other, or both, made us laugh nearly every day, something Ray was especially proud of. Whenever I cracked up at something he said or did, he would tell me, "I still got it, Mom."

Their humor and personalities were as different as night and day, but together, Ray and Martha were a comedy duo, skillfully playing off one another. Ray was more of a song and dance man, captivating audiences with silly, animated stories. Martha was Ray's straight man, her delivery more refined. She was quick, sharp and full of surprising one-liners. Her comments made Ray stop and think—then respond with something even more outrageous to go along with whatever she threw at him. While Martha's comedic timing was smooth, her retorts witty and deliberate, Ray never looked at her as a threat, stealing his thunder. Rather, he delighted in his partnership with Martha.

Whenever I heard a news story that featured a remarkable individual who pulled through a life-altering circumstance with a sense of humor, I wondered if I would have been able to do the same. Would I ever laugh again if I were to lose my eyesight or be confined to a wheelchair? Could I bring joy to others through humor if I, myself, faced horrific challenges? And then Ray and Martha came along and showed us how humor can make the intolerable tolerable. They both had a knack for putting a funny spin on their daily observations. For example, after cleaning the bathroom one evening, I looked in on the kids to say good night.

"Growing up looks boring," Ray stated from the lower bunk.

"What are you saying? Scrubbing toilets doesn't look fun?"

"No, it doesn't. Being an adult looks boring. All you do is work and pay bills."

I laughed and said, "You've got a point. But there's a lot to look forward to."

"Well, I don't want to grow up. I want to stay a kid forever," my Peter Pan son declared.

"Just think, though. You'll learn to drive a car. Go on dates and school dances. Go to college and find a job. Eventually, move out and have a place of your own."

"I don't want to go to college. I hate studying."

"Well, you don't have to attend college. You could go to a trade school."

"What's that?"

"A vocational school where you learn a trade, like plumbing. Or bricklaying, like Grandpa Buzz. He went to trade school."

"Really? How come no one ever told me about trade school? Is that where mechanics go, too? Like the guys at Carver Auto Body?" Carver Auto Body was a small shop a few blocks from our home. All the kids in the neighborhood were drawn to the shop because they had a pop machine outside the building. Sometimes, after buying a soda, Ray stopped in to talk to the mechanics, too.

"Sure. You could go into auto mechanics, if that's what you're interested in."

"I'd like that. Then I wouldn't have to read boring textbooks. Just notes like, 'Fix tire.'"

I chuckled while Ray continued with his ambitious plans. "And I'm going to live in a trailer so I don't have to pay bills."

"You're killing me, Ray." I couldn't help but think of Chris Farley's *Saturday Night Live* sketch. The motivational speaker who lectured, "If you don't apply yourself, you'll end up living in a van … down by the river." "I hate to burst your bubble, Ray, but you still have to pay bills. You have to buy the trailer, pay for the land you put it on, and pay for electricity and water."

"Well, then I'll just buy a cheap trailer, park it in the back yard, and hook up to your water and electricity."

I shook my head. "You're killing me."

"Hey, you're just mad that you didn't think of it yourself. You've been paying bills your whole life." Ray smiled.

Just before turning out the lights, Martha shared her plans for her future living arrangements with her preschool friend. "When I grow up, I'm going to live in the woods with Audra … in a tent."

"See? She's smarter than you too, Mom."

~

Rusty and I were inspired by Ray's and Martha's strength and lightheartedness at home. But I was fortunate to also get a glimpse into our children's school days.

When Ray was in third grade, I went back to school to finish my teaching degree at the University of Wisconsin, River Falls. Martha liked to tell everyone that she was in college, too, as her preschool was on campus. Upon graduating, I was hired to teach third grade at Carver Elementary. Martha was about to start kindergarten and was excited to have both her brother *and* her mom at school. Ray? Not so much. It was his final year at Carver, a top dog fifth grader, and he wanted nothing to do with me at *his* school.

"I'm glad you got a job, Mom," he said, "but why does it have to be at Carver?"

Ironically, while I ignored Ray in the hallways so as not to embarrass him, he would smile and wave whenever he spotted me, calling out, "Hi, Mom. How's it going?" Sometimes he also gave a friendly warning to my students. "I hope you're being good for my mom. I mean Mrs. Garvey."

I loved teaching at Carver and especially treasured those little moments when I got to sneak a peek into Ray and Martha's world outside of home. I was pleased to see that they behaved in the hallway, had an abundance of friends on the playground, and were respectful to their teachers. Most of all, I enjoyed hearing the wonderful laughter the Garvey children seemed to evoke. My third-grade students clamored to run errands for me if it meant dropping something off to Ray's or Martha's classroom. To Ray's class, because he always gave them a silly message to bring back to his mom. And to Martha's classroom, because my students were infatuated with her funny little accent, insisting my daughter was from a different country. Martha's speech-language pathologist, however, would argue that her difficulty with *r*-controlled vowels and *s* sounds was nothing to make light of.

Best of all are my memories of ending our school day together. I can still see Martha rushing down the hallway as soon as the last bell rang, anxious to join Ray in my classroom. And I can still hear Ray's laughter when he saw the ridiculous outfits his dad had allowed Martha to wear to school. While I prepped for the next school day, Ray and Martha usually kicked back on my classroom reading couch and hung out together. I can still picture them sprawled out on the couch, laughing and sharing stories about their day.

Darla Garvey

That year, when the three of us were together at Carver, was one of the best times in my life. My children and I were part of the same community, and it felt like home. My colleagues were my friends, but they were also my children's teachers. Often times they shared a quick Ray or Martha story, if only in passing in the hallway. Like the day Ray's band teacher stopped to tell me about Ray's first private music lesson. We weren't sure how serious Ray was about playing the trumpet, so rather than invest in a new horn, Rusty took Ray to a pawn shop and bought a second-hand trumpet. When his band teacher asked where Ray had gotten the old horn, he said, "Me and my dad bought it last night … at a *porn* shop."

Another benefit of my job was being present during special school events that I might otherwise have missed out on. Like Martha singing in the choir. Or the day Ray spoke at a school-wide assembly. He was one of four fifth-grade students chosen to deliver a speech on what he'd learned in Drug Abuse Resistance Education, or D.A.R.E. class. That day I watched my son walk across the stage to the microphone with equal parts confidence and caution. At the end of his speech, Ray shared a list of strategies Officer Fraser, his D.A.R.E. instructor, had provided on ways to say *no* if someone offered you drugs. "And if all else fails," Ray stated, "take a cold shower." After the assembly, Patti Life, Ray's teacher, rushed over to me and whispered, "Seriously? Take a cold shower?" She busted out laughing.

"Well, clearly he wasn't listening in class. What was it supposed to be?"

Patti stopped laughing just long enough to say, "Turn a cold shoulder."

Ray and Martha's teachers seemed to appreciate their humor and outgoing personalities. So much so that they really didn't think of them as having a serious illness. There was only one teacher who had the occasion to peek behind the curtain and see the ugly truth about cystic fibrosis: Mr. Harv French.

In the fourth grade, Ray was in Mr. French's class. He was a popular teacher with all his students, Ray no exception. Harv was a stocky man with a full head of thick gray hair. His stern look, offset by a kind smile, was an effective combination for a teacher. I think Ray looked up to him like he did his grandpas. In turn, Harv appreciated Ray's spunk and humor —most of the time.

Harv retired at the end of that year. I often teased that Ray must have done him in. Yet the following year he came back to Carver to chaperone the fifth-grade class trip to Deep Portage Conservation Reserve in Hackensack, Minnesota. Specifically, to oversee my son's care. It would be Ray's first overnight experience at a camp, and he made it quite clear that he was ready for three nights with friends—and no parents. When we learned there wouldn't be a nurse at camp, I offered to chaperone. Ray's response was quick. "Why can't I go without you, Mom? I'm not your little boy anymore."

Ultimately, Ray got what he wanted. I stayed back and Harv chaperoned. But Harv had no idea what he was getting into. Of course, as his former teacher, he was aware of Ray's health—in general. Harv knew when Ray was battling a cold, heard his distinct CF cough in the classroom, and marked him absent on days he was out sick. He excused Ray from class a little early to take his enzymes in the nurse's office before lunch. Harv knew about cystic fibrosis, and yet he didn't. When Ray eagerly weighed in on a book discussion of *Charlotte's Web*, Mr. French focused on Ray's point of view, not cystic fibrosis. When Ray was busy making his classmates laugh at some ridiculously embellished story, Harv saw a bubbly, happy kid, not a disease. He only saw determination, not self-pity, in the eyes of a young boy who refused to walk the mile-long run in gym class, even if he was coming in dead last. And, unless Harv were to hook Ray up to a feeding tube at night, he would have thought Ray went to bed like any other boy.

So Mr. French thought that watching over Ray at camp was going to be a piece of cake. However, just before the trip, Harv came to our house to get trained on Ray's care. I had placed Ray's medical equipment and prescription meds on the kitchen table before Harv arrived. When he saw what Ray would have to pack for the trip, he was shocked. "Ray has to bring all this?"

"Yeah, and this doesn't even include Ray's G-tube supplies. We decided he can skip tube feedings while he's at camp. He'll be rooming with five other boys in a cabin, and he doesn't want to be on display each night."

After I explained details about my son's care and Ray demonstrated how the vest worked, Harv seemed more at ease. He even chuckled when Ray warned, "You might not want to stick around when I do the vest at camp, Mr. French. Because, well, it's kind of gross. I hack up loogies."

Martha and I met Ray in the school parking lot when he returned from Deep Portage. As soon as Martha spotted Ray coming off the bus, she ran into his arms for a big hug. I pulled Harv aside and asked how things had gone. "Ray is one tough kid," he said to me. "With all that he had to manage with cystic fibrosis, he was still at the center of every camp activity. He didn't miss out on a single thing. To be honest, though, I did have to wrangle him in to do the vest. But only because he didn't want to break away from his friends. Not because he was defiant."

A short time after their wonderful outdoor adventures at Deep Portage, Mr. French stopped by with a gift for Ray, a large hardcover book: *Wayne Gretzky: The Making of the Great One*. It was much more than just a book about Ray's favorite hockey player. It was a gift that showed what Ray meant to Harv. Inside, he'd inscribed this letter:

Dear Ray,

There are heroes like Wayne Gretzky because of their special talents, and we all hear of their successes and they receive much adulation. Then we have what appear to be ordinary people; few hear about their challenges in life that they meet head on without an audience and accomplish more than we realize and understand. Some of us are privileged to meet people of this kind. We find out they are really extraordinary and heroes in their own right. Ray, you are one of these people—you are my hero. I wish you the best of luck. I hope we are able to keep in touch.

Your friend,
Harv French

Keep Running

In the fall of 2000, during Ray's sixth grade year, he came down with a terrible chest cold, or what his doctor referred to as a pulmonary exacerbation—meaning he was producing more mucus than he normally did. We kept him home from school and increased his vest treatments to four times a day, and a prescribed oral antibiotic was added to his medications.

Each morning I woke my son up before I left for work, made breakfast, and got him started on his first breathing treatment of the day. Rusty took care of lunch and Ray's second treatment before he left for work. I returned home from teaching and took over with dinner, homework, and more respiratory therapy.

During each treatment Ray doubled over in a series of coughing fits—struggling to bring up thick, green mucus from his airways.

On top of his grueling routine, Martha still had to do her vest treatments as well. It seemed as if sterilizing a daily supply of nebulizer cups had become my second career, but organization was key to getting through each day.

That week we had relied on Ray's friends, Jessie and Laura, to drop off his daily homework. School work had never been a priority for Ray. Completing assignments when he had missed classroom instruction made school work an even bigger challenge. His focus was further hindered by fatigue and the simple fact that he was in pain. It was too much for him, and a sense of defeat was palpable.

After eight exhausting days, our at-home efforts failed. Ray was admitted to University of Minnesota-Fairview Hospital.

His sputum cultures showed a heavy growth of pseudomonas, a bacteria that plagues CF patients and leads to stubborn lung infections. I was terrified simply hearing the word pseudomonas. *Was this the beginning of irreversible lung damage for our son?*

Long-term intravenous antibiotics were needed to treat pseudomonas, so Ray had a peripherally inserted central catheter (PICC) line placed. A long, thin catheter was inserted into a vein in Ray's arm. The tip of the catheter was positioned in a large vein just above his heart. The cardio-vascular team explained to us that the first place the heart pumps blood to is the lungs. Thereby, powerful antibiotics would be delivered straight to Ray's lungs—a much more aggressive and effective treatment than oral antibiotics.

Rusty was with Ray the day the PICC line was placed. After school, Martha and I had rushed to the hospital, where Ray eagerly described the entire procedure to us. Then he climbed out of bed to show his sister how he could still get around. Martha had watched closely as her brother carefully coiled up the long IV tubing and secured it to a hook on the IV pole so as not to trip over it. Then off they went, down the hall to the hospital playroom. Rusty and I trailed behind and took note of a young brother and sister talking and giggling as if pushing an IV pole was a perfectly normal thing.

With each passing day Ray's health slowly improved, and he began to get restless. One night, while I sat at his bedside grading papers and Ray flipped through TV channels, he suddenly blurted, "I'm sick of this place. I wish I could go home."

"You will soon enough, Ray. Hang in there."

With tears in his eyes, he said, "I miss my own bed. I miss Martha and Dad. And I miss Boone, too."

Just then Ray's nurse entered the room to disconnect him from the IV.

"When's his next IV infusion due?" I asked.

She looked at her watch. "He doesn't have to hook up again for three hours."

"How about his next vest treatment?"

"The respiratory therapist will come in shortly after the IV runs."

When she left the room, I closed the door behind her. I dug in the closet and grabbed Ray's winter jacket and tossed it on his bed. "Put this on. I'm busting you out of this joint."

"No way, Mom. Are you serious?" His eyes lit up.

I set his shoes on the floor next to the bed. "Hurry, slip these on."

Ray giggled for a minute before his smile faded. "What if we get caught, Mom? I'll get in trouble."

"Don't worry about it. Anyone asks where we were, I'll tell them we went to the cafeteria."

"With my coat on?"

"I'll think of something. You'll be fine."

With that, Ray slipped his jacket on and laced up his shoes. I cracked the door open and looked down the hallway. The coast was clear. Not a nurse in sight. We scurried to the elevator, pressed the button for the lower-level lobby and successfully exited the front double-doors of the hospital. Now we only had a short walk to the parking ramp and we would be on our way home. I took Ray's hand and started to run, but as soon as he had breathed in the cold air, he doubled over—coughing uncontrollably.

Wrapping my arm around his shoulders, I said, "I don't know what I was thinking, Ray. This was a terrible idea. I'm sorry, but we have to turn back."

Still doubled over—trying to catch his breath—Ray waved me on. "Keep running, Mom. Keep running!"

"Are you sure?"

"Go get the car. I'll wait over there on that bench." He pointed.

On our drive home Ray couldn't stop laughing. It was as if he had just pulled off a heist and was now speeding away in the getaway car. He began plotting out how he was going to sneak in the house and surprise Martha and his dad, but the second he stepped inside our home, he called out, "Hey guys, I'm home."

Martha ran to her brother and hugged him. "You're really home?"

"Yep. They let me out early," Ray teased.

Rusty threw me a look and whispered, "What the hell did you do?"

"Relax. I'll get him back before anyone notices."

Ray's visit was shorter than he would have liked, but it had lifted his spirits and that was all that mattered.

When we returned to his hospital room, he quickly hung up his coat, kicked off his shoes, and slipped back into bed without anyone noticing. He was pretty proud of himself for pulling off his escape.

A few days later he was *officially* discharged, but he still required another week of IV antibiotics at home. Even though a nurse checked in on Ray every other day, we were responsible for his round-the-clock IV treatments. Neither Rusty nor I was comfortable with this task. I was especially terrified that I would do something wrong that would put our son's health at risk. *What if I accidentally pushed air through his PICC line when flushing it out with saline? What if I didn't prepare a sterile field correctly and infected his IV site?*

Ray, however, took everything in stride. One day he even insisted on going to the pharmacy with me. He was in the middle of dosing an IV drug at the time. The drug store was about to close, and I couldn't wait for the antibiotic to finish running. He would have to stay home, I decided.

"But I want to come with you, Mom."

"It's just a quick trip to the drug store. It's not like you're going to miss out on anything."

He argued that he could certainly ride with me because he was no longer tethered to an IV pole like he had been in the hospital. Rather, his meds were now administered using an elastomeric pump—a hand grenade-shaped ball that was pre-filled with medication and connected to the IV line that extended from Ray's arm. The device was pressurized and slowly deflated as the antibiotic ran through the PICC line. Ray referred to it as *the ball*.

He liked how he could place the ball in a fanny pack while it was dosing, allowing him the freedom to move about the house.

"I really want to go with you, Mom," Ray insisted.

His determination was impressive, so I gave in. On the way to the drug store, Ray said, "Isn't this ball cool? I wonder who invented it."

I couldn't get over this kid's bravery. Rather than dwell on the reason he needed the IV drug in the first place, he appreciated how it was being delivered into his body. And truth be told, Ray didn't care one bit about going to the drug store that day. He just wanted to prove that he *could*.

In large part, I believe Ray took it all in stride because he had no idea at that time that a one-and-done need for a PICC line was not in the cards for someone with cystic fibrosis. The disease is progressive, and repeated lung infections, frequent hospitalizations, and IV antibiotics are a normal part of CF life. Still, we were grateful that Ray's attitude and humor set a precedent for Martha when she faced her own CF complications and hospitalizations. Like her brother, Martha even broke out of the hospital once—sneaking off to attend a Minnesota Wild Hockey game at the Xcel Energy Center in St. Paul.

Fancy the Fox

To a child, vacations are an exciting adventure. For an adult, it's an escape from the daily grind. But for our family, the daily grind came with us. There is no escaping cystic fibrosis.

In March of 2001, we had planned a ski trip to Lutsen, a ski resort town in Northern Minnesota. Unfortunately, Ray came down with a cold just as his spring break was getting under-way. I considered canceling our reservations at the Caribou Highlands Lodge, but Ray bumped up his vest treatments to four-a-day and quickly recovered from his cold, miraculously avoiding another hospitalization. Thus we were able to salvage the last half of our almost-canceled ski trip.

Because Rusty doesn't ski, he decided to stay back and work. I had to remind myself that CF care wouldn't be any more difficult at the lodge than it was at home. Still, traveling without Rusty was a lot for me to juggle. Just the simple act of packing gave me a temporary case of OCD. Ski goggles, long underwear, or mittens could be purchased if left behind. Spe-cialized CF drugs and medical equipment were another story.

After checking our bags half a dozen times, we finally hauled everything out to the car and closed the trunk. Ray hopped up front with me, already wearing his ski hat. Martha got com-fortable in the back seat with a stack of books, drawing paper, and crayons. She always kept busy with some sort of activity. Ray, on the other hand, was content just to listen to the radio.

It was late in the afternoon when we settled into our room at the lodge. From our balcony, we watched the skiers take their final run of the day. Ray, however, was more interested to see how his latest prank would play out. As luck would have it, a group of rowdy college boys had the room across the hall. We could hear them in the hallway—laughing, swearing, and discussing which bar would most likely accept their fake IDs. Ray was a little too fascinated with their antics, watching through the peephole in our door. At one point, Ray noticed that the guys had taped a sign to their door which read "Only pretty girls welcome." Ray found a pen, tiptoed across the hall, and made changes to their sign. He crossed out the word *pretty* and wrote *ugly* and then changed *girls* to *boys*. All night long Ray kept an ear out for their return, continually watching through the peephole. He couldn't stop giggling when he heard the ruckus in the hallway—the inebriated college boys insisting that they were going to find out who had messed up their sign and kick their ass. Ray could not have asked for a better reaction.

Ray and Martha horsed around until late that evening, so I let them sleep in. I was especially concerned about Ray needing his rest so soon after having a cold.

When he finally woke up, he was furious. "Why did you let us sleep so long, Mom? We could be skiing by now."

"It's okay, Ray. I'm going to buy half-day tickets. We'll still get in a lot of skiing today."

"I wanted to ski for the *whole* day, not a *half* day."

"We can make it a full day tomorrow. What do you want for breakfast?"

"I don't care about breakfast. I'm getting my ski clothes on."

"You need to eat breakfast and do your therapy first."

Martha rolled over in bed and looked at me with sleep in her eyes. "You'll go after Ray, okay?" I said. She pulled the covers over her head.

Ray protested, "Are you serious? We have to do our therapies? That'll take too long."

"There's plenty of time."

Ray stomped around the room, picked up the vest that was lying in the corner, and flung it across the room. Then, at the top of his lungs, he screamed, "My life sucks!"

I immediately hurdled over a coffee table, grabbed Ray by his shoulders and pinned him to the wall. Through gritted teeth, I slowly punctuated, "Your life does not suck. Don't you ever say that again. Do you understand me?"

Ray looked absolutely stunned to suddenly find himself in my grip. Before letting him go, I repeated, "Your life does not suck, Ray."

With tears in his eyes, he picked his vest up from off the floor, slipped it on, and hooked himself up to the compressor. I went to the kitchen to prepare his neb cup. When I brought it to him, he jerked it out of my hand. Placing the mask over his face, he let the elastic strap snap around the back of his head. Grabbing the remote control off the coffee table, the same one I had just leapt over, he turned the TV on and cranked it up—full volume.

I knew I had overreacted, but Ray's statement terrified me. Everything I did—every day of *my* life—was to make sure *his* life did not suck. My biggest fear was that someday he would think that it did. My heart broke, watching his body shake from air pounding against his chest. I wondered what my son thought of me. *Why did I lose my cool? Why am I always the head-strong parent when it came to treatments?* Rusty would have let him skip his therapy, reasoning that his lungs would get a workout from an afternoon of skiing. Ray had even mentioned this during his outburst. "Dad wouldn't make me do this."

"Yeah? Well, he's not here, is he?" I answered, almost resentful that he wasn't. "You are feeling better because you've been *doing* your therapies, not because you've been *skipping* them."

As soon as we stepped outside, it was as if the "my life sucks" incident had never happened. The rest of our day was an adventure.

It was late in the ski season, sunny and warm, yet there was an abundance of snow, some still clinging to tree tops. Carrying our skis and poles, we trudged through the snow toward the lift line. That's when we noticed the chairlifts were only two-seaters. Ray was afraid of heights and disappointed the three of us could not ride up together. So I asked the chairlift attendant to keep an eye on Martha while I took Ray on his first chairlift ride to get him acclimated to the height.

Unlike her cautious brother, Martha was more daring and grew impatient with my ski lessons, insisting that she could ski without my help. I backed off and prematurely let my beginner skier go down the hill on her own. Ray and I watched as Martha picked up way too much speed, seemingly forgetting how to stop. Suddenly she veered off the ski trail, slipped under bright orange mesh fencing, and disappeared.

"Holy crap, Mom!" Ray yelled.

I frantically skied to the place where we had last seen her, Ray not far behind. Peering down a steep embankment, we found Martha lying on her back and partially buried in snow.

"Are you okay, Martha?" I shouted down to her.

Smiling up at us, she hollered, "That was fun."

Things improved after Martha's crash. Skiing with better control, we graduated to bigger runs. Our ski group grew larger, as well. We met up with my friends Mark and Janene Slagle and their children, Sam and Jessie. After the lifts closed, the Slagle family joined us for a swim at our lodge. The four kids were thrilled to discover that half of the pool was inside, while the other half was outdoors and surrounded by mounds of snow.

Another night, my friend Cathe Carbone came up and met us for dinner, adding more laughter and fun to our vacation.

My children really liked Cathe. She and Ray were especially close, given that cracking wise was a strong suit for both of them. It was hard to tell which one was quicker witted because their back-and-forth banter hit at lightning speed. We dined at a little rustic bar and grill that night. Halfway into our meal, the bartender approached our table and asked the kids to keep an eye on the back patio door, which opened to a large wooded area.

"Why?" Ray asked the bartender.

"There's a little red fox that comes to the door every night about this time. She eats bread right out of my hand. I named her Fancy the Fox. Wait until you see her." The bartender smiled.

"Can we feed Fancy the Fox, too?" Martha asked.

"I don't think she'll let you get close to her. Took her a while to trust me. But you can watch me feed her."

I'll never forget the look of awe as Ray and Martha stood just behind the bartender, watching Fancy the Fox nibble bread from his cupped hand.

After an active day of skiing, swimming, and meeting Fancy the Fox, the kids did their therapies in front of the fireplace, too tired to fuss. They settled into their beds while I crawled into mine. I could hear Martha snoring, but before Ray drifted off to sleep, I whispered from across the room, "Hey, Ray."

"Yeah?"

"Did you have fun skiing today?"

"Yeah, it was really fun."

"How about Martha skiing off the side of the mountain?"

"Oh, my God. That was scary."

"I'm glad she didn't get hurt."

"She's crazy. She just lay there and laughed."

"She *is* crazy," I agreed. "I'm glad you're not afraid of the chair lift anymore."

"Yeah, but I still wish I could ride up with you once in a while."

"Me too. But Martha can't reach the chair without my help."

"It's okay," Ray said.

"Wasn't it fun meeting Fancy the Fox?" I asked.

"That was so cool. I've never seen a fox up close before."

"Me either. How about that outdoor pool? That was a nice surprise, wasn't it?"

"That was awesome."

"Hey, Ray."

"Yeah?"

"Does your life still suck?"

"No. I'm sorry, Mom. I love you."

"I love you too, buddy."

Upper Afton Road

When we got back from Lutsen, my friend Jeana called to see what I was up to. I told her all about our ski trip and how much fun the three of us had had together.

"How do you do it, Darla?" Jeana asked.

"Do what?"

"Take everything on and still manage to make things fun for your kids?"

"Trust me, Jeana. This ain't no Hallmark movie over here. But we got lucky with Ray and Martha—both are pretty exceptional."

"Yeah, but they didn't just get that way on their own. You and Rusty had something to do with it." Then she asked, "How did you get so tough?"

"I'm not that tough Jeana. I just do what any mom would do for her kids."

"No, not every mother could handle it."

"You love your kids. You just do it."

"No, it's not that easy," Jeana argued. "Listen, I have three sons. They're all perfectly healthy and … I'm in A.A." She chuckled.

Jeana always made me laugh, but when I hung up, I stopped to seriously think about what she had said. Cystic fibrosis is a crappy illness that requires a ton of daily maintenance, but when things were going well, we worked together and embraced every minute. Did that make me tough? I hadn't given it much thought before, but Jeana had caused me to reflect on my own childhood. Was there something in my past that had prepared me for this life?

~

I grew up in the Battle Creek area of St. Paul, in a modest but very nice brick rambler that my father had built. He was hardworking, social and vivacious, with a quick sense of humor. If laughter erupted in a room, Buzz was generally the cause of it. On the other hand, if you crossed him, you never had to guess if he was upset. Yet he was quick to forgive and forget.

Mom was more reserved, even tempered, and reliable. Without too many questions, she calmly provided shelter and comfort from any storm we were riding out.

My parents were wonderful in so many ways, but like Bill Murray's film *Groundhog Day,* life was pretty routine and predictable on Upper Afton Road. Mom served dinner for her husband and four children at the same time every night—shortly after Buzz came home from work. Each night, like clockwork, he dropped his lunch box at the front door, walked into the kitchen, kicked off his work boots, and slipped out of his cement-covered pants. Then he plunked down in his chair at the head of the table—in his underwear.

Mom immediately picked up his pants and tossed them downstairs to be washed, brought his lunch box to the kitchen sink to rinse out, then asked the same question while carrying his dirty boots to the front closet. "Why can't you take your boots off on the rug?"

Buzz, the stereotypical Archie Bunker type and clearly the man of the house, usually responded, "I bust my tail all day. I'll take my boots off wherever I want."

Mom was in constant motion, working around the house. I wondered why she never told him she was busting her tail, too. While Buzz laid brick, she stayed home and took great pride in keeping everything tidy. You'd be hard pressed to find a tissue in a wastebasket or an unmade bed.

My parents were solid and consistent, our home filled with expectations and structure: dinner time, bedtime, and a curfew. Homework was to be completed independently. That was my job, not theirs, they told me. We were Scandinavian Lutherans. Going to church was mandatory. Swearing was not allowed. If I said *God* instead of *gosh*, a swift reprimand came my way with a look that could kill. Yet Buzz said "goddamn it" on a daily basis. The "do as I say; not as I do" policy was in full swing at our house.

Each morning, I stood on the corner of Upper Afton Road and Miller Crest Lane with the neighborhood kids, waiting for the school bus to take us to Battle Creek Elementary. I was quiet and shy, rarely talking in class. Teachers wrote comments on my report card like *Darla seems withdrawn.* Or *Darla doesn't participate in class discussions.* I was so shy that I only responded with a shrug when teachers called on me. The sad thing is, I always knew the answers. I got good grades, but without providing verbal proof of any sign of intelligence in class, I'm sure my classmates viewed me as slow. Or at least that was my assumption.

In fifth grade, life as I knew it came to a screeching halt. I had my first of many grand mal seizures. I was on the home stretch of a basketball relay race in Mrs. Clark's phy-ed class. I wasn't the most skilled basketball player, but I do remember pulling out ahead of everyone during that particular race. However, I never crossed the finish line. One minute I was dribbling the ball. The next I was out cold, lying on the gymnasium floor.

I woke up with something stuck in my mouth: a small wooden paddle that always hung from Mrs. Clark's keychain. At that time, people thought a person having a seizure could swallow her tongue if you didn't put something in her mouth to hold it down.

My entire class circled around and stared at me. They looked as scared and confused as I felt. Suddenly, two paramedics broke through the crowd, lifted me onto a stretcher, and carried me out to the ambulance. Mom was there too, which was both a comfort and a surprise. My parents only had one car, and Buzz was at work. I wondered how Mom had gotten to school, but mostly I wondered what the hell had happened.

I stayed the night in the hospital, where they performed an electroencephalogram, or EEG, a test that measures and records the electrical activity of the brain. Diagnosis? Epilepsy. Treatment? Barbiturates. Side effects? Lethargy. If I had been quiet before, barbiturates certainly didn't help. Often times I fell asleep in class from the anticonvulsant drugs. Over the years, the dose was increased every time I had a seizure, slowly turning me into a zombie. I guess it didn't occur to my parents to ask the neurologist about changing the dose or going on a different drug, even when I complained that I never, ever felt normal. Their generation did as the doctor ordered.

Back then, epilepsy was taboo. In fact, my parents never even used the word, which made it seem all the more shameful. I had something no one wanted to talk about. With the word off limits, my parents said things like, "You're okay. You just had an *episode*." Or, "You're okay. You just got a little *too excited*." Episode? Too excited? Perhaps it was their way of protecting me from worry, but downplaying seizures was almost insulting. I wanted my parents to help me understand what was wrong with me, not sweep it under the rug.

That same year, in fifth grade, we had a substitute teacher one day. After taking attendance, she said, "I have a note here from your teacher to keep an eye on one of you. Raise your hand if you have epilepsy."

Classmates sitting closest to me whispered, "That's you, Darla." Unfamiliar with the term, I refused to raise my hand

and claim the label. Growing impatient, the substitute called me up front, pointed to a word in my teacher's note, and asked, "Do you have this?" I stared blankly at the note. It was written in cursive, and I couldn't read it. Annoyed by my silence, she demanded an answer. "Is this you? Do you have epilepsy?"

I glanced around the room. Everyone was nodding *yes*, so I shrugged and said, "I guess." The substitute looked at me as if epilepsy equated to stupidity.

So, as it turned out, epilepsy wasn't exactly a self-esteem booster, and public seizures were not a crowd pleaser. Seizures brought shame and embarrassment from the very onset of my illness. They overshadowed my childhood with dread and fear. Dread of when the next seizure would hit. Fear of where I'd be when it did. I don't suspect any ten-year-old deals well with becoming an epileptic overnight, but for a shy kid like me, it was brutal. Shy kids don't like to be noticed. People notice seizures.

I had at least a dozen seizures during my three years at Battle Creek Junior High. The worst one took place, again, in the gym. We were starting a gymnastics unit. Our phy-ed teachers, Miss Schleck and Miss Fry, had set up stations: uneven bars, balance beam, pommel horse, and the ever-popular trampoline. Everyone was excited about gymnastics because it beat the hell out of crab soccer. Look it up. It's a thing.

That day, when it was my turn for the trampoline, I jumped to get some height. Suddenly, in mid-air, I felt the God-awful strange feeling I got right before I had a seizure. I didn't have time to safely lower myself. It happened in a split second. One minute I was jumping. The next minute I was waking up on the mats placed around the trampoline. I had landed hard, too, no thanks to the ineffective thirteen-year-old spotters standing around the edge of the trampoline.

No one ever said anything to my face about my show-stopping seizures, but I felt the silent judgment, convinced I was the butt of their jokes. Walking down the school hallway, I imagined kids whispering, "See that girl? She's the one who spazzes out all the time."

I was too young to realize that every teenager has her own set of problems to worry about. A giant zit, a hole in her pants, a failing grade. No one cared what I was going through. Me, and my embarrassing seizures, weren't even on their radar. But it would take years before I discovered that the only one really bothered by epilepsy was me.

I entered Harding High School in the mid-1970s—bell bottoms, tube tops, lava lamps, and mood rings. It was the golden era of vinyl records and some of the best rock-n-roll music of all time: The Rolling Stones, Steve Miller Band, and Led Zeppelin, to name a few. You could buy a cheap beater car, fill the gas tank for a few bucks, and drive around listening to music all night.

Cable TV and streaming services weren't around yet. We watched weekly network shows in real time. Shows like *Sonny and Cher*, *Laugh-in*, and the *Carol Burnett Show*. And we waited all year to watch *The Wizard of Oz*. If you missed it, you had to wait for it to come around the following year.

Best of all, I grew up before there were such things as helicopter parents and cell phones. I had a lot of freedom, walking or biking anywhere in the city. My parents didn't know where I was half the time. Nor did they seem to care, as long as I was home before the street lights came on. Parents in the 1970s were pretty much hands-off like that. Vague answers to their questions were almost preferred. "Hanging out" was a real thing. It was an acceptable answer if parents asked what you were up to. "Just hanging out."

Education was more relaxed, too. There was no real pressure to go to college and no serious consequences for skipping class a time or two, or in my case, a couple dozen. Teachers allowed you to make your own decisions—and mistakes.

Those of us who went to keg parties in the woods, or occasionally smoked pot, were still considered fairly decent kids. And smoking cigarettes wasn't necessarily a sin. In school, we made ceramic ash trays as Christmas gifts for our parents. Smoking was part of the culture, glamorized and practically encouraged. Commercials for every brand of cigarette were advertised on prime time TV and regularly dangled from the mouths of talk show hosts and movie stars. Giant billboard ads featuring the Marlboro Man dotted highway landscapes.

At Harding High School, mounds of cigarette butts piled up outside each doorway, as students thought nothing of stepping outside to have a smoke between classes. Teachers didn't seem to mind either. After all, they were guilty of the same bad habit, smoke rolling out of the staff lounge throughout the day. I occasionally lit up myself, mostly when I went to parties and had a few beers. Which wasn't necessarily a crime either. The drinking age in Minnesota was 18, and if you were a little underage—well—close enough. I look back on that decade now with fondness. A lot of freedom. A lot of fun. A simpler time. But I'll admit, I pushed the envelope.

Never in a million years did I think I would write about epilepsy when I spent so much of my life trying to hide it. In fact, I never talked about my illness. My closest friends never knew that every single day I worried about having a seizure. Maybe I should have talked about it, because internalizing was a burden. But in my house, we didn't talk about our feelings. For the love of God, who wanted to hear how you felt? So, rather than talk about how shitty I thought epilepsy was, or how lousy I felt drugged up on barbiturates every day, I pretended nothing was wrong with me and acted with reckless abandon. It would be a whole lot easier to blame my rebellious behavior on the '70s; after all, I was just doing what every other teenager was doing. But I wasn't like every other teenager. I had an illness, and I had limitations. Instead of acknowledging that, I overcompensated for the stigma I felt and started running with the fun crowd, staying out late, foolishly never listening to my body—or my parents.

I continued to have seizures throughout my teens and well into adulthood, always at an inopportune moment: a Christmas work party, a wedding dance, skiing in the mountains, or running through an airport. As embarrassing as it was, I'm grateful I was never alone when one took place. Someone was always there to help me. This was never more critical than the summer of 1981, when a seizure nearly ended my life.

Lake Phalen

I woke up alone with an oxygen mask covering my face, an IV in my arm, appalled to discover a catheter was catching my urine. As I scratched my scalp, sand fell onto my hospital gown, reminding me why I was in intensive care at Ramsey County Hospital in St. Paul. *Maybe*, I thought, *they don't bother bathing the ones who aren't expected to survive.* With heavy lungs and unbearable pressure, I questioned if I'd make it much longer. Unable to take a deep breath without sharp, excruciating pain, I had to calm myself and settle for short, shallow breaths. My mantra became *Don't freak out. Just suck in what you can.*

Suddenly, I heard an alarm blaring. "Code blue! Code blue!" The sound of footsteps raced across the floor, and voices escalated as two doctors and a nurse rushed into my room. I wasn't alone after all. I had a roommate on the other side of a curtain, and he or she was in trouble.

"What the fuck! She was stable," one doctor shouted.

"Who was here? Who came to see you?" the nurse asked.

"Come on, damn it. Tell us what you took," the second doctor demanded.

I heard a woman's voice. Nothing intelligible, really—just moaning and groaning.

Then I heard the first doctor holler, "Screw it. Start pumping her stomach."

The commotion carried on for quite some time; then everything fell silent. Moments later, a young woman was wheeled out from behind the curtain. She looked sedated, comfortable in her bed. I took note of her long dark hair and angelic face, just before spotting a tag dangling from her toe. When the nurse saw that I was watching, she quickly pulled a sheet over my roommate's head before rushing her out the door. *Jesus Christ*, I thought, *I'm on the toe-tagging floor.* Then I drifted off, no strength beyond my own pain to think any more of the dead dark-haired beauty.

Later that day, I came out of a fog. Or maybe it was the following day. I had no idea. Each time I re-entered the world, I spent a second or two figuring out where I was and why I hurt so much.

Sometimes I was alone. Other times a doctor or nurse hovered over me, talking as if I couldn't hear them. Occasionally my friends were off in the corner of the room, crying and hugging one another. One afternoon, I awoke to the family minister praying over me, which was of no comfort whatsoever. It only heightened my fear. Was he saying a *final* prayer?

Most alarming was the day I woke up gasping for air, only to find Rusty with my oxygen mask in one hand, a Stridex medicated pad in the other. He quickly smeared the pad across my nose, cheeks and forehead. Snapping the mask back in place, he said, "Sorry, Darla, but you needed that." He smiled, kissed my forehead, and left for work. I wanted to slap him for startling me, but I had to love the guy for trying. Rusty was the only one who thought enough to wash me.

This time Buzz was with me. Between breaths, I managed to force out a few words, muffled behind an oxygen mask. "Who ... found ... me?"

"I did." He looked down to hide the tears that were already welling.

I wondered how that was possible. I had heard him swim past me. Drawing in short breaths, I waited for more to the story, but he didn't offer anything. Struggling to find enough air, I asked, "How ... did you ... know?"

"I just knew. I swam out to where I last saw you. I dove under, over and over, looking for you." He stopped for a second before stating, "I don't want to talk about this right now."

I closed my eyes and rested. Then I gathered up strength to ask one more question. "How long ... was I ... under?" I'm not sure why this mattered to me, but it did.

"I don't know. Three minutes. Maybe a little longer." Waving a hand to end the conversation, he said, "That's enough. We can talk later. Just get better." He patted my arm and left me alone to wonder, *What isn't he telling me?*

Exhausted from our short conversation, I closed my eyes and tried to remember the details of that day.

Sitting at the kitchen table on a hot August morning, I contemplated a way-too-crunchy bowl of Grape Nuts. My family had just returned from church, and I was desperately trying to avoid a lecture on my evil ways, acting as if I didn't have a hangover. Staying out late, drinking beer with Rusty and his buddies, had seemed like fun at the time. So fun, in fact, we'd closed down a little hole-in-the-wall bar on the East Side of St. Paul, staying for last call. Rusty and his friends had a comedic art for embellishing each other's old stories, making them a little less accurate but new again. I had no problem listening to them reminisce about their boyhood adventures for the six hundredth time. Apparently, I had no problem throwing back a drink or two either.

My younger brother and sister had begged Mom and Buzz to take them to the beach that morning. Wanting peace and quiet, I hoped my parents would cave in to their request and leave soon. I wanted nothing more than to crawl back in bed. But then it occurred to me that since my old Chevy Caprice wasn't running, I should go with them. If not, I'd be stuck in the sweltering house all day. I hollered to Buzz just before he walked out the front door, "Hey, if I take a dip with you guys, will you drop me off at Rusty's after?"

"Sure. Grab your suit. We'll wait for you."

I had recently moved back home after I found out my roommate was pregnant. I had no desire to live with a newborn and asked if I could come home until I found a place of my own. So it had been awhile since I'd joined my family on an outing.

The beach at Lake Phalen was crowded. It seemed the entire city of St. Paul had had the same idea to cool off. Bodies sprawled on towels covered nearly every inch of sand. The roped-off swimming area was shoulder-to-shoulder people. Weaving in and out of the sunbathers, Mom led us to a small clearing close to the water. She wasn't much of a swimmer, so she stayed on shore, watching my brother and sister play in shallow water. I kicked off my sandals and immediately headed into the lake, Buzz close behind. We dove into the water for an exhilarating plunge. Suddenly I felt invigorated, giving no more thought to my hangover.

"Hey, do you want to race me?" I challenged Buzz.

Running a hand through his wet, thinning hair, he threw a competitive smile. "Out to the rope and back?"

I nodded.

"You're on!"

Buzz had been on the swim team at Mechanic Arts High School back in the day, and he was still a strong swimmer then in his mid-forties. I hardly stood a chance but foolishly thought it was worth a try. Side by side, without a word, we took our first strokes. It was a fair start but a slow one until we swam out beyond where anyone could touch bottom. No longer concerned about bumping into the waders, I put my face down in the water and picked up speed. Good freestyle form was my only hope in keeping up with Buzz. When my outstretched hand bumped the rope, I turned to see where he was. Treading water, he mockingly tapped the rope, throwing a dirty grin. He was toying with me, out-swimming me with no effort whatsoever—planning to kick my butt on the return lap.

I let go of the rope, flipped over on my back, and kicked as hard as I could. With arms extending overhead like a windmill, I gave it my all.

Buzz's long, smooth strokes sliced through the water with such grace, I hardly heard him pass me by. I thought how I'd splash him in the face for teasing me—just as soon as I caught up to him. I pictured him laughing, saying, "Did you really think you could beat your old man?"

But I never met up with my dad. Instead, the clear blue sky above me disappeared. My body betrayed me, first taking my sight. Then my hearing vanished. Dark and silent, the familiar aura just before having a seizure washed over me, a warning there was only a split second before losing consciousness. Limp arms and legs submerged. Helpless, my head slipped under water as I took in a big gulp. Sinking to the bottom of Lake Phalen, I thought, *I'm only twenty-one. Is this really how it ends for me?*

I shuddered at the memory of that day, the certainty that I was a goner. Then, in my wrinkled hospital gown, I drifted off to sleep.

Later that day, Mom came to see me. She reluctantly shared a few details of Buzz's frantic search for me. At one point, he spotted a lifeguard in a rowboat nearby and desperately called out, "Help! I can't find my daughter."

The lifeguard asked, "How old is your daughter?"

Shocked and angered by his question, Buzz yelled, "She's a grown woman. Goddamn it. Just help me."

"Maybe she's on the beach," the lifeguard casually replied.

"No. She was just here. She went under. Help me!"

Mom described how Buzz had caught a glimpse of me floating up to the surface near the rope. He swam out, grabbed me by my hair, and dragged me to where he could stand. Exhausted, on tiptoes, he struggled to hold my head above water. The lifeguard finally assisted, performing mouth-to-mouth, while Buzz continued to hold me up. Together, they brought me to shore. "You weren't breathing," Mom said. "A crowd gathered around while the lifeguard administered CPR. I had no idea it was you lying on the beach, until I caught a glimpse of your bathing suit and saw your dad collapsed in the sand. He was mumbling through sobs, 'It's too late. I didn't get her in time.'"

After Mom left my hospital room, I tried to piece together more of that day. The next memory I had, after sinking under water, was that of my head pounding in protest to a loud shrieking sound. I thought I was home in bed, my alarm clock blaring. Jostling about and gasping for air, I quickly realized this couldn't be my bed. I didn't know where the hell I was but, Jesus, I couldn't breathe. It was as if someone had dropped a grand piano on my chest, strapping it down for good measure. The pain was unbearable. I couldn't catch a breath. As I struggled to open my eyes, salty tears reached my lips. I cried in agony, still unsure of what was happening.

Like a dissipating cloud of smoke, my vision began to clear. Rolling to one side, I made out a pair of men's black shoes. Someone was sitting next to me. I tried to lift my head to see who it was, but I was too weak. Suddenly the man's feet flew up in the air as a bucket of water splashed to the floor, drenching his shoes.

"Oh, God. Is she okay?"

Turning my head, I followed that familiar voice. I made out just the shadow of Buzz as his face slowly came into focus.

"Oh God, oh God. Hang in there, babe." He waved his hands in the air like a frightened character in a horror movie, seeing the villain for the first time. Typically a man in complete control, there was terror in his eyes I'd never seen before. I stared at him, trying my best to figure out what he was reacting to. Eventually getting a grip, Buzz sounded more like himself. "You're going to be okay. We're almost to the hospital."

I took quick, shallow breaths that shot sharp pain through my chest and back. It was hardly enough air to sustain me. I felt myself going out but fought to stay conscious. It became apparent that I was in an ambulance. It was sirens blaring, not my alarm clock. I realized the water hadn't come from a bucket, but rather from me. I had thrown up on the medic's shoes and was about to do it again. When I finished, the medic placed a mask over my face and told me to breathe. "Just relax," he said.

Feeling as if he were smothering me rather than offering oxygen, I panicked and took a weak swing at him. He braced my shoulder down and held the mask firmly in place. Defeated, my hands rested at my sides, where I felt my wet, sandy bathing suit. I pieced it together. The race. The seizure. Sinking under. My dying thoughts. I had to tell Buzz it was a seizure. He should know. Struggling to find my voice trapped inside the pain, I raised a finger, signaling him to come closer. He waited while I took three quick breaths, saving them up to speak. "I'm sorry ... I didn't go ... to church today," I managed to push out.

"Oh, Darla." Tears rolled down Buzz's cheeks as he reached for my hand, but I never felt his touch. Instead, I had the sensation of floating, drifting further and further away from my father. Like a theater curtain was drawing shut, Buzz faded away.

My next memory was that of a bright ceiling light, beaming above a man with bushy red hair. He was too close to my face to see him clearly. Patting my arm, he said, "Hang in there, kiddo. You're going to be okay, Darla." He sounded familiar. He knew my name. When he took a step back, I recognized him.

Dan Slagle. He had graduated a couple of years ahead of me, a certifiable class clown. I wondered if he should be trusted in an emergency room, yet here he was, and he almost seemed to be in charge.

From somewhere behind me, I heard Rusty's voice. "Can I see her?" I wondered how he had known I was in the emergency room. I later learned Mom had gone to get him before driving to the hospital, thinking he should see me. Maybe one last time.

"You've got one second," Dan ordered.

Speechless, Rusty approached my side, hair sprouting up in every direction, his blue eyes puffy. His unshaven morning-after mug was a reminder of how stupid I'd been to stay out all night, then push it hard the next day, racing my father. *Oh God, Buzz. What did I put him through?* I would have been wise to lay low that day. My seizures were generally triggered by lack of sleep and/or physical exertion. And a stupid hangover had definitely tipped the scale.

I tried to speak—to tell Rusty about the seizure—but nothing came out, and he was quickly pushed aside. I was alone now, struggling to breathe. Fear set in as doctors and nurses swarmed about. Even in that terrifying moment, there was a sense of self-blame and shame as to why I was there. If I'd had the strength, I would have explained to everyone in the emergency room: *I'm not an idiot. I know how to swim. I had a seizure. I couldn't help it.* Instead, adding insult to injury, I coughed and threw up all over myself.

~

I spent nearly a week in ICU, in and out of consciousness, before moving to a different floor. One night I asked the nurse's aide who brought me dinner if she knew how long I'd been in the clink.

She answered, "Eight days … I think."

I managed to sit up for a meal of chicken broth and Jell-O. Unfortunately, I couldn't keep it down. That night, I discovered the food tray had a drawer that flipped open, a small mirror attached to the inside. Pausing for a moment, I dared myself to take a peek. Slowly I placed the oxygen mask on top of my head, like a pair of sunglasses, to study the stranger in the mirror.

I looked sick. Not cold and flu sick, but dying sick. It was the end of summer, and my body was tanned a deep golden brown. Yet somehow my face was the color of cotton. Each physical feature seemed to contradict another. Dark circles framed light blue eyes. Dry, split lips stood out against greasy skin. My ears appeared somehow larger next to hollow cheeks. A nurse told me I was down fourteen pounds—weight I didn't need to lose. My collarbone protruded above the neckline of my hospital gown. Long legs, once strong and muscular, now appeared child-like poking out from under the sheets. No wonder people dropped their mouths and choked back tears when they visited.

Suddenly feeling light headed, I repositioned the oxygen mask, bumping sand from filthy hair. I shoved the food tray aside, curled up in the fetal position, and dreamed of taking a nice hot shower.

To help remove water from my lungs and clear my airways, a respiratory therapist rapped his hands on my torso like an angry bongo drummer. As painful as it was, it forced me to cough up disgusting liquid into a bedpan. Most alarming was the blood. There was always blood in what I brought up. The therapist pounded until I waved him off. I had a breaking point, and it was obviously much sooner than he liked. Each time I called it quits, he said, "Okay, Darla. I'll stop, but next time we're going longer." And he meant it.

"You're at high risk for infection," he told me one day while I complained during a treatment. "In fact, I hate to tell you this, but you're not out of the woods. Right now your lungs are like a heavy sponge. You've taken in a lot of water, and they could collapse," he warned.

"Yeah, well, you don't know what this feels like," I barked. Coughing—moving all that junk out of my inflamed airways —was like passing a razor blade through tender tissue.

"I know. It sucks. But you have to work with me."

Lying in that hospital bed, I could never have predicted that eight years later, I would administer the same treatment to my son and eventually to my daughter as well. And I would be just as adamant as my respiratory therapist was—lecturing, coaxing, arguing and bargaining for Ray and Martha to complete their treatments. And both of them would protest, in much the same way as I had, often pleading to cut their BDs short. "Mom, can we please be done now?"

I imagine the time between seizures was a vacation for my parents, but cystic fibrosis was all day, every day. Rusty and I couldn't minimize it by saying something like, "You're okay. You just have the sniffles." Instead we educated our children about CF, providing more and more information as they matured. Just enough to make sure they understood the importance of their care, but not so many details that they were overwhelmed or fearful of their future.

I had lived recklessly and nearly lost my life over a foolish decision to race Buzz. I wanted Ray and Martha to make better decisions than their mom. I tried not to direct their every move, but I did stress that they honor what their bodies were telling them and judge for themselves how far they could safely push it. A common phrase in our home was *Go ahead and have fun, but pace yourself.* However, if I'm being honest, it was a message lost on Ray and Martha. It was nearly impossible to hold them back. But I'm grateful they engaged in life the way that they did, because being shy is socially paralyzing. We miss out on so much if we live our lives inwardly.

I saw a new neurologist after leaving the hospital. When I told him what seizure drug and dose I was taking, he asked, "How have you been functioning?"

"I don't know, but I'll tell you what. I've been tired for eleven years."

"No doubt," he said. "You're on a high dose of a heavy barbiturate. I'm going to wean you off and put you on something more appropriate." Turns out there was a better option for me, and for the first time since my diagnosis, I felt clear headed. However, I wasn't completely seizure-free until I was thirty years old. My neurologist followed me closely throughout my twenties, constantly tweaking my medication, until he found the perfect recipe that stopped my seizures altogether.

I never told my children that I had epilepsy. I guess I thought they had enough on their plate. They didn't need to worry about their mother too. Instead, I focused on *their* illness and advocated for them. I questioned every drug and procedure their doctors prescribed—not going on blind faith. After all, sometimes doctors get it wrong. And sometimes, when you communicate, they get it just right.

Early on, our kids learned how to stand up for themselves, something I didn't master until I was much older. Probably not until high school, when some kid had the nerve to say, "You know, every time you have a seizure, it kills off some of your brain cells." I fired back, "Well, good thing I was born a genius, because even with all my dead brain cells, I'm still smarter than you." We both cracked up, and I discovered that if I was funny enough, no one would laugh *at* me. Self-deprecating humor and sarcasm became effective tools, helping me to cope as I got older. But I swear, Ray and Martha had the ability to laugh at themselves straight out of the gate.

When Ray was maybe three or four years old, a neighbor boy invited him to play on his jungle gym with some other kids on the block. Everything was going just fine until suddenly, out of the blue, Ray decided to pull his pants down and show his privates. The boy's mom immediately marched Ray home and told me what he had done. She looked absolutely disgusted with my son. Maybe disgusted with me, too, like we were the weird family on the block with the creepy flasher kid.

I immediately took Ray inside and explained to him how we keep our clothes on in public. Ray just shrugged it off like it was no big deal. Alarmed by his casual reaction, I took the shame route and ended our talk with, "Don't you understand? You can't run around naked, Ray. Are you crazy or something?"

"Well … I'm only half-crazy, because I was only half-naked." He giggled.

This became a common theme throughout his life. Not the naked part, but the stubborn, consistent way Ray reasoned that his actions or words weren't intentionally hurtful, therefore, no big deal. As a first-time mom, I was concerned that his behavior would reflect on me, but in a way it was refreshing— like he needed to remind the world to get a sense of humor. Ray rarely allowed anyone to get under his skin. Whenever I tried to reason with him, by saying something like, "Listen, buddy, this is how the world works," he would respond with, "Well, maybe that's how it works for you, Mom. Maybe that's how you think, but it's not how I think."

So, Ray was Ray, and there wasn't a lot anyone could do to change him. He liked who he was.

Like her brother, Martha took everything in stride and didn't embarrass easily either. One morning before she left the house to catch the school bus, I noticed that only the front of her hair was brushed smooth.

"Martha, please take a quick brush to the back of your hair," I pleaded. "It looks like a rat's nest."

"Well … too bad for the kid who sits behind me," she stated, before rushing out the door.

I do not come anywhere close to matching the self-confidence and character that Ray and Martha possessed, but if I were to answer my friend Jeana's question, "How did you get so tough?" I would say, in some strange way, epilepsy—the very thing I despised—gave me strength.

While I can't pretend to know what it's like to actually have cystic fibrosis, there was a time in my life when my lungs were compromised and I relied on IV antibiotics and a respiratory therapist to help clear my airways. It took many months after being discharged from the hospital before I could walk any distance without sucking wind or feeling light headed. It was only a small taste of what it feels like to not breathe easily, but maybe just enough to heighten my empathy for Ray and Martha. There's no single benefit to having epilepsy. But in my case, perhaps there was one. I realize now that growing up with a chronic illness influenced how I parented. I know what it's like to feel different, and I made damn sure my children never felt shame for something that was not their fault.

I believe there is a thread that weaves itself through childhood into adulthood, and those early experiences shape who we become. Piece by piece, we build upon our life experiences —the good ones and the bad ones—and gradually, we each become the person we were meant to be.

Arcade Street

With very little interest and a twenty-five-cent investment, I set a beer down on the table in front of a complete stranger. "Here, you look thirsty," I said to him. Before I could walk away, he invited me to sit. During our short conversation, I asked what he did. He smiled and said he was an inner-city lumberjack. Turns out he was a college student and trimmed trees during the summer months. He also said he was on the football team and was studying law enforcement to become a police officer. I immediately thought, *a cop and a jock—two strikes against him.*

I wish I had a classier story of the first time we met, but I don't. It was "quarter beer" night at the Parkside Lounge. I was all of twenty years old, wasting another night at another dumpy bar on St. Paul's East Side. I had been asking my friend Mary to take me home for quite a while. She said she would, if I first said hello to Rusty Garvey. She swore he was a nice guy.

From across the barroom, I took a moment to study this so-called nice guy. His disheveled shoulder-length hair was questionable. It was hard to say if his dark mop of waves was an asset or a nuisance in need of grooming. I noticed a large tear on the sleeve of his worn leather jacket and decided the jacket had probably seen as many barroom brawls as he had.

"Are you kidding me, Mary?" I protested after my quick assessment. "There's no way I'm talking to that guy. I can see from here he's nothing but trouble."

"No, he's a nice guy. I think you'd like him. He's really funny."

"Seriously? He looks like a big goon."

"Just go over and say 'hi.' Then I promise we can leave," my matchmaker friend insisted.

If anyone would have told me I was buying a cheap glass of beer for my future husband that night, I would have laughed. But in 1987, Rusty and I were married. Nothing fancy. Just a small chapel wedding at First Lutheran Church in the Swede Hollow neighborhood of Dayton's Bluff on—where else? St. Paul's East Side.

It's funny to think about it now, but that night at the Parkside Lounge, Rusty looked like a rebel—maybe even a criminal. Yet he surprisingly had his act together. I still looked like the wholesome girl next door, but I was a hot mess with no clear direction in life. It was Rusty who questioned my ambitions, or lack thereof, asking, "How come you're not in college?"

In high school, when I wasn't sleeping through my classes, I was ditching them. My grades were so poor my counselor insisted I join an on-the-job-training program if I wanted to graduate. He said he had already set up an interview for me at a law firm. When I told him I had no interest in OJT or secretarial work, he slid my less-than-impressive transcripts across his desk and said, "Let's face it, Darla. You're not college material." So my fate was sealed: office procedure classes in the morning and my afternoons spent in a stuffy law office.

Between my high school counselor and my parents, college was never discussed. So I assumed I was not cut out for higher education. When I met Rusty, however, my trajectory changed. With his encouragement, I enrolled at the University of Minnesota and began working on my generals. Later I would earn a bachelor's degree in elementary education from the University of Wisconsin, River Falls, and then went on to grad school at Hamline University in St. Paul. I had a recurring dream where I walked into my old counselor's office at Harding, slapped my *impressive* college transcripts on his desk, and said, "Not college material, huh?"

I have always marveled at Rusty's unwavering determination to succeed, and I'm grateful he insisted I set the bar higher for myself. Yet, given that I was raised in a two-parent family that provided a great deal of care and stability, it's surprising that my motivation to better myself would ultimately come from a guy who was living above a bar on the *lower* East Side.

~

For the first five years of his life, Rusty lived in Des Moines, Iowa. His family was as typical as any other family living in the 1960s. His mother, Roberta, stayed home and took care of Rusty and his younger brother and sister, while his father, Jim, managed a grocery store.

Family games were played, dinner was on the table each night, and bedtime stories were read. Christmas was met with the usual excitement of any young boy. Sugar cookies, Santa Claus, and decorated Christmas trees.

Rusty's birthday parties were special, too, celebrated with his grandparents and childhood friends. Roberta even kept a scrapbook, photographing and documenting Rusty's milestones—including his first day of kindergarten in Des Moines. But family life as he knew it would soon unravel.

Rusty's father lost his job at the grocery store—a nice way of saying he got fired. He found a new job and moved the family to Hiawatha, Iowa, where Rusty attended first grade. Jim's drinking picked up, another job was "lost," and another move was made, this time to Cedar Rapids, Iowa. Only eight years old at the time, Rusty had already attended three different schools, and a fourth one was on its way. Fired from yet another job, Jim moved his family to Hackensack, Minnesota, where he and his wife owned and operated the Chat & Chew Café. Before and after school, Rusty and his siblings ate breakfast and had dinner at the café.

Running their own business now, there was hope that Jim and Roberta would finally find success. But working long hours together put a strain on their marriage. And tensions grew deeper as Jim took to the local bars after work and Roberta, who never drank, went home alone to care for her children. At her wits' end, Roberta made a decision to escape her failing, unhappy marriage.

One summer evening, she piled her kids into the car, claiming they were going to the laundromat. Sitting in the back seat on a mound of dirty clothes, Rusty watched out the window as they drove down Main Street, past the bank, past the laundromat, and past the Chat & Chew. In the rearview mirror, he noticed tears streaming down his mom's face and realized they wouldn't be plugging quarters into a washing machine that day.

Two things occurred to Rusty as they drove out of Hackensack for the last time. One, he was barefoot. And two, he didn't get to say goodbye to his dad, who was left passed out on the couch.

Roberta took her children back to Des Moines, Iowa, and stayed with her recently divorced mother until she could figure out her next move. Eventually Roberta would also divorce. A single mother of three now, she moved to White Bear Lake, Minnesota, just east of St. Paul. There Roberta rented a place that had actually been someone's garage. Temporary makeshift homes like this, lousy meals or no meals at all, became the norm. Even when his parents were married, moving had been a familiar event. The pattern continued after the divorce—Roberta running from bill collectors, chasing the next failed business dream, or marrying the next man too quickly.

Saying goodbye to newly made friends was a heartbreaking trend, leaving Rusty hesitant to connect. No sense getting too attached, he reasoned. After all, history would undoubtedly repeat itself—another move imminent. In fact, Rusty never completed a whole year at the same school, and often times there were month-long gaps between leaving one school and enrolling in the next. He was always the new kid, sometimes ahead of his class, sometimes behind. Eventually, always behind.

There was one brief period when Rusty had a fairly nice home after Roberta's father passed away. She used her inheritance to buy a house in the Battle Creek neighborhood of St. Paul. That year, Rusty met Jerry McNally, a boy who lived a few blocks away. Jerry and his buddies would become some of Rusty's closest friends during that period of his life.

Rusty was also on the junior high wrestling and football teams. So, with new friends and organized sports, he was more optimistic than he had been in a very long time. But his sense of security and belonging would be short lived.

On Rusty's thirteenth birthday, after spending the afternoon downtown with McNally, he came off the city bus and noticed something strange lying on his front lawn: big, black heaps of something that appeared to be debris. As the boys got closer, they discovered there had been a fire. Rusty's home was severely damaged, and the black mounds in the front yard were charred remains of chairs, couches, beds, and tables. Firefighters had put out the house fire and had removed smoldering items from the home, spraying them down with their hoses to prevent a fire spark.

Every good thing Rusty finally had in his life was gone. Everything. Every stitch of clothing. Every personal possession. Even his dog hadn't survived the fire. And, all but for a few pages of Roberta's scrapbooks, his childhood in photographs had been erased.

Without a home now, Roberta's transient lifestyle picked up again. Luckily, they were never too far away from Jim Garvey, who had moved from Hackensack to St. Paul to be closer to his children.

Sundays became the one consistent day in Rusty's life. It was the day when he could visit his father—now living above the Arcade Street Bar on the lower East Side.

Arcade Street is a hustling, bustling St. Paul throughway connecting Swede Hollow Park to Lake Phalen—roughly a three-mile blue-collar stretch of corner bars, family-run businesses, a rundown YMCA, massage parlors, and the Arcade Movie Theater, which showed its last film in 1978.

Back then, the clapboard-style homes' owners were mostly white working folks, many of whom earned a modest living working at one of three places: the Whirlpool appliance factory, the 3M plant, or the Hamm's Brewing Company.

Rusty's Sundays were mostly spent listening to music on the jukebox and playing pinball at the Arcade Bar with his brother and sister. All the while, Jim tossed back a few drinks with the regulars. Other times, Jim dropped his kids off at the movie theater. Once in a while, he took them to Catholic Mass at Sacred Heart Church on Sixth Street—always a few minutes late. And a couple times a year, Jim brought his children to his home town of Boone, Iowa, to visit their grandparents.

When Rusty was fourteen, there was talk of making yet another move, this time somewhere in Florida. Roberta was on her second of four marriages by then, a half-brother now in the mix. Bound to her gypsy ways, Roberta enticed her children with the promise of making their own money—selling cotton candy at a carnival—and opting out of school until the carnival season was over. But the thing was, Rusty *wanted* to go to high school, and he wanted to continue playing sports. The last thing he wanted was to be part of another one of his mother's "starting over" schemes. Especially if it meant leaving Minnesota and not spending Sundays with his father.

Determined to put an end to the constant turmoil, Rusty made a life-altering decision and told his mom, "I'm not running with you this time."

After some discussion with Jim, Roberta brought her oldest son to the Arcade Bar. Before she drove off, she handed Rusty a check that bounced when he later tried to cash it.

Holding a plastic trash bag containing his meager belongings, Rusty walked up to the third floor of the Arcade Bar with his new dog. Jim frowned as soon as he opened the door to his small boardinghouse room. "I didn't know the dog was part of the deal," he said.

A functioning alcoholic, Jim worked at the Whirlpool factory by day, and bartended, bullshitted, and tossed back whiskey by night. A lifestyle he'd chosen—or maybe it had chosen him —but not one conducive to parenting a young teenage boy. Yet he welcomed his son, the two of them squeezing into one small, dingy room—a shared tenant's bathroom and shower were down the hall. The paint on the walls was peeling, heavy cigarette smoke hung in the air, and a sheet of plastic covered a drafty window in what was now Rusty's new home.

With only a worn couch to sleep on, Jim added a used mattress for his son. There was hardly enough space for the two of them, much less a dog who, unbeknownst to Rusty, was pregnant. The litter of pups were sold off and the mother dog was sent to live with a bar patron.

Eventually, Rusty and his dad moved across the street above Governor's Bar, which was equally as rundown and dreary as the flophouse room above the Arcade Bar. But it was more suitable, with two small bedrooms and a private bathroom. A step up, even considering they had to stand on a wooden crate while showering so as not to fall through the rotted floorboards.

In August of 1974, Rusty reluctantly enrolled at Johnson High School, also on Arcade Street, about a one-mile walk from the bar. He wanted to go to Harding High School instead—the school where Jerry McNally and his Battle Creek friends would be attending—but that was out of the question. It would cost Jim a hefty sum to send his son out of the neighborhood school boundaries, money he didn't have. So, once again, Rusty was in transition, parting ways with old friends and attending a new school without a single friend.

It was through football and wrestling that Rusty found acceptance at Johnson High School. In 1976 he was part of a championship football team. In an important play-off game, Johnson beat Harding High School—their biggest rival—by one point and went on to win the Twin Cities Football Championship, which led Johnson to the state tournament.

By his senior year, the teenage boy who was once an unknown on the lower East Side became the captain of his high school wrestling team and was the leader of a football defensive unit dubbed "Garvey's Gorillas."

"Six Degrees of Kevin Bacon" is a popular expression based on the concept that any two people are just six acquaintance links apart. On the East Side, one might argue that there is only one degree of separation. Even though the East Side is a large inner-city community, it's as if everyone living there is linked in some form or another. And for some reason, an East Side tie seems to last forever. That's certainly the case for Rusty. His closest Johnson alums are Jerry Splinter, Scott Behr, Jon Zarins, and Scott Kruse. The five guys are still tight today, some forty years later. They're masters at telling a simple five-sentence story, laughter erupting after each line as if they're telling it for the first time. Their old tales always begin with, "Remember when…?" and inevitably end with someone being a son of a bitch.

"Remember when we used pick you up for school at the bar and every morning we walked past that old guy's window?"

"Yeah, the lonely old guy who had the room down the hall."

"We felt sorry for him because he sat at the table with a bowl of cereal in front of him, looking all depressed."

"Exact same position every morning—resting his forehead in his hand."

"Turns out the poor son of a bitch had been dead for a week."

I asked Rusty once if it had been difficult living in a rough neighborhood above a rough bar, even with the best of friends. The traffic, the music, loud drunks and bar fights. And sharing a room with his dad, not to mention the mice. Then I went so far as to ask if he'd ever felt like it wasn't enough.

"At the time, it was the best I'd ever had," Rusty was quick to answer. "I never really *had* to go to school when I lived with my mom, but my dad made sure I got off to school."

"That's nice," I said.

"No, it wasn't." He laughed and shook his head. "I woke up to blaring polka music every damn morning. Before he left for work, my dad used to set his clock radio to the polka station … at full volume. Then he would walk back to the bar on his early morning 'coffee' break to make *sure* I got up for school."

"Oh my God. Did he really come back to shag you out of bed, or just to have a little bump?"

"Both." Rusty laughed. "He also left a dollar on the table every day for school lunch. And he always left a pot of stew or something for supper. Kept it warm—sitting on top of the heat register—before he went downstairs to the bar."

Rusty went on to say that, even though his dad was always there for him, Jim's long hours at the factory and his nightly habit of hanging out at the bar meant he had to learn to fend for himself. Each week, for example, he lugged a basket of dirty clothes to a laundromat on Payne Avenue, about a half-mile walk from the bar. He told me about the day when he made an unfortunate decision. While his clothes were drying in the machine, he sneaked into the Payne Reliever—a strip club across the street. When he finally returned to the laundromat, every stitch of clothing he owned had been stolen. "Serves you right." I laughed.

Based on Jim's lifestyle, I suppose if you didn't know him, you'd think he was a less-than-stellar father. But you'd be wrong. He was Rusty's saving grace, providing structure and discipline that had been missing from his life—albeit in an unconventional way.

Sometimes I think of Rusty when I hear Neil Young's "Keep on Rockin' in the Free World." There's a part in the song where Young sings about a child never going to school, never finding love, and never getting to be cool. If not for Jim, Rusty could have been that kid, but he wasn't. No longer hopping from town to town, school to school, Rusty finally had a real home and a sense of community. He did get to go to school, finishing all three years at Johnson High School. He went on to play college football at Inver Hills Community College and later earned a football scholarship at the University of Evansville in Indiana.

Rusty did get to fall in love, and although he gets embarrassed if anyone dares to mention he was voted homecoming king, he did get to be cool.

Those formative years, living with his dad on the East Side, had a lasting effect on Rusty. They even directed his career path. While he had other opportunities to work in different cities, Rusty ultimately took a job with the St. Paul Police Department. He started out as a beat cop in the Payne Avenue-Arcade Street area and provided community policing in the familiar neighborhoods where he'd once lived.

For many of the residents in the area, he wasn't just Officer Russ Garvey; he was Jim Garvey's son. This gave Rusty a leg up. He had East Side credibility and could de-escalate situations that might otherwise have had a different outcome with a lesser-known cop.

Jim Garvey would live with us during the final year of his life. He was diagnosed with throat cancer and later developed an inoperable brain tumor. We converted my office into a bedroom and cared for him at home. The upside to this arrangement was that Ray and Martha got to see their grandfather every day.

Eventually Jim had surgery to remove the tumor in his throat. Rusty was working the night before his dad was admitted into the hospital, but Jim and I sat outside on our back patio, talking late into the night. There was a possibility Jim's surgery would also include a laryngectomy, which meant he would lose his voice. So that night, Jim told me all about his life, including how he felt about his oldest son. "Rusty was a good boy," he said. "He never gave me any trouble. I'm very proud of him."

That was the last time I heard Jim's raspy voice or his adorable squeaky laugh. He did, in fact, have a laryngectomy, leaving him with a hole in his neck. He learned to talk with the aid of an electro larynx, a battery-operated device that produces sound to create an artificial voice.

Eventually his care proved to be too much for us, and Jim was moved to Our Lady of Good Counsel, a facility in St. Paul that provides care to terminally ill cancer patients. A month later, Rusty would say goodbye to his father—the man who had made an incredible impact on his life.

When it came time to plan Jim's funeral, Rusty suggested we hold the service at First Lutheran Church. "We can't have the funeral there," I told him. "That's not what your dad wanted."

"How do you know what my dad wanted?"

"We talked the night before his surgery. Trust me, he didn't want a Lutheran service. He repeated to me more than once, 'Remember this when I go: I am Catholic.'"

Jim's wishes were honored, and a Catholic priest presided over the memorial service at Anderson Funeral Home on Arcade Street, in the community where Jim had worked and lived for a significant part of his life.

In all the years I've known Rusty, I've never heard him say one disparaging word about his upbringing—never sensed an ounce of self-pity. Somehow he made even the saddest childhood memories humorous. Leading by example, Rusty passed along that positive attitude and resiliency to Ray and Martha. A common message from father to his son and daughter was this: "Whatever you do, don't quit."

I think sometimes when you start out with little, you value more. That certainly seems to be the case with Rusty. He appreciates the simplest of things and taught our children to do the same. You could give Ray or Martha new socks and they'd slip them on their feet as if they had never before owned a pair.

Rusty's gratitude showed up often, but it was never more apparent than the day he mowed our lawn for the first time. When he finished cutting the back yard, he took a seat in a lawn chair and cracked open a beer. He sat there for hours, just staring out at the lawn. When I finally stepped outside to ask if he was ever going to get to the front yard, he smiled and said, "Doesn't it look nice?"

"It's just grass, Rusty." I laughed.

"You don't understand. It's been a long time since I've had a yard."

So, with green grass and a new brick home, things looked pretty good for us on Ferndale Street. Rusty was thrilled that our kids attended neighborhood schools in *one* school district where lasting friendships were being made. Rusty encouraged community involvement, most often through local sports organizations. Both our children were skaters, playing hockey for Tartan Area Youth Hockey Association, with Martha moving up the ranks, playing defense on the girls' high school hockey team.

Rusty rarely hung out at the bars with other cops after his shift. Instead he came home, took his uniform off, and left his work behind. In fact, he rarely talked about police work. When he was home, he was just Dad.

As long as Ray and Martha put forth their best effort, he accepted their athletic and academic outcomes, often with a sense of humor. He couldn't help but appreciate Ray's philosophy in both sports and school. If he lost a wrestling match, Ray proudly stated, "At least I didn't get pinned." If he earned a C on his report card, he let that roll off his back, too, saying, "A C is better than a D."

You'd think, being a teacher, I'd place academic achievement at the top of the list, but I was most proud of my children for being decent human beings. Good grades are nice, but a straight A student with poor manners would be more concerning. While Rusty agreed with me, he still preferred when teachers cut to the chase and told us how our kids were doing in school.

During a parent-teacher conference one year, Martha's teachers went on and on about how respectful and kind she was. She had earned the Peace Award, and they couldn't stop talking about what an outstanding young lady she was. While Martha and I beamed with pride, Rusty grew impatient with all the accolades. He just wanted to see her grades and get out of there. On our drive home, Rusty asked Martha, "How the hell did you get so nice?"

She shot back, "Sometimes good kids come from bad parents."

I couldn't stop laughing. I mean, really, who gets scolded for being nice? And what little girl can put her dad in his place with one quick, snappy retort?

If one ignored the health problems and our twisted sense of humor, our family looked pretty much like any other family. Our home was filled with laughter, anger, passion, tension, joy, and frustration, but mostly, profound love. We were happy and life was good—until the day it wasn't.

Tonight's My Night

It was early April, 2001. Spring. The season for new beginnings. I quickly finished arranging a basket of flowers at the kitchen counter while glancing at the clock. Daffodils and lupines replaced the silk daisies that had seen better days. I was in the mood to brighten up the house after a long, greedy winter had stolen a chunk of our spring.

I needed to call the kids home soon so they could get ready for church. It was Maundy Thursday, the Christian holy day before Easter. Ray was going to receive his first communion at King of Kings Lutheran Church in Woodbury. Martha was playing in the neighbor's back yard, but I didn't know where Ray was. His backpack was tossed on the front porch, which meant he'd never made it inside the house after school. I started making some calls and found Ray at his friend Pete's. I reminded him of his first communion. Before hanging up the phone, I heard Ray tell Pete he could play when he got back from church.

A few minutes later, Ray burst through the front door. "Mom, I'm home."

"Oh, good," I called to him from the middle of the staircase. "Martha is getting dressed, and you need to come up and find something nice to wear, too."

Ray trailed up the stairs behind me and asked, "What's the deal with the flowers, Mom?"

"They're replacing the dirty white daisies in the bathroom." I stopped at the top of the landing. "Wouldn't that be a good name for a band?" I asked.

Ray threw me a blank look.

"Think about it. That would be a great name for a band. You watch. Someone is going to use it, and in a few years you're going to ask if you can go see The Dirty White Daisies in concert."

He rolled his eyes, the silent signal only a twelve-year-old boy can send to let his mother in on a little secret. *She's nuts.*

I was about to ask Ray how he'd gotten his pants so muddy, but he shut his bedroom door to change.

As I glanced in the mirror, it was clear the bathroom wasn't the only thing that needed freshening up.

A few minutes later, Ray stood outside the bathroom door and asked, "How's this, Mom?" He was wearing tan corduroys and a sweater.

"That sweater looks really nice on you. Why don't you wear it to school anymore? I forgot you even had it."

"Do you know how embarrassing it is to walk down the hall and see some other kid wearing the exact same sweater?" he stated.

I made a mental note not to shop at Target with the rest of America.

He started down the stairs, then stopped and peered back into the bathroom. "What are you doing?"

"Just touching up my makeup. I want to look nice for church too."

"What for, Mom? No one's going to look at you. Tonight's my night."

"Oh, they always look at the mother, Ray. People can take one quick glance at the mother and determine if the entire family is crazy or not."

He studied me briefly. "For real?" As soon as he saw the beginnings of my grin, he shook his head. "They do not." Then he repeated, "Well, no one's going to look at you. Tonight's my night."

Later, Rusty told me that Ray had said something similar to him. He went downstairs and asked his dad what he was doing in the laundry room. When Rusty told him he was ironing a pair of dress pants for church, Ray said, "Don't bother, Dad. No one's going to look at you. Tonight's my night."

As we drove to church, I wondered if Martha should be with us, too. Her friend Brooke Heutmaker and Brooke's mom, Bev, had stopped over as we were all getting ready to leave, asking if Martha could go to a movie. I thought she should be with her brother when he received his first communion, but Rusty saw it differently. "What's wrong with letting her see a movie?" he asked. "This night is about Ray anyway. Martha will be bored. Let her go to the movie."

I caved in and handed Bev a few extra bucks to buy Martha a hot dog at the theater. This would be her lousy supper. I felt guilty since we were going out for dinner with my parents after church. But Martha seemed happy with our decision.

We met Mom and Buzz inside the church doorway, then stopped at a table where a woman was handing out red carnations to the kids receiving communion. I quickly pinned a carnation to Ray's sweater before we filed into a pew at the back of the church. Just then, Harv French, Ray's fourth grade teacher, entered the worship hall. I was surprised to see him. I'd had no idea he attended the same church, but then again, we weren't exactly regular church-goers. I waved Harv over and he took a seat next to Buzz, then reached across to shake hands with Ray. Ray proceeded to tell Mr. French he was going to have wine tonight, causing Harv to chuckle.

When the usher motioned for us to stand and approach the altar, Ray stopped abruptly. Hospitalized with a lung infection earlier in the year, he hadn't been able to attend all his communion classes. Now he was nervous.

"What do I do, Mom?"

"Just catch up to Grandma. Do what she does. I'll be right behind you." I watched as Ray held out his cupped hands to receive bread—the body of Christ. Then he took a communion cup from the minister and choked back wine—the blood of Christ. For the second time that night I wondered how he had gotten so dirty. Every single fingernail was caked in mud. I had a moment of guilt, thinking how I never quite had my act together. I hadn't even seen to it that my son washed up properly for his first communion.

My parents joined us for dinner at Famous Dave's after the service. Ray wanted to eat quickly and hook up with his friends again, and Famous Dave's was on the way home.

As usual, Ray was the entertainment at the table. My drink hadn't arrived yet, so I asked Buzz if I could take a sip of his beer. Ray said, "Grandpa, hurry. Put some backwash in your beer. That's what I do at school so no one drinks my milk." That led to a lunchroom story. Ray told us the day before, when he'd set his lunch tray down at a table, a girl had said, "You can't sit here, Ray. This table is for the popular kids." Ray said he plunked his tray down and told her, "I'll sit wherever I damn well please."

A little stunned by Ray's language in front of his grandparents, I leaned over to Rusty and said, "So much for going to church." But I wasn't the least bit surprised by Ray's reaction to the self-proclaimed popular girl. He had had very little experience with rejection. Most people were drawn to him, so the very thought of someone telling him he wasn't good enough to sit at her table didn't sit well with him.

I said goodbye to my parents outside the restaurant while Rusty and Ray went to get the car. When they pulled up to the curb, Ray gestured for me to get in the back seat. Now that he was old enough to legally sit in the front with air bags, he made a big deal of it—an even bigger deal if it meant I had to squish into the back seat.

As I reached for the car door handle, Rusty pulled ahead a couple of feet. Ray threw his head back in a fit of laughter. I reached for the door handle once more, and again Rusty pulled ahead. Ray's laughter nearly brought him to tears as this continued the entire length of the parking lot. When I finally got in the car, I told them they were both annoying as hell, which made them laugh all the more.

On our short drive home, Ray turned up the radio to sing along to a rap song, which surprised me. He had more of an appreciation for the oldies.

"I didn't think you liked rap music. I can't believe you know all the words to this song."

Ray stopped singing long enough to say, "They play rap on the school bus. This one's pretty good." Then he turned the radio up even louder and danced in his seat. I watched his head moving to the beat of the music and smiled. The kid had rhythm.

It was dark as we pulled into our driveway. Rusty told Ray it was too late to hang out with his friends. And I asked if he'd run down to Brooke's house and bring Martha home.

He hopped out of the car and started to run across our front lawn to Brooke's, hollering over his shoulder, "Hey, wanna race me?"

At the same moment, Rusty asked if I'd get the mail and tossed the mailbox keys to me. I caught the keys in one hand and called out to Ray, "I guess not! You already took off without me."

I watched Ray run across the grass into the dark until all I could see were the white bottoms of his tennis shoes. Then I walked across the street to the mailbox. I glanced over at the Heutmaker house, just three doors down. Their front door was open and their porch lights were on. I remember thinking,

"That was fast. Ray must have been in a hurry to tell everyone he drank wine."

I walked home and tossed the mail on the kitchen counter. Rusty was on the phone, and from the nature of his conversation, I assumed he was talking to another cop. I whispered, "I'm going to head down to Brooke's and thank Ken and Bev for watching Martha." Rusty acknowledged me with a nod.

The night had turned cold, so my walk became brisk. I was just approaching the edge of Brooke's lawn when something caught my eye. I couldn't make out what it was until I got a little closer. There in the grass was Ray, lying flat on his back, his arms and legs spread wide open. I detected a slight smile on his face as I got a little closer. I looked around, expecting to find Martha in the same position somewhere near Ray. I imagined Ray had told her, "Quick, Martha. Get down. Here comes Mom. Let's scare her."

I called out to Ray, "What the heck are you doing, you nut?" Again, I scanned the yard. "Where's Martha?"

He didn't respond.

I leaned in to get a better look at his face. His eyes were slightly open, just a crack, but his eyelids weren't even flickering. He was doing an excellent job of holding still. I leaned in and stared at his face, waiting for him to start laughing. He could never beat me in a stare down, and he was already wearing a small smile.

"Oh, you're good at this, Ray. You're real good. But I can tell you're going to laugh."

Still no response.

Growing impatient, I said, "Okay, buddy, the joke's over." I took a step or two away to call his bluff. "If you don't get up, I'm going to call 911."

Even Ray, a seasoned prankster, wouldn't let me go this long. Suddenly, in a panic, I knelt down beside him and placed a hand on his shoulder. He was out cold. How was it possible I could not know?

I stood up and spun around in a circle of confusion. For a second I couldn't quite convince myself that Ray needed medical attention, but a wave of adrenaline rushed over me, forcing my legs to move. I ran to Brooke's front porch. Ken was standing on the top step of his split-level entryway. I opened the door and hollered, "Call 911! Ray collapsed in your yard! I'm going to get Rusty!"

It felt so wrong to leave Ray, but I told myself it was going to be okay. I looked over my shoulder as I ran home. Ken was already at Ray's side, and Bev was standing outside on the doorstep with the phone in her hand. My bases were covered. I kept thinking, *I have to get Rusty. It's going to be okay. I just have to get Rusty.*

On my frantic flight home, I decided Ray must be having a seizure. *That must be it*, I told myself. *He's just having a seizure. Figures!* I had passed down the CF gene and now epilepsy too. I was a genetic cesspool.

I followed Rusty's voice down the hall to the kitchen. All I said was, "RAY!" Then I stumbled back out the front door.

Rusty sprinted past me, trying to stuff the cordless phone in his back pocket. I watched him run, the big clumsy phone bobbing around in his pants pocket as he gained speed. It was then that I stopped pretending Ray was having a seizure, even before I heard Ken say that Ray wasn't breathing. Even before Rusty began CPR.

I glanced up at the Heutmakers' house and noticed Brooke's older sister, Jessie, was watching from the door. I prayed Martha wasn't watching too. Ken seemed to read my mind. He called out to his daughter to get back inside and keep Martha and Brooke in the basement. Jessie stood frozen in place. Ken screamed, "Now!" She peeled herself away from the front door and did as her father ordered.

Bev, still on the phone with the 911 dispatcher, called out to me, "What does Ray have?"

"What do you mean?" I hollered back.

"What illness?"

"Cystic fibrosis."

As soon as I said it, I wished I hadn't. I didn't want the medics to focus on the wrong thing. I knew this had nothing to do with CF. Mucus can build up in the lungs over time, but the person doesn't suddenly stop breathing. His heart doesn't suddenly stop beating. Ray was just running. His lungs were fine. Something else was wrong. Maybe, I thought, he was choking on something.

"Is he breathing yet, Rusty? Please tell me he's breathing," I cried out.

Between compressions and breaths, he managed to answer, "Not yet, but I've got him. I've got him."

I fell down on all fours and pounded the cold, wet ground. "Come on, Ray! You can do it, buddy. Come on. Just breathe."

I rubbed Ray's legs while Rusty continued to work on him. "Are you sure you checked his airway? Is he choking on something?"

Without breaking rhythm, Rusty nodded yes. He had checked. I couldn't judge the time. One minute or five might have gone by before Rusty turned Ray on his side and he spit up. I jumped up and cried out in relief, "Yes, finally!"

I was horrified when Ray didn't draw a breath. I was sure after he spit up, he'd start coughing and breathing, just like in the movies. But his body was still limp. Rusty rolled Ray onto his back and continued CPR. I dropped down in a heap next to my boy.

Rusty started pumping Ray's chest with frantic force. "Be careful. Don't hurt him," I cried.

Several times during mouth to mouth, Rusty turned his head to the side and spit out the vomit that continued to spew from Ray's mouth into his own. I didn't like what I was seeing but tried to convince myself that his throwing up was a good sign. Any second Ray's airways would be clear and he'd breathe again.

Strangely, I noticed that my feet were cold and wet. I wondered how I could sense anything about my own body right then, but somehow my shoes had come off and my socks were soaked. Ken appeared at my side and pulled me to my feet. He held on to me and told me help was on the way. Ray was going to be okay.

"Can you keep Martha when the ambulance comes?" I asked.

"We've got her, Darla. Don't worry about Martha." Then he repeated, "Help is on the way. Ray's going to be okay."

"Will you tell Martha that? Tell her Ray's okay. Tell her he's going to the hospital but he's all right."

"I will."

But silently, I corrected myself. *He's not all right. He's not breathing.*

I finally heard the siren as an ambulance rounded the dimly lit corner of Ferndale Street and Highwood Avenue. The truck seemed to crawl the rest of its way before coming to a stop. I ran toward the ambulance waving my arms like a wild woman, but no one stepped out of the truck. I knew Bev had told them Ray wasn't breathing. Why were they acting like this was a broken leg call?

I continued jumping up and down and waving my arms in the air until, finally, the back door opened and three paramedics, two male and one female, came out of the vehicle. I don't recall if I said anything to them. I don't suspect I had to. It's probably the most foolproof part of their training. Follow the most hysterical person on the scene and they'll lead you to the victim. I directed them across the lawn several yards to where Ray was lying. They knelt down and gathered around Ray, pulling medical equipment from a bag. They told Rusty to step back, but he wouldn't stop working on Ray. They repeated their command: "Step away!" Rusty reluctantly peeled himself off his son and sat back on his knees.

I held my breath. I held my breath for my son, longing to give him my air. I held it in my lungs and waited. Waited for the medics to do something. Rusty felt it as well. Too much time was slipping by. He shouted, "He needs air. He needs another breath. Come on. Give him a breath!"

One of the male medics stopped what he was doing, looked directly at Rusty, and said, "Don't worry. I know what I'm doing. I'm a professional."

I was too dumbstruck to speak, but I remember thinking, *Oh my God! Our boy needs help, and tonight we get the guy with an ego problem.*

Rusty's booming voice filled the night air. "I don't care who the fuck you are. I'm his dad. Do your job!"

I sensed the presence of neighbors gathered on the lawn next door but didn't bother to look because I was fixated on a defibrillator the female medic now held in her hand. There was a sense of hope right then, a piece of equipment that could save our son. My father had told me that I had been under water at Lake Phalen for over three minutes before the lifeguard started CPR. Maybe there was time yet for Ray, too. Maybe the medics could still revive our son.

Kneeling down at Ray's feet, I rubbed his legs, the only part of his body available to me. The medics warned me to step away as they placed the paddles on Ray's chest. I lowered my head and silently begged God, *Shock his little heart and keep him alive. Please, oh God, please let this work.*

Then I heard the male medic say, "Again."

My prayers quickly turned to cursing. "Damn it. Come on. Goddamn it." The defibrillator hadn't worked. I watched as they shocked Ray again. No change. No breathing. No life.

I don't recall how many more times they tried to jumpstart Ray's heart. I had long since buried my head in my hands. When I finally looked up, Ray was being lifted onto a stretcher. The female medic walked along one side of Ray, pumping a hand-held resuscitator while the other medics hoisted the stretcher into the back of the ambulance.

Rusty crawled in the back of the truck with Ray. The medics told me to ride up front. The driver hopped in the truck without looking at me. He sat silently and waited for everyone to get settled in the back before putting the truck in gear. His silence was disturbing, a clear sign that he knew as well as I did that this wasn't going well.

From inside the ambulance I saw Ken and Bev planted in the middle of their lawn. In a moment they would have to go inside their house and face Martha. *My poor little Martha.*

On the way to Woodwinds Hospital, only a few miles from our home, I turned back once to check on Ray. From the front seat I couldn't see his entire body. I couldn't see if his chest was moving. But I didn't have to. The chilling look of terror in Rusty's eyes said it all. I turned around in my seat, closed my eyes, and prayed once again. *Please God, please. Let my son live. You can't take him. You can't take my boy.*

When the ambulance came to a stop outside the emergency entrance, I jumped out and ran to the back of the truck. Rusty came to my side and took my hand as the medics hoisted our son out on the stretcher. Ray's body jostled slightly to one side, then bounced back in place as the wheels of the bed scraped the ground. A sea of people in scrubs suddenly engulfed him.

I half expected to see Ray's eyes open, searching for his mom and dad. Questioning what was happening to him. "What's going on? Where am I?" And I half expected to answer him, "You just had a seizure, Ray. You're going to be fine."

Instead, we watched as the medics rushed our unresponsive son past us. Ray was wheeled into a small emergency room. A pale, limp curtain hung to one side in a failed attempt to provide privacy. Gripping hands, Rusty and I stood back from Ray while a team of frenzied emergency staff tended to him. It seemed like half a dozen people were working on Ray. Hands and arms flailed about, orders shouted. There were people giving injections and compressions, pumping a resuscitator. All the while the room seemed to be shrinking.

A sliver of space opened up between the hospital staff and Ray. For one brief moment I caught a glimpse of his eyes rolling back in his head. I covered my mouth and gasped in horror. Ray's eyes were empty. Completely void of life. For a split second I willed him to go. If he wasn't going to be the same, if he wasn't going to be *Ray,* then let him go. As soon as the thought flashed through my mind, I wanted to erase it. *Take it back. Take it back. What kind of a mother wills her son to go?* But even in that moment, I knew the answer. The kind of mother who loves her son and knows he's already gone.

But no matter what I had been thinking, nothing prepared me for what happened next. The medics simply stopped. Everything fell silent. The light in the room seemed to fade, and all movement, all the urgent bodies frantically scurrying about a second earlier, became still. Everyone pulled away from the table, leaving Ray exposed and alone, a tube still protruding from his mouth. They couldn't help him. That's what they told us. "We're sorry. We can't do any more for him."

Rusty nodded as if he understood and accepted their words, but I shook my head and protested. "You can't quit on him! How do you know when enough is enough? Do something!" I cried.

The doctors and nurses lowered their eyes and left the room without a word. Rusty let go of my hand, draped his large body over our son and sobbed. "You worked too hard for this, Ray. You worked so hard."

I ran to a bathroom outside the room and vomited.

A little later, a nurse came in the room and removed the tube from Ray's mouth. Then she asked if we'd like Ray's feeding tube removed as well. I thought about what we had promised Ray. How he could have it removed when he got in high school. Then it would be up to him to eat that extra cheeseburger or drink that extra milkshake to maintain his weight. Light headed, I clung to the bed rail for balance and thought, *Oh God. He doesn't even get to go to high school. He didn't even finish sixth grade. He didn't get to grow up.*

"The tube can come out," I said. "But let me do it." I wanted to tend to my son. Take care of him one last time. Ignoring my request, the nurse quickly took a syringe and drew the fluid from the tube, removing it herself. Then she asked if we'd like her to put a Band-Aid over the hole in our son's stomach. I nodded. "He's just a kid," I told her. "Every kid needs a Band-Aid."

I was vaguely aware that Rusty had left the room. Maybe he had gone to throw up like I had earlier. I held Ray's hand in mine and studied his beautiful little face. His features were perfect. I had often told him how handsome he was, and he'd tell me, "You have to say that. You're my mom." I lost a little bit of credibility when I told him that even his eyebrows were handsome.

And his hair—he had the most gorgeous head of thick blonde hair. When we were driving in the car, sometimes I would reach over and stroke the back of his head, telling him his head was begging me to touch it.

I stared at Ray's nose. He was relieved his nose was like mine. He didn't want a large nose with a bump on it like his dad's, no matter how often I told him a bump adds character. Occasionally Ray asked me to feel the bridge of his nose. "Dad says a bump is starting to grow. Do you think so, Mom? Feel it."

Ray's mouth was closed now, his curvy lips hiding the large white teeth responsible for his incredible smile. I traced his strong jawline with my eyes, stopping at his chin. His chin had a slight cleft in it like his grandpa's. Ray referred to it as his butt chin, but Grandpa Buzz would rather he had called it a dimple.

My son's dark blue eyes were shut. I wished I could wake him up, look into his eyes, and tell him I loved him. Yet, in a sickening way, I didn't want to see his eyes. I couldn't bear the thought of not seeing the light in them, the light that set him apart. The light that made me proud he was mine.

I closed my own eyes and, in a crazy attempt, willed the world to change back to what it had been a short time ago.

Letting go of Ray's hand, I wiped my eyes dry. When I reached for his hand again, I stopped and stared at the mud caked under his nails and thought how my son had just died with dirty fingernails.

Suddenly Rusty appeared at my side. "Darla, you need to call your mom and dad. You have to tell them . . ."

"Tell them what? Their grandson is dead? I can't do that. I can't." I sobbed uncontrollably.

"Darla," Rusty pleaded.

"No, I can't call them. I just can't."

With a crippling wave of nausea, it dawned on me. "Oh my God, Rusty. How are we going to tell Martha? We have to tell her that her brother died? This is so wrong."

Rusty lowered his eyes and whispered, "She can stay at Brooke's tonight. She doesn't need to know yet."

Tonight Martha's world would be the same, if only in her sleep. Come morning it would be forever changed.

"Your parents are in the lobby." A nurse's voice broke through my thoughts. Slowly, I turned and glared at Rusty. He had given out my parents' phone number.

"I'm sorry, Darla. They need to know. Better meet them in the lobby. Warn them. They don't know Ray's . . ." His voice trailed off.

I found myself in the lobby, completely unaware of how I'd gotten there, my parents rushing toward me, their eyes full of concern. In unison their voices hummed in my ear. "What happened? Is Ray okay?"

I stood before them, shaking my head. Eventually I murmured in no particular direction, "We . . . lost him."

Cutting through my disconnect, I heard my dad cry out, "Oh, God, no." His knees buckled and he fell back against the wall, slithering halfway down before catching himself. He managed to balance himself like a three-legged dog. If the room wasn't spinning, I might have helped him.

Mom stood silent, shocked, tears streaming down her cheeks. We were like three wounded soldiers on a battlefield, sprawled out on the ground just beyond each other's reach. I turned away and floated down the hall, my parents following behind. Words could not prepare them for seeing their young lifeless grandson lying on a hospital bed, a sheet pulled up to his shoulders. I dropped into a chair in the corner and watched my family through a bewildered haze.

Rusty and I left the hospital only when staying—watching our son's cold body change—became more difficult than leaving. When we got home, Rusty dragged Ray's heavy denim quilt off his bed and onto ours. We huddled beneath it and unsuccessfully tried to sleep. In the morning I staggered to the phone and dialed. Our neighbor Ken picked up on the first ring.

"Ray ... Ray didn't make it," I whispered through sobs.

"I know. I'm so sorry."

He knew? How? Panic rose inside me. If he knew, did Martha? Afraid of the answer, I hesitated to ask, "Is ... Martha ... awake?"

"No," Ken said.

I squeezed my eyes shut, relieved.

"Do you want me to wake her, Darla?"

"No. Let her sleep. Call me when she's up. I'll come get her."

Sooner than I wanted to, I found myself following the same path Ray had run the night before. I stopped in my tracks and stepped around a large patch of grass, flattened where I had found him. I swallowed hard and pressed on.

Martha was at the front door getting her shoes on. Bev and Ken stood silent. I couldn't look them in the eye, keeping my gaze to the floor.

In an innocent, cheerful voice, Brooke said, "Bye, Martha."

"See ya, Brooke." Martha smiled, delighted with her first sleepover.

I took Martha's hand, steered her away from the lawn, and led her down the driveway to the street. Suddenly feeling too visible to the world, I picked up my pace. Martha's seven-year-old steps quickened—two to my one. Bouncing along at my side, she looked up and asked, "Where's Ray? Is he in the hospital? Are we going to see him today?"

Scrambling for an answer, I muttered, "I'll tell you when we get home. Dad wants to talk to you first." I wanted to stop walking. Protect her from finding out. Delay time. Better yet, go back in time.

With her feet barely inside the door, Rusty scooped Martha up in his arms, then set her down on the kitchen counter. Startled to find herself there, she searched her dad's tearful eyes. With lips already quivering, she asked, "Where's Ray?"

Rusty rested his forehead on Martha's head and wept. "Ray went to Heaven."

I was surprised by his quick answer. We hadn't talked about how we would tell Martha.

She swung her head my way, eyes filled with shock and fear. "For real, Mom? For real?"

With tears streaming, I nodded.

She pushed her dad away, hopped off the counter and ran to the living room, where she buried her face in a cushion of the couch. In a muffled voice I heard her sob, "I want Ray! I want *my* Ray. I want *my* Ray!"

"You think their dying is the worst thing that can happen. Then they stay dead."

~ Donald Hall
Poet Laureate of the United States

Stages of Nothing

I cannot tell you everything about the hours or days following Ray's death now, after all these years, any more than I could have told you about it at the time. Every second of my existence was spent in a cloud of disbelief. I guess I was in the first stage of grief: denial.

I once read that denial is a defense mechanism that buffers the immediate shock. We block out the words and hide from the facts. The article stated that it's a temporary response that is supposed to carry you through the first wave of pain. I guess that makes sense, but in the end, it didn't make a damn bit of difference to me. So what? There are stages to grief. Understanding that doesn't change the end result. Death is death. Pain is pain.

I pretty much hated when people talked about the process of grieving or healing. Some people said that Ray wouldn't want me to be sad. I beg to differ. He wouldn't have expected anything less. I could imagine him saying, "Geez, Mom. I died and you're not even sad? Didn't I matter?"

When your child dies, there's no other option than being sad. Destroyed, really. The strange thing is, there was a night—about a year before he passed away—when Ray asked me just that.

"Mom? Would you be sad if I died?" I was tucking him in, about to say good night, when out of the blue he asked that question.

"Ray. Don't even say that."

"Well, would you cry if I died?"

161

"I would never be the same, and all I would do is cry."

"For real, Mom?"

"For real. So don't even talk about that."

In our home, words like *longevity*, *fatal*, or *life expectancy* were never uttered. Not once. Doctors and nurses, family and friends, teachers and parents were warned to never speak in those terms either. We treated cystic fibrosis as something one had to combat to maintain good health *until* they found a cure, not *if* they found a cure. Life was to be lived with joy and hope, not gloom and doom. But I could not help but wonder if Ray had had a premonition or something.

After Ray died, no one really knew what to say to us, so it was to their credit for even trying. But sometimes it seemed there wasn't a single word in the English language that would bring me solace. Maybe I was stuck in one of the other five stages of grief: anger. Apparently in the anger stage you lash out at inanimate objects, strangers, or even family and friends. I remember being absolutely resentful of Boone, who lived to be sixteen. More than once Boone tricked me. I'd hear his footsteps coming down the hallway toward the kitchen and think, "Oh, good. Ray's up. I can start breakfast." Watching Boone, instead of Ray, saunter into the kitchen made me want to hurl a frying pan at the dog's head. I loved that dog. He was part of our family, but oh, how I hated him in those moments. How dare he outlive my son. Pets die. Twelve-year-olds don't die. And yet they do.

Frequently, people shared their religious beliefs, saying things like, "God needed an angel." Perhaps they thought it was a compliment—to compare Ray to an angel—but it only angered me. What kind of a God needs a twelve-year-old angel to help run his kingdom? Even Martha was bothered by such a notion. When someone told her that Ray was now her guardian angel, she answered, "No, he's not. He's my helpful ghost." I had to hand it to her. She knew her brother better than anyone. *Helpful ghost* was a more fitting way to describe Ray than an *angel*.

Other times people said that Ray's work on Earth was done and the Lord had called him home. I'm sure they meant no harm, but it was a statement so callous-sounding to my ear, they might just as well have said, "Oh well, it was his time to go." That might be an acceptable thing to say about a ninety-year-old in poor health, but not a twelve-year-old boy. Ray was just getting started.

But by far the most upsetting religious viewpoint was, "God only gives what you can handle." Whenever someone said that to me, I wanted to slap him across the face.

Many people stated the obvious—that losing a child is the worst kind of loss there is. Sometimes adding this alarming statement: "And you will *never* get over it." A distasteful blunder regularly followed up with, "But you will never forget Ray." Like that was some consolation.

Sadly, "you will never get over it" was the most truthful statement of all. Gives a whole new meaning to "the truth hurts." And "you will never forget Ray" was quite possibly the most untruthful statement of all. I knew I would not forget my son—as a whole. But I worried I might forget *specifics* about him. The funny or poignant things Ray said. The sound of his voice or his laugh. His adorable wide-eyed look of amazement at even the smallest of things—his appreciation for life always present. Would these things be lost over time?

On the inside of Ray's closet wall, I had kept track of his and Martha's growth. Periodically I had the kids stand with their backs to the wall, placed a book on top of their heads, and drew a line. Side by side, their new height was displayed as the years passed by.

One day, after hearing someone say that I would never forget Ray, I ran in a panic up to his bedroom. Flinging Ray's closet door open, I stared at the makeshift growth chart. The last recorded measurement was dated March 18, 2001, less than a month before Ray died. He stood at four feet, nine inches tall. I pressed my body up close to the wall, holding the side of my hand on the March 18 line. I wanted to see where my son had measured up to me. I had forgotten—*specifically*. That day, I discovered he was about shoulder height to me. Would I have remembered that without the growth chart?

On March 18, Martha had measured three feet, ten inches. I tried to imagine where she'd stood next to her brother. Perhaps at his shoulders. The same as Ray had stood next to me. Would I forget what the two of them had looked like when they walked side by side as they so often did?

A lot of people said that God would answer our prayers and bring us peace, but I was too angry to pray for peace. I've never been too good at praying in the first place. I almost feel silly doing it, like I'm talking to myself. I start out with good intentions, but ultimately I cut my prayers short with something like, "Just do what you need to do to fix me, Lord. Amen." But that night, on the way to the hospital, I prayed with all my heart. *Please, God. Don't take my boy.* I suspected Ray was already gone by then. Maybe a little too late for praying. I don't know.

I have always questioned religion. To me, Bible stories are fables used to teach a lesson, but they are no more truthful than "The Ants and Grasshopper." After losing Ray, my questions multiplied and finding answers seemed impossible. But ultimately, I knew I had to find my way with or without believing in a God. The thing is, it's easy to believe when life is good, when the path is smooth. That's when people say they are blessed. Just as easy not to believe in a God when one hits a rough patch in the road. That's when people ask, "Why, God, why me?"

Religion aside, one thing that really helped to ease our pain was when friends and family shared a special memory of Ray. Through their stories, we realized that our boy had made an impact on others, and we weren't alone in our loss. Just simply hearing Ray's name helped. But I knew people weren't going to continue stopping over to share a Ray story. They would move on with their own lives. When the phone calls stopped coming as frequently, when Ray's name was mentioned less and less ... well, that's when I realized I was on my own. I could not rely on someone else to figure out what my future would be without my son.

I don't know how other mothers do it. I've struggled. I've struggled a lot. I fight to be happy, if that makes any sense. Happiness no longer comes naturally like it once did. I have to consciously make the decision to look for the good things in my life. Some days I don't see that very clearly. Most days I still hurt tremendously, and I'm so very lonesome for Ray. People often say that time heals all wounds, but for me, the more time that goes by, the sadder and more lonesome I feel. I equate this passing of time without my son to how a mother whose child is off at war must feel. The longer the war drags on, the sadder and more lonesome she must become.

I questioned if there was something different I could have done *that* night. Would Ray still be alive if I had raced him? I can't help compare that night to my near-drowning experience at Lake Phalen. Buzz raced me like I had asked, and he was there to save me when I disappeared under the water. Why didn't I race Ray? If I had been at his side when he stopped breathing, would the outcome have been different? It's an un-settling and eerie thought—to think what could have been my last words to Buzz actually were Ray's last words to me. "Do you want to race me?"

To this day I beat myself up, wondering if Ray would still be here if I had realized he needed medical attention immediately, instead of believing he was just pulling a prank on me. My father instinctively knew I needed help in the water that day. Why didn't I have those same instincts to recognize that my son needed help? I shared these tortuous thoughts with Buzz once. He comforted me by pointing out, "It's not the same, Darla. I knew you had seizures. You didn't know anything was wrong with Ray that night, so how could you possibly know he was in trouble?" Then he added, "Besides, that kid was always horsing around."

Still, these questions have haunted me over the years. Apparently questions like mine are part of another stage in the grieving process: bargaining. But the thing is, I don't feel stages of grief. I feel everything all of the time. A stage, to me, means *temporary* or a *phase*. But a loss like the one I suffered is permanent, which is quite the opposite of a stage. Denial. Anger. Bargaining—all the questions I carry—have remained, permanently. I haven't even touched on depression, but I will argue that depression isn't a stage either. Depression slips in whenever the hell it wants.

Sometimes I think I've come a long way. Other times I feel the most I've done over the years is tightly secure a bandage over the gaping hole in my chest so I don't bleed out. I've been able to stabilize my injury and control when and where I react to the pain. I don't know where that puts me in the process. Acceptance? It doesn't really matter. It doesn't change the fact that there's a big ugly wound under the bandage. No series of stages of grief changes the truth or explains it away. We don't come out the other side *completely* healed. They shouldn't even call it a healing process in the first place. Maybe just *life*.

One thing I do remember about those early days was the terrifying disconnect I felt to everything and everyone, my family included. The thought of not being close to the most important people in my life scared me.

I had a large extended family. Dozens of aunts and uncles and twice as many cousins who frequently reached out to me. I also had a group of amazing friends that I knew I could call on, day or night. My friends and family were there for me, but grief had such a strong hold, I couldn't give anything back to them. My broken heart felt like a burden, so I kept to myself much of the time.

After Rusty told Martha that her brother had gone to Heaven, there was no turning back. Somehow saying it out loud made the absurd true, sending a seven-year-old girl to bury her face in the couch cushions, crying out, "I want *my* Ray!"

Before anyone dared to come over or call, the three of us were alone. Together, but alone. No one knew what to say. I held Martha on my lap and tried to comfort her, but she only stayed for short periods of time. She pushed herself away but then had no idea what to do once she left my lap. There was no comforting each other, and there was no comfort in being alone. This would become our norm in the weeks and months ahead: *together alone.*

Joe Dirt

When the phone rang that first morning without Ray, the three of us froze for a second before I picked up without thinking. Michelle McDonald, Ray's middle school classmate and his boyhood crush, asked, "Is Ray home?"

It was Good Friday and a group of Ray's friends were supposed to go to the movies, Michelle included. She was probably calling to confirm plans. I regretted answering the phone the second I heard her voice. With a sickening pit in my stomach, I heard myself say, "Ray's not here." In a shaky voice, I quickly added, "Right now." The words sounded vile and downright silly to me. A cover-up that hardly reshaped the truth.

Before Michelle could say another word, I quickly asked, "Is your mom around?"

"My mom's at work."

Julie, Michelle's mom, and I had been friends since junior high school. She worked in the kitchen at Carver Elementary, and she had known Ray since he was in kindergarten. She was kind and compassionate, always offering him seconds in the hot lunch line, aware of his weight issue. On non-school days, Julie worked at an Adventure Connection program in the school district. I asked Michelle for her mom's work number and ended our conversation abruptly.

My heart sank, remembering how excited Ray had been about his movie plans, especially excited because it was a co-ed activity. He had talked about it with us at Famous Dave's.

"I can't wait until tomorrow," Ray said.

"What movie did you and your friends decide on?" I asked.

"*Joe Dirt*," he told me.

"The one with David Spade?"

"Yeah."

"I'm sure it will be amazing." I rolled my eyes.

"I don't care. Michelle is going to be there," he replied with a huge grin.

Ahhh, Michelle. That was all that mattered. Michelle would be there. A few weeks prior, I had been about to throw a load of clothes into the wash when Ray came running down the stairs to the laundry room in a panic. "Mom. Where are my jeans?"

"On your legs."

"Very funny. The ones I wore yesterday. Where are they?"

"I don't know. Probably in this pile somewhere."

"Tell me you didn't put them in the machine."

"No. I'm washing whites. Why? What's the big deal with the jeans?"

"There's something in the pocket I need to get." He searched the pile of dirty clothes until he found the jeans he was looking for. As he dug around in a front pocket, several pens and a highlighter dropped to the floor.

"Why do you keep those in your pocket? I'm constantly picking them up off the floor."

"Because Ms. Beske will kill me if I don't have a highlighter."

"Then leave them in your school locker."

He shrugged, hardly concerned about a highlighter or a pen. Growing more anxious by the second, he finally pulled a small wallet-size picture from a back pocket of his jeans.

"Whew. It's still here."

"Who's the picture of?"

"Michelle McDonald."

"Oh, can I see it?"

"Yeah, but you can't read the back."

He held the picture at a safe distance from my face as an adorable blonde girl with a beautiful smile stared back at me.

"Wow. She's really cute, Ray."

"I know." He smiled.

As Ray walked up the stairs, I heard Rusty ask to see the picture, too. Later he would tell me that Ray was aiming too high.

Hanging up the phone with Michelle, I collapsed on a kitchen chair and sobbed. I cried for Michelle. I cried about *Joe Dirt*, the stupid movie Ray would miss out on. I cried because he would miss out on every single activity from here on out—his entire future gone. And I cried because we would never get to see the man he would have become.

Eventually I regained enough strength to call Julie. I don't remember how I told her about Ray. I only remember worrying about Michelle. In a moment she would learn about her friend. Feeling weak and dizzy, I ran to the bathroom and vomited. This would become a daily affair. Me and the toilet.

Pieces of Time

A dark, eerie feeling loomed over our home, strangely providing a protective barrier from the outside world, if only for a short time. Soon enough, the phone calls picked up. The doorbell rang. Questions poured in. Without knowing the cause of Ray's death, people were left to wonder what had happened, coming to their own conclusions, which generally pointed toward CF. We were dumbfounded ourselves, without an answer to provide.

In those quiet moments before chaos erupted, I made a call to Harv French. I needed to inform Principal Sharon Sandberg that I wouldn't be at school on Monday—unlikely for the rest of the year. I didn't have Sharon's phone number, but I had Harv's. The thought of breaking the news to him made me sick.

"Harv."

"Is this Darla?"

"Yeah, it's me," I muttered through sobs.

"Are you okay? What's wrong?"

"Oh God, Harv." I paused. Then without much thought, I said, "Ray ... died ... last night." My words sounded so grotesque I wanted to apologize for them.

"Excuse me? I don't think I heard you right. Did you just say…?"

Bawling now, I confirmed, "Harv, we lost Ray. I'll tell you more later. Right now I need you to call Sharon. Tell her I won't be coming to work on Monday." Then I quickly hung up, trusting Harv would follow through.

Collapsing in bed, the most ridiculous sentence replayed in my head, over and over again. *Ray died last night. Ray died last night. Ray died last night.* I crawled out of bed and threw up.

Later, Harv would tell me he questioned if he had heard me correctly, terrified he was spreading a horrible rumor. Nonetheless, he made a call to Sharon, as well as to my Carver colleagues. A calling tree was set in motion, reports of Ray's death eventually reaching the entire Maplewood Middle School staff.

A stream of neighbors and family members trekked in and out of our home over the next several days. They brought food, kind words, and flowers, and they reached out to Martha in the most thoughtful ways. It's strange to think about it now. I know I embraced each and every visitor, grateful they were there for us. Yet it's almost as if my mind went into overload—allowing only so much in before it shut down. My brain seemed to pick and choose at random which person's words or actions stuck. Maybe that's typical of people reeling from a tragedy—the inability to absorb everything. After short periods of interaction, I mentally checked out, my thoughts turning inward, wondering if any of this was real. Additionally, I couldn't engage in conversation for long if Martha was out of sight. Panic rose whenever I lost track of her, even in our own home.

So, while some memories remain fuzzy, lost in the chaos, other moments are crystal clear. I will never forget the stunned, painful expressions on Janny and Daryl's faces as they walked across the street to our house on Good Friday. I was on our front porch, saying goodbye to I don't remember whom, when I heard their front door open. As if in slow motion, I watched them walk across our front lawn—Justin and Tyler at their parents' sides, little Katelyn on Janny's hip. To this day, I can see the look of fear and trepidation in the boys' eyes, and it still breaks my heart. I knew for certain, in that very moment, that theirs would not be an easy recovery. Justin, Martha, Ray and Tyler—a familiar foursome no more.

The only thing I remember saying to Justin and Tyler in our exchange that day was that Ray had loved them. And I remember Rusty thanking the boys for being Ray's friend.

Another clear memory is that of Scott Richards and his daughter, Audra, riding over on their bikes. Rusty and I spoke to Scott in our driveway for a bit before he handed us a letter detailing his fond memories of Ray. A letter so sweetly written, it would later be read at the funeral. That day, Scott, who has three daughters, told us, "I didn't get to experience a boy. But if I had a son, I'd want him to be just like Ray."

One evening, Gary Ales, Rusty's former high school teacher and football coach, dropped by with his wife, Jean. Rusty was touched that Mr. Ales had taken the time to reach out and console us, sharing his own experience in the death of a child. Years earlier, Gary and Jean had lost their teenage son, Kevin. One comment Gary made that day still stands out, a bit of advice we listened to and followed. He told us not to pack Ray's pictures away, but rather display them proudly. "Don't tuck away the memory of your boy," he warned. "Keep his pictures out, and talk about him as often as you can. That's what we do. We talk about Kevin to keep his memory alive, because he mattered." And with that, Gary pulled out a picture of his son from his wallet. I studied the face of a young, handsome boy, his life cut short like Ray's. I felt the Ales' pain but also took note of their strength.

Among the many phone calls from people offering their condolences and support, two especially stood out. The first was a phone call from Ray's sixth grade language arts teacher, the wonderful Ms. Barb Beske. The first thing out of her mouth came almost in the form of a scream: "What happened?"

"We don't know," I said before offering a few details of that night. Then Ms. Beske said, "You know, every year there is one student who stands out. That one special kid who makes me appreciate why I got into teaching in the first place. This year, that student was Ray. Hands down. I absolutely loved that kid."

"Thank you," I told her. "I really appreciate that. He loved you too, Barb. Always came home with a Ms. Beske story."

Through sobs, she said, "And I have Ray Garvey stories that I'll never forget." She added, "Is there anything I can do for you, Darla?"

"No, I don't think so," I answered. "But thank you for asking."

I was about to hang up when something suddenly came to mind. "Wait. There is something."

"What is it?"

"I know your students journal every day. Do you think instead, they could write letters to us? Maybe share a special memory of Ray? I'd love to read that. Maybe it would help them work through this, too. You know? If they had a way to get some of their feelings out."

"I think that's a great idea. I'll be sure to encourage the kids to write to you."

Ms. Beske delivered on her promise. In the days that followed, letters from Ray's classmates poured in. Most talked about how funny he was, many referred to him as their best friend, and everyone said how much they would miss him. I had been consumed with worry how Ray's young classmates and closest friends would cope when they heard the news. What must the halls and classrooms of Maplewood Middle School have looked like on that first Monday after Easter break? The following letters provide some insight.

Monday
04-16-2001

Dear Mr. & Mrs. Garvey,
I would like to tell you about my day. At 7:39, I entered the bus. I sat at my usual place by my friend, Nick. He looked sad. When I sat down he told me about your son, Ray's death. At first I didn't believe what he was telling me. Then, we were at another stop and my other friend, Jeremy, showed me an article and read it aloud to me. Nick was right. Ray did die. I started to cry when I got to my locker. I hardly knew Ray but deep in my heart, I loved Ray. He was a special kid.

He always sang Elvis songs during ZAP time and he always made the girls happy. When I went to my science class, I passed Ms. Beske. She was really sad. Everyone who saw her crying, went over to comfort her. Ms. Beske really liked Ray.

Ever since I started on the bus, my day was terrible. How could something like this happen? The things that I know is that God will watch over him for you and Ray will always be by your side. I'm so sorry that Ray has passed away. Everyone misses him already. We love Raymo!

Always,
Alex

I'm not sure how Ray got the nickname Raymo—perhaps he gave it to himself—but the moniker had stuck to the point where some of his teachers entered Raymo Garvey in their gradebooks. So a lot of children wrote about their friend, Raymo.

Hey Ray,

I don't know how to say this but the girls at school are really going to miss you because they're all crying. I don't know if you can see this, but Megan made a book about you. You sure have touched a lot of kids so someday, I'll see you, okay Raymo.

Your best friend,
Kevin Schulze

P.S. I'll spike my hair for you.

Kevin's mom, Paula, went to high school with Rusty. His grandpa, Wes Barrett, was a bricklayer and Buzz's friend. The Barrett family knew our son as Ray, not Raymo. Even so, when Kevin talked about his new middle school friend, Raymo Garvey, they wondered if he was talking about our son. They told us later that Kevin looked up to Ray, even copied his hairstyle.

Ray had left his bike at his friend Andy's house sometime before he died. One day I found the bike propped up against our front porch, a bouquet of flowers tied to the handlebars with a simple note that read: "Remember the good times." Andy also wrote a beautiful letter to us.

Dear Garveys,

Ray was one of my best friends. We had a lot of good times together. Every day at school we would be partners. Like say hi to each other, be partners in gym class, give each other high fives, made each other laugh, did stuff together, made up songs, and were like brothers. Some favorite times were at lunch when he ate chips off from the floor. When Peter Moore, Dustin Propp, Tyler

Fierst, Ray's neighbor kids, and I played street hockey, we all had a great time. Ray was a funny, great friend to me.

He was nice to others, he had courage, he liked to do new things, he wasn't afraid of anything, he acted cool, and had a great attitude. He was also tuff, didn't take no crap from anybody, and was a great sports player. He taught me to have courage, to be tuff, to try new things and be a better person and funny person. Also be more braver.

Ray was one of my best friends I ever had and it was really sad to have him pass away but he will always be in my heart and I'm sure yours and I will never forget that really funny great friend of mine, Ray Garvey. He was sure a great one and I'm really sorry he passed away.

From your friend and Ray's best friend,
Andy Carlson

Many of Ray's classmates had only known him for a few months, sixth grade being their first year together. So it was meaningful to read how Ray had made an impact on his new friend Tiffany in such a short period of time.

Dear Mr. and Mrs. Garvey,

I had a couple of classes with Ray and all in the subjects I didn't like but Ray made them fun. It was a privilege to have Ray in my class. Ray was very popular. He was sweet and kind. I'll miss looking over at Ray's desk and seeing an incredible creation of God's. I'll miss you RAY GARVEY.

Love,
Tiffany

A lot of his classmates wrote about a day they would never forget, the day Ray sang and danced in front of the entire class. Ms. Beske had informed me about it at parent-teacher conferences earlier in the year.

When I met with her to discuss Ray's progress, she started with, "Umm ... did Ray tell you what happened in class the other day?"

"Oh, no. What did he do?"

"Well, I don't know if I should tell you or not." She smiled.

I was relieved. Couldn't be too bad if she was smiling. "Now you have to tell me," I insisted.

"Well, I always play music in the classroom when the kids journal. I played a CD of Elvis the other day. Ray immediately started bopping to the music. Eventually he started singing under his breath, too, while he wrote in his journal."

"I guess that doesn't surprise me. He's a huge Elvis fan."

"Well, it surprised *me*. I mean, what sixth grader even knows who Elvis is? I asked Ray how he knew Elvis, but before he could answer, my students jumped in and said that Ray knows every Elvis song and requests Elvis music at school dances. They also said he could dance like Elvis. So I challenged Ray to come up front and prove it."

"I'm guessing he did?" I chuckled.

"Yes, he immediately got up and out of his seat and took on the challenge. He sang and danced just like Elvis. It was the most adorable thing I ever saw. Maybe I shouldn't have done it," Ms. Beske added, "but I called all the other sixth grade teachers into my classroom and had Ray perform a second time. It was so darn cute, I wanted them to see it."

"I'm sure you made his day. I'm surprised he didn't tell me about it himself." Then, for some reason I asked, "Just curious. What song did he perform to?"

178

" 'I'm All Shook Up,' " she replied.

A few days after Ms. Beske's call, we received a sympathy card. In it, she wrote the most beautiful tribute to her young student, signing it:

Ray, you left me all shook up.
Love,
Ms. Beske

The second call I distinctly remember came from Dr. Carlos Milla. He blurted out the same question as Ms. Beske and in much the same way. "What happened?"

I wondered how he had already learned that his young CF patient had died. I wanted to ask him, but instead I responded with the words I would continue to repeat over the next several weeks. "We don't know what happened."

I told Dr. Milla that Ray wasn't sick. That he was feeling fine. I told him how he had been running and how I'd found him lying in the grass, flat on his back.

"I saw him last month. His heart and lungs checked out fine. His pulmonary function test was excellent. He was a healthy boy. I just don't get it."

"I know. He was filling out so nicely, too. The G-tube was working. He felt really good, really strong."

Dr. Milla agreed, then asked me, "Was there a storm that night?"

"No."

"Any electrical wires down?"

"No."

"No lightning?"

"No, why?"

"Because it sounds like he got zapped. This isn't what happens with cystic fibrosis."

"I know."

"Sounds like he got zapped," he repeated. "His heart just stopped. But I don't understand how this could have happened."

"Me either."

"I know this is a tough question, but have you thought about an autopsy?"

"No, I haven't. I don't think I want to do that, though." I cringed at the very idea.

"I understand. It's hard to think about, Darla. But it could give us some answers."

"I'll talk to Rusty. I'll call you back."

After a difficult conversation, Rusty and I decided not to have an autopsy performed. We couldn't handle the idea of anyone cutting into our boy. But later I asked Rusty, "What if the same thing could happen to Martha? What if it's something genetic? Something we could prevent if we knew what it was."

Rusty sat quietly, thinking.

"We can't lose her too, Rusty. We need to know what happened."

A few minutes later, I called Dr. Milla and told him he was right; we needed answers. He made arrangements for Ray's body to be transferred to the University of Minnesota, where their doctors would perform the autopsy.

Peace in the Valley

We sat quietly in the living room with Martha, all three of us in some weird trance. I had hardly recovered from the autopsy decision when Rusty broke through the silence. "We're going to have to start planning."

I stared at him blankly.

"You know," he said, "the funeral."

I couldn't focus on anything, much less make another decision. Everything felt heavy. All I could do was fight nausea and cry. My heart hurt so badly every time I looked at Martha. What was going on in that little seven-year-old brain of hers? As an adult, I could not process Ray's passing. How could she?

Martha has always been a deep thinker—always wringing her hands and pacing the floor while she processes her thoughts. Whenever I witnessed this, I knew a big question or a big confession was sure to follow. She was doing it now, pacing and wringing her hands.

"Is Ray the same size in Heaven?" she asked.

And there it was. The big question.

Remarkably fast, Rusty answered her, "I think you get to be whatever size you want to be in Heaven."

"Then Ray's the same size," Martha reasoned. "He liked being small. He could hide in small places."

Rusty seemed so strong, so present. In that one moment, he offered Martha more than I could. I was not grounded in any sort of reality. I felt like I was half dead myself, watching and listening from afar. My thoughts were scrambled, my voice was trapped inside my throat, and my whole world seemed distorted.

For a second, after Martha's question, I thought about the size of caskets. I'd seen small caskets in movies when a child character dies. Did they come in different sizes? Small, medium, and large? Babies, adolescents, and adults? I didn't know. Ray had told me himself that he wasn't my little boy anymore. I decided he should definitely have a full-size casket.

A short time later, there was a knock at the door. It was the neighbor girls, Laura and Pam, offering to take Martha to play. I was never so grateful for Martha's friends. Perhaps they could give her a few minutes of normalcy.

Martha was hardly out the door when Rusty began talking about churches, cemeteries and funeral homes. We had to make decisions on all of these things, he said. I became angry at his practicality even though he was right. We needed to plan.

We butted heads on the very first detail: where to hold the service. I insisted on King of Kings Lutheran Church in Woodbury, the church where our kids went to Sunday school and Ray had received his first communion. Rusty thought the funeral should be held at First Lutheran Church in St. Paul, where my parents were members.

"Your mom and her church lady friends can help plan the lunch," Rusty said.

"How do you know my mom is even up for that?"

"We can talk about that later." Rusty switched gears and suggested we take a drive out to Union Cemetery in White Bear Lake, where we had buried his father four years earlier. "Let's take a drive out there and see what you think."

It sounded like something you'd say if you were looking to buy lake property, not check out a place to bury your kid. But soon enough, we gathered Martha from the neighbor's and brought her to my parents' house before heading to White Bear Lake.

~

The Tuesday before Ray died, he had come home from school all excited. Busting through the front door, he called out, "Hey, Dad, this kid at school is selling his go-cart. Think we could buy it?"

"I don't know about that, Ray. You'll just get yourself in trouble with a go-cart."

"I'd be careful, I promise. It would be so much fun, Dad."

"How much is he asking for it?"

"A hundred and fifty bucks."

"I'll think about it."

"Come on, Dad. What if someone else buys it?"

"I'm sure your friend isn't going to sell it overnight."

The following day, Ray marched in the house and slammed the front door, his face bright red. "Where's Dad?" he demanded.

"Outside. Why, what's wrong?" I trailed behind Ray as he flung the patio door open and yelled, "Dad, guess what? My friend sold the go-cart to someone else. I could have had it if you would have looked at it *yesterday*."

~

The cemetery was smaller than I remembered. A single horseshoe-shaped driveway encompassed the entire grounds. It wasn't pristine by any means. It seemed only flat stone markers were allowed. Flower pots sat crooked, attached to stakes in the ground, less than impressive. I thought our son should have something more grand—a tall marble monument sitting atop lush green grass. Plus the cemetery was far from our home. I wanted him closer. I did not want to hurt Rusty's feelings, but this was not the right place for our son.

Jim Garvey's stone marker sat near an old oak tree. "Look, no one else is buried next to him," Rusty pointed out as we walked up to his dad's gravesite. "Ray would be next to his grandpa. It's the nicest spot with this oak tree here," Rusty reasoned with a shrug.

I wanted my son next to me, not in the ground next to his grandpa. I walked over to the oak tree, taking cover there should I throw up yet again, a new hobby of mine.

"I don't know, Rusty. I don't know." I burst into tears.

"I don't know what to do either." Rusty wrapped his arms around me. "It's just that my dad's here. I don't know where else to go."

Still embraced in his arms, I cried even harder.

Looking over my shoulder, Rusty suddenly said, "What are the odds of that?" He spun me around and pointed toward the street.

I could not believe what I was seeing. A young boy in a red baseball cap was zipping down the road on a go-cart. A black-and-white checkered flag attached to the back of the cart whipped back and forth in the wind. The boy looked to be about Ray's age, twelve or so. I took note of his red ball cap again. One of Ray's favorite hats was a red San Francisco 49ers ball cap. He wore it everywhere. The boy rounded the corner and turned down a side street, and then—almost ghost-like— he disappeared as fast as he'd come.

"Maybe it's a sign," Rusty said.

I brushed away tears. "Yeah. Maybe Ray does belong here, next to his grandpa."

So that was settled. Union Cemetery. Check.

We next drove to Schoenrock Monument on Jackson Street in St. Paul. Rusty was again using the same resources he had used for his dad. I seemed to be along for the ride, unable to navigate the world without him.

184

We parked the car and walked a block to the entrance of Schoenrock. I nearly gagged.

"Hang in there, Darla. We have to pick something out."

I drew in a deep breath as he held the door open. A large man in bib overalls greeted us from behind a long counter. When he extended his hand to shake Rusty's, I noticed his thick fingers were calloused, his nails dirty. He was a grave-digger, I decided, and I recoiled.

Rusty told him why we were there.

The man said he was sorry and then asked in what cemetery the marker would be placed.

"Union Cemetery," Rusty said.

"The one in White Bear Lake?"

"Yeah."

"I was just out there this morning," he told us. Then he smiled as if it were a wonderful coincidence.

We wandered around the showroom as if picking out kitchen tile for a backsplash, not a slab of stone to mark our son's gravesite. When Rusty spotted a blue granite sample, he said, "How about this one? Ray liked blue."

"Yeah," I told him, "he liked a bit of flash, too." The stone was sparkly, and I could not help but think of Elvis and his blue suede shoes.

So the blue sparkly one it was. Stone marker. Check.

The large man in bib overalls asked for the spelling of Ray's full name, as well as his birth date and date of death. He wrote it down on a slip of paper. I took note of our son's short life, written down on paper in black and white, the dates far too close together.

Next the man asked if we wanted anything else carved into the stone. He showed us pictures in a book—stone etchings of crosses, angels and roses. I looked over Rusty's shoulder as he flipped through the book.

"Wait," I told him, "turn back to that last page."

Rusty flipped the page. "You like this one?" he asked, pointing.

It was an etching of a valley with the sun's rays shining above it. The words "Peace in the Valley" were written along the side.

I nodded.

"Why this one?"

"Because Ray had an Elvis gospel CD in his music collection. 'Peace in the Valley' is one of the songs on it. And he was a ray of light. I like the sun in this carving."

We decided to add a line along the bottom of the stone: "Forever Our Ray of Sunshine."

I let Rusty take the reins on a lot of the funeral planning. I even caved on the decision to hold the service at First Lutheran Church after he told me that many St. Paul police officers had volunteered to assist in the funeral procession. However, there were two details I insisted upon. One was that we place a vase of red carnations on each luncheon table, the same flower I had pinned on Ray's sweater at his first communion. The other was that we play "Peace in the Valley" and "Precious Lord Take My Hand." And they had to come from Ray's own CD. It had to be the gospel according to Elvis, the king of rock and roll.

From Schoenrock Monument, we drove to the Anderson Funeral Home on Arcade Street, less than a block from Johnson High School. There were nicer funeral homes in the Twin Cities, but this was the one where Jim Garvey's service had been held. I didn't know what to expect for Ray's visitation, but I was certain the size of Anderson's would not suffice. I did not express my concerns, though. I was too busy fighting that awful out-of-body sensation again, Rusty talking to a funeral director all the while.

Soon enough we found ourselves in another disturbing showroom in the basement of the funeral home. This time caskets were lined up in rows. We roamed around for a minute before Rusty pointed to a blue one. I nodded *yes* as another wave of nausea hit.

The funeral director asked how old our son *was*, but I could not answer. I was far too focused on his use of a past tense verb.

Rusty sadly replied, "Twelve."

Then the funeral director asked, "Do you want a child-sized or adult-sized casket?"

So they did come in different sizes.

He told us the child-size one would be less expensive. "No," I spoke up before he read prices from a comparison chart sitting on his desk. "We'll take the full-size one."

Blue casket. Adult-size. Check.

From the funeral home, we drove back to my parents' house to pick up Martha. By this time, I was physically and emotionally drained. I sat at the kitchen table for a while, my mom pushing food. I hadn't eaten in two days, not since Famous Dave's, our last meal with Ray. Yet I didn't feel hungry in the least.

"I have to show you something, Darla," Mom said. She directed me to the refrigerator, where a magnet held a small piece of paper. "I found this under the refrigerator." She pointed. "Just a corner of it was sticking out. I don't know how long it's been there." I'm sure she wondered how she could miss something out of place given her thorough cleaning habits.

Martha followed me to the fridge and stood close at my side while I read the note to myself:

I love you Grandma.
Love Ray

I studied the note. Martha watched me carefully. I read it twice before I looked my daughter in the eye. Her expression was one of innocent guilt. The handwriting was not Ray's.

"Don't tell her, Mom," she whispered. "I just wanted Grandma to feel better."

I wrapped one arm around Martha's shoulder and brought her close to me. I wondered how it was she had thought not only to forge the love letter from Ray in the first place, but also to plant it under the refrigerator—a portion of the note showing just enough to be found. How had she found it in her broken heart to comfort someone else?

When we got home, Justin and Tyler invited Martha to play at their house. Again I was grateful for her friends, and I'll confess, it was a welcome reprieve from the pain that hit me whenever I looked into the sad eyes of our little girl.

Rusty was on a mission to wrap up the funeral plans, asking that I come to the kitchen table to help write our son's obituary. I couldn't think straight long enough to construct a single sentence, opting to find a photograph for the obituary instead. I searched through albums and boxes until I came across a photo my mom had taken the summer before. She had snapped the picture at Battle Creek playground after one of Martha's softball games. The sun was setting behind Ray, providing a beautiful background. It was not a professional picture where he was dressed up in his Sunday best. His hair wasn't even combed. Rather, Ray was wearing an old faded t-shirt and had what he comically referred to as "carpet head." Occasionally Ray would place the palm of his hand on top of his head, then repeatedly rub his hand in a circle until his hair twisted into snarls. Carpet was the look and feel of his hair when he deliberately messed it up like this.

I brought the picture to Rusty and set it down on the table. Visibly choked up, he said, "Carpet head. That's perfect."

Then he asked that I read what he had written—poignant words from a father lamenting the loss of his son. He had written of Ray's accomplishments and captured his character and his personality in the most loving way. I was impressed with the consideration Rusty had paid to all of the sports organizations Ray had been involved in, as well as the schools he had attended. He explained that he wanted to mention places where Ray had spent time, reaching out to those who might have crossed paths with him. He also thanked the University of Minnesota Cystic Fibrosis Center, our friends at Carver Elementary, and the St. Paul Police Department. I don't believe I made a single change to his tribute.

The Medalists

That same evening, the Saturday before Easter Sunday, Cathe Carbone was among the people visiting our home. Cathe shared some special memories of Ray, most of which included all the crap they had given each other. So there she was, mourning the loss of her little smart aleck pal.

"Did I ever tell you how Ray referred to you?" I asked my friend.

"Oh, no. I can only imagine."

"He really liked you, Cathe. Told me you took the 'gold.'"

"He did?" she asked, tears welling up.

I went on with the rest of the story, telling Cathe how, out of the blue, while doing his homework, Ray said, "Cathe's really cool. She takes the gold."

"Yeah, you two are something else together," I'd admitted. Then I had asked him, "If Cathe takes the gold, what about Sue?"

Whenever my friend, Sue, called the house and Ray answered the phone, he'd yell, "Mom! Sooey, Sooey, Sooey's on the phone," like he was calling the hogs home. He loved teasing Sue no matter how often she told him to knock it off.

Ray thought for a second before answering my question. "Sooey takes the bronze."

I busted out laughing. "So Sooey bumps down to third place, huh? Who takes the silver medal then?"

"I don't know. But Cathe takes the gold. Sooey gets the bronze," Ray insisted.

When I finished the story, Cathe wiped away tears and said, "Ray was the golden one. I loved that kid." Then she asked, "Do you have an Easter basket for Martha?"

"Oh my God, no." I hadn't even thought about Easter.

Rusty made Easter special—always placed a trail of jelly beans outside Ray and Martha's bedroom doors leading to their baskets as if the Easter bunny had left it for them. Every year the kids followed the trail of candy to their baskets, then headed outside for an Easter egg hunt.

"Don't worry, Darla. I'm on it," Cathe said. "I'll pick up a basket and some toys and Easter candy for Martha. I'll drop it off later tonight so she has it in the morning."

As it turned out, several other friends brought Easter baskets for Martha, too. But Easter without Ray proved to be too much for her. That morning Martha half-heartedly followed the trail of jelly beans to her baskets and sadly glanced at their contents. Then she reluctantly went outside to hunt for eggs with the most forlorn look on her face. She placed two plastic eggs in a basket, broke down in tears, and ran inside to her bedroom.

The following day was Monday, April 16, the day of Ray's visitation. Tim McIntosh and Don Mickus, Rusty's college football buddies, unexpectedly flew in from Indiana. They said they couldn't stay for the funeral but needed to be with us, if only for the day.

I stayed home with Martha while Tim and Don accompanied Rusty to the funeral home to help set up a display of our son's accomplishments. Special photographs of Ray, artwork, sports trophies and medals, as well as his karate belts, were placed atop several tables.

Later, when Rusty came home, he told me that Ray's achievements were well represented. Then, in almost a whisper, he said, "I saw him, Darla."

I sat on the couch, speechless. It had never occurred to me that he would have the chance to view our son without me, and I was offended that he had. Rusty saw my disappointment and said, "I'm sorry." Then he added, "I should warn you. He doesn't look quite the same. Maybe it's because of the autopsy."

"Please stop. Just stop talking." I buried my face in my hands and sobbed.

After a minute, Rusty took a seat next to me and carefully said, "I hope you don't mind, but I put something in Ray's pants pockets."

"What are you talking about?" I snapped, still upset about Rusty's viewing of Ray.

"I put a pen and a highlighter in his front pocket."

Wiping my eyes dry, I almost smiled.

"There's more. I put Michelle's school picture in his back pocket."

Somehow, having this little secret between us softened my anger. Then something occurred to me. "Rusty. We don't have pallbearers."

"Oh, my God. How did we forget that?" Rusty shook his head. "Who should we ask?"

"I don't know. We shouldn't even be doing this. Ray's eighty-year-old golfing buddies should be figuring this out."

"I know. It's a shame," Rusty said. "But what are we going to do? We can't have his twelve-year-old friends carry the casket."

God, how I hated that word. *Casket.*

"Maybe we should focus on people that Ray connected with," Rusty suggested.

"Like who?"

"How about Mark Sletner? Ray really liked seeing him run from Boone at dog trials. And he thought Mark was pretty cool because he also had a black belt in karate."

"Yeah, Mark's an excellent choice," I agreed. "He was so good to Ray . . . and Martha."

"Okay. Let's think. Who else? Has to be someone Ray was drawn to."

"Scott Richards," I said without hesitation. "Ray and Scott shot the breeze like they were old buddies." I reminded Rusty how Ray liked coming with me whenever I picked Martha up from playing at Audra's house. Partly because he could flirt with Audra's cute older sisters, Hayley and McKenna. And partly because Scott's wife, Amy, always offered delicious snacks. But best of all, he liked listening to Scott's stories, especially if they involved a good prank. Like the time Scott planted a fart machine under his principal's overhead projector and set if off during a staff meeting. Needless to say, a fart machine had been added to Ray's list of must-haves.

Next we decided on Rusty's life-long friend, Jerry Splinter. Ray had taken to him like family. Jerry always dropped off Christmas presents for our kids, but I'm not sure what Ray liked more—Jerry's gifts or his incriminating stories about his dad.

We chose Tim Wolfe, one of Rusty's college friends. Ray and Martha loved going to Tim's house to play with his children, Sam and Megan. Tim and his wife, Kari, made every visit special.

"Okay. Four down. We need two more pallbearers," Rusty said.

We sat for a minute, thinking. Then I blurted out, "I've got it. The medalists."

"The medalists? What are you talking about?"

"Cathe and Sue," I said. Then I shared the story of the gold and bronze medalists. "I think it's important to include my girlfriends," I told Rusty. "After all, they were part of Ray's life, too."

193

Final Farewell

We were almost late to our own son's visitation. Who does that? Rusty had taken his pants to the dry cleaners', and they weren't ready yet. Our friends Kari and Tim Wolfe and Kristie and Tim Parkos were at the house. I don't even recall why they'd stopped in on their way to Anderson Funeral Home, but there they were, witness to the pants saga. I was anxious and complaining that we were going to be late, while Rusty calmly waited for the dry cleaners to call, insisting we had plenty of time. I hadn't expected to be angry that night. Heartbroken, sick to my stomach, yes, but not angry. Why had Rusty waited until the last minute to take his pants to the cleaners? Why the hell couldn't he find something else to wear? And why wasn't he as upset about it as I was?

Martha was pacing and wringing her hands like she does. She had never been to a funeral or a visitation before. Now she was about to see her brother for the first time since he'd died. I couldn't help but wonder what her and Ray's last exchange was—a question I would ask her much further down the road. She would tell me that she'd picked up a pair of gloves from a chair in the living room and Ray had said to her, "Those are Peter's." And that was it. Those were his last words to his sister before heading off to his first communion.

I hugged Martha periodically as we were getting ready, but I don't remember if I said or did anything more remarkable than that to prepare her for the night. What I do remember most clearly is Rusty's damn pants. Maybe it was a necessary evil—to focus on something stupid to take my mind off the dreadful.

My parents were already at Anderson's, standing at the entrance, when we walked in. Mom said, "We waited for you. We haven't gone in yet." Just then the funeral director motioned for us to enter through large double doors leading to the viewing room. He gave Rusty, Martha and me a moment, closing the door behind us.

I'm not sure how to describe the next few minutes, and maybe I don't need to. I'll hold on to those private moments and just say this. It felt like one of those strange dreams where you can only reach out and grab intermittent flashes of reality and the rest makes no sense. The only problem? It wasn't a dream at all.

When the double doors opened, a long line had already formed, leaving us little time to pull ourselves together. Somehow Martha slipped away, gravitating toward friends and family. I can't say I blame her. Her standing with us all night was an unrealistic expectation, but I worried about her. Who was comforting her? What if someone said something to upset her? She was only seven, fragile and confused. I wanted to protect her, but we were bombarded by the crowd, and she fell out of sight.

While Rusty stayed in the moment, telling people how much they had meant to Ray and thanking them for coming, I was busy thinking—*this person or that person wouldn't be here if it wasn't true.* Ray must really be dead. Periodically, I had to glance at my son to remind myself why I was standing in a goddamn funeral home.

Grace Zemski, my friend Chuck's mom, was the very first person in line. She took my hand and asked, "What happened to your son?" The big mystery question, repeated throughout the night.

When I saw Lyle and Nancy Swanson, I burst into tears as Lori had to nearly hold her dad up, his knees buckling as he reached out to hug me. Her mom, Nancy, also distraught, relied on a cane for support. The kids and I had spent a weekend at the Swansons' cabin the summer before. Lori has two sons, so you'd think Ray would have naturally hung out with her boys, but he immediately took to Lyle, shadowing him the entire weekend. He sat next to Lyle whenever we ate, fished with him at the end of the dock, and hopped in the hot tub with his new buddy. That weekend, Lyle pulled me aside and said, "Darla, you've got quite a boy there." On the way home, Ray said, "I like that guy. Is he always that nice?" I said, "Yep, always." So Lyle, a wonderful, caring man, was beside himself with the loss of his little sidekick, Ray.

The most devastating moments, however, were those of Ray's young friends walking through the line, clutching onto their parents' hands, crying uncontrollably. I knew it would be difficult to see all the children—the neighborhood gang, Ray's classmates and teammates—but it was beyond painful. Rusty found ways to reach out and comfort Ray's friends, reminding them of something funny they had done together. He told the children, "It's okay, don't be afraid," when he saw how scared they were to approach the casket. And, if all else failed, he pointed out the table where Ray's fart machine was, suggesting that setting it off would be an appropriate tribute to their prankster pal.

Midway into the visitation, Martha came to us and said she was hungry. Of course she would get hungry. Why hadn't I thought about that? Gratefully, someone overheard her, ran across the street and brought back a McDonald's kid's meal.

Recognizing the night was growing far too long for a little girl, the Holm family offered to take Martha home with them, where she hung out with Pam and Jim until we came for her.

Well over a thousand people passed through the funeral home that night. It's impossible to recall all the heartfelt words exchanged, but it seemed the most offhanded remarks were strangely of comfort. Remarks like that of our neighbor Chris, who said, "Ray was a little smartass." Rusty and I burst into laughter when he added, "That kid constantly gave me crap for being thirty years old and still living with my parents."

~

A couple years prior, Seth's family had moved from the neighborhood to a new home in the town of Lake Elmo. It crushed Ray to say goodbye to Seth as they pulled out of their driveway for the last time. The boys found time to hang out together when they could, but it wasn't like the good old days when all they had to do was cross the street to begin their day together. Before the evening came to a close, a gentleman approached us and said he was a friend of the Ronsberg family and that his son knew Ray from playing hockey in Seth's new backyard. He had recognized Ray's name in the obituary and contacted Stu and Kari to inform them. He said they were in Lake Placid, New York, at Seth's hockey tournament and they were trying to change their flight to come back for the funeral.

My heart sank, trying to imagine Kari and Stu breaking the news to Seth. Weeks later, they told us about the moment when they'd sat Seth down in their hotel room and told him about Ray. Kari said the next several minutes were beyond brutal. When Seth calmed down long enough to ask what had happened, they told him it probably had something to do with cystic fibrosis.

Seth got angry and asked, "How come you never told me Ray could die from CF?"

Kari explained, "Rusty and Darla didn't want people to treat Ray any differently."

Seth cried and insisted, "You should have told me. You should have told me!"

Stu eventually asked, "What difference would it have made?" Seth responded, "I would have spent more time with him."

~

Stu, Kari, Seth, and Sidnee came straight from the airport the next morning, just minutes before the funeral service began. When I saw them at the front of the church, standing next to the open casket, I rushed down the aisle and embraced Stu and Kari. Then I knelt down to comfort and hold Seth in my arms. He was surprisingly brave, holding it together better than I was. Reaching into his pocket, Seth pulled out a wallet-size picture—a photo of himself in his hockey uniform. "Darla, can you give this to Ray?" he asked.

"Sure," is all I managed to say before placing Seth's picture on Ray's chest, his best bud now close to his heart.

I found Rusty and Martha standing at the back of the worship hall. By now the church was packed as tight as teeth. Just before we made our way to a front pew, Rusty stopped halfway down the aisle, where Amy Richards sat with her three daughters. I overheard him ask, "Can we borrow Audra?" I guess he thought it would be of some comfort for Martha to have a friend at her side. The two girls sat in the pew in front of us. I spent much of the service watching Martha, wondering how she was handling everything. I wanted her at my side, but I think Rusty did our daughter a favor.

I also couldn't take my eyes off of all the children sitting in the choir loft. Earlier, unbeknownst to me, Rusty had directed Ray's friends to sit together in the loft—sort of VIP seating. Not only had Rusty thought of Martha and the other children, he'd stayed up all night writing about our son, a message my brother delivered during the service. Rusty had written about what made Ray special, describing what our son had gone through each day and how he'd faced his challenges head on. He stressed that Ray had lived a good life, had a great attitude, loved making his friends laugh, and never gave up. He also announced that we were still in the dark, unsure of how Ray had passed away. I was shocked. I had no idea my husband had been up writing late into the night. I remember thinking, "Why am I so disconnected? Why can't I think?"

Much of the service was a collection of memories shared by Ray's teachers. Their stories drew tears as well as laughter, which seemed appropriate when describing Ray. Patti Life, an amazing teacher who understood and appreciated Ray, got up to read first.

As one of Ray's teachers, I would like to be able to tell you that Ray loved coming to school because he loved to learn, loved to read and write, and that he was fascinated with fractions. But who am I kidding? Raymo came to school because that's where his friends were.

If you wanted to learn what was happening: who liked who, who was going to dump who, all those important things, Ray was the guy to ask. He was in on everything.

He liked to surprise us. One day, he came to school with his hair dyed. He did it himself in the bathroom. The dye was running down his cheeks and forehead. I couldn't help but laugh.

He loved making us laugh. He played a bird in the fifth grade play and dressed himself in yellow feathers, white tights and boxer shorts. The boxer shorts were a bet he made with his father.

Ray would suddenly break into dance in the middle of class. He did an excellent twist. He'd giggle uncontrollably with some secret joke of his until the whole class was laughing along with him. He was a favorite to sit by, the King of the Futon, and everyone's friend.

Ray strutted into our classroom every day with his smile that announced, "Here I am everybody!" And that's exactly how I picture him going into Heaven. *Here I Am Everybody!"*

My close friend, Lou Ann Henderson, spoke next.

I had the honor of working with Ray for six years at Carver Elementary. I was his music teacher.

When I think of Ray, I think of a big smile and a happy heart. He was one of those kids that just made you feel good to be around him. One of my first memories of Ray was when he was in first grade and I was out for dinner at Applebee's with a few of my non-teacher friends. Well, we were gabbing away and I looked down, and there staring up at me with those shining eyes and that big grin was Ray. He just looked so thrilled to see me. He had that way about him. He made you feel special. So I said, "Well, hello, Ray," and he just smiled at me with that big grin to say, "Hi." The reason I remember that so much is because after he left, my friends went on and on about how cute he was and how LUCKY I was to be a teacher. And that is so true —Ray was one of those kids that really made you realize how great it was to be a teacher.

Ray continued to brighten my days when he came to my classroom for music, and there are many fond memories. But last year was another highlight when he had one of the starring roles in the musical production "Of Mice and Mozart." He looked so great in his costume of big, fluffy yellow feathers. Maybe some of you noticed a couple pictures of Ray in his canary costume. Now, maybe some other fifth grade boys would've had a hard time putting on big webbed feet and feathers, but not Ray! He made the most of every single moment in life and played the part of Mozart's canary as only Ray could do it...with his whole heart!

Ray also sang in the Carver school choir, and as Darla and I have shared, he may not have had the best voice in the group, but his enthusiasm was infectious. He may even have sung a little off key once in a while, but he sang with every fiber of his being and with his whole heart and soul.

So, Ray, we are SO much going to miss you! And I know you're up there right now. Maybe even singing in the choir with Elvis. I just want to thank you so much for touching my life. Your life will continue to inspire all of us to live our lives to the fullest, just like you did. And to sing our own songs with our whole heart and soul.

Ray really liked his second grade teacher, Jackie Robinson. One day, while riding in the car, Ray heard Paul Simon's "Mrs. Robinson" on the radio. He changed the lyrics to: "And here's to you, Mrs. Robinson. *Students* love you more than you will know. Wo wo wo." I told Jackie about Ray's rendition of "Mrs. Robinson" and how he wanted to come to her retirement party with his friends and sing it for her. She laughed when I assured her that Ray didn't have a creepy Dustin Hoffman crush on her, but he was going to miss her. Jackie decided she couldn't bring herself to do it, so Harv French shared her thoughts on Ray.

Ray was the ultimate salesman. He taught his second grade class all about cystic fibrosis. He brought in the vest he had to wear during his treatments. By the time he was done speaking, all his classmates were saying, "Cool." They wanted a vest too!

With Ray it was "take a walk on the wild side." If there was a spitball to be thrown, a food fight to indulge in, or a mud puddle to jump in, Ray was always part of the action. He had an innocent way of looking at you that made you feel that ... well ... maybe it wasn't as bad as it seemed. He would cock his head, put on that famous smile of his, and captivate you with his charm. Ray ran with the big dogs, but he never forgot the underdog. He was very sensitive to the feelings of his classmates. If someone in class had been made fun of by another student, Ray would speak up and come to his rescue. He was as gentle on the inside as he was tough on the outside.

Ray had a spirit and a spark to him that is rarely seen in a child so young.

In closing ... Ray, I'm singing back to you now ... So, here's to you, Mr. Garvey. Everyone loves you more than you can know.

Harv read a beautiful poem and shared some special memories of his former student, including his lovely "hero" inscription in the book *Wayne Gretzky: The Making of the Great One.*

I held it together as best I could, listening to the stories of my son, but completely fell apart the second the Elvis music played, while a slide show of Ray projected onto a large screen at the front of the church.

Too soon, the service was over. Knowing I would never see Ray's face again, I felt profoundly lonesome as I watched Mark, Scott, Tim, Jerry, Sue and Cathe carry our son out to the hearse. I dreaded the thought of going home later to officially begin our lives without Ray.

Somehow, Martha slipped away from us again as we left the church for the cemetery. I don't know how it happened, but she wound up riding with my parents. She even took a seat between her grandparents during the short prayer service at the cemetery. Perhaps it was harder to be with her mom and dad, a physical reminder that we were now a family of just three. I stood off to the side, staring at my little girl, thinking, *She looks cold. She needs her mom. I should wrap my arms around her.* Yet I couldn't move, my feet cemented to the ground. In that moment, I felt like a failure, questioning if I'd ever muster up the strength to be the mom she needed.

When we got back to church, I heard a number of people talking about how impressive it was to see all the squad cars at every intersection during the drive to Union Cemetery. They said they had never seen so many police officers directing a funeral procession. Strangely, I didn't notice a single squad car that day.

Near the end of the church luncheon, I spotted a group of my friends sitting together at a long table. I took a seat with them and, probably inappropriately, said, "True to form. The East Siders are the last to leave the party … even without a cooler of beer."

Truth be told, I can't thank my friends enough for sticking around that day and staying in my life for the long haul. There are those who drifted away, some the least expected. And there are those, like my girlfriends, who gratefully remained. I know it wasn't an easy task for them—to continue their friendship with a messed-up, grieving mother. I was about as desirable to visit as an old lady in a nursing home who has lost her mind. So the support of my friends is not lost on me. Without a doubt, my life would be a whole lot worse without them. And

I hate to think where I'd be without Rusty and Martha. I was slow to come around, I'll admit. But there was a small defining moment, several days after the funeral, when Rusty first attempted to direct me down a better path.

~

Martha crept into our dark bedroom one morning, drapes tightly drawn. We were still lying in bed, reluctant to face another day without Ray. Slowly, she tiptoed to my side of the bed. I squinted at her, only one eye open. Silently she stood near me for a minute, seemingly afraid to disturb her own mother. With an awful, uneasy look, she quietly backed out of the room and carefully shut the door behind her. I rolled over and didn't even bother to call her back in to ask what she wanted. Sometime later, she gently opened our bedroom door again. Hesitantly, she whispered, "Mom? I'm hungry ... and ... I'm thirsty."

I'm ashamed to say it, but I did not respond to my daughter. Defeated, she tiptoed out of the room, this time with a sad look of neglect. Everything that had once been fulfilling felt heavy now—like a burden. I didn't want to be responsible for any part of the day. Not even responsible for my seven-year-old.

Barely awake himself, Rusty nudged me with an elbow. "You have to get up, Darla."

"I don't have to do anything!" I snapped.

He elbowed me again, this time harder. "Yes, you do. Someone still calls you Mom."

And with that, I forced myself out of bed and sauntered downstairs, where I found Martha on the couch, wrapped in a blanket, the TV on. Her eyes lit up when she saw me, and my stomach churned for being such a selfish shit.

I wondered how long she'd been awake, wandering around the house, before she dared to wake me. In that moment I was keenly aware that my little girl was now an only child. And, on top of not having her brother, she had been left alone with two distraught, largely unavailable parents.

She followed me into the kitchen and hopped on a counter stool, watching as I opened the refrigerator door. I scanned the sparse contents for a minute. "Hmmm, not much to pick from." We hadn't made it to the grocery store, still pecking our way through contributions. It seemed lasagna was the go-to condolence dish, several pans dropped off by family or friends. Much appreciated, but Martha was tired of it.

"Hey, have you ever tried lasagna?" I teased. "I can heat some up for you."

Martha wrinkled her nose and then smiled. Resting her chin in her hands, she waited for a better offer. It had been a while since I'd seen her smile. It was nice. I don't remember what I ended up fixing that morning, but I got up and ate breakfast with my daughter. And that moment, in that one day, was good. *Someone still calls me Mom.*

Maundy Thursday

Rusty pulled a pair of white athletic socks off his feet and tossed them onto the bedroom floor. "Whose socks are these?" he complained.

"Obviously they're yours."

Baffled, he shook his head. "No, they're not even the brand I wear."

Routinely, these ill-fitting socks were washed and placed back in Rusty's sock drawer. And time and again, he grumbled, "Seriously, who the hell's socks are these?"

This went on for many weeks after Ray passed away. Besides the socks, there was a pair of unfamiliar tennis shoes in the front closet. I asked some of the neighborhood kids if they had left a pair of shoes at the house, but no one claimed them. So there they sat, tucked away in the front closet.

Then one day, Denise Fierst, a friend who lived around the corner from us, asked if I knew what Ray and her son, Tyler, had been up to the night Ray passed away. I told her all I knew was that the boys were playing near the new development on their scooters before heading over to Pete's house. That's where I'd found Ray, when I was calling him home to get ready for church.

Denise described what Tyler had told her about that night. The story explained, not only the mystery socks and shoes, but also why Ray's fingernails were so dirty when he received his first communion. At some point, Denise asked Tyler to write the story for us.

Whose Shoes Are These?
By Tyler Fierst

On Thursday after school, Ray, Pete and I went down to Carver Auto Body on our scooters. We each got two pops because they're only 50 cents. Then we scootered up to New Century. From there we went to the park in the center. Ray and Pete had to go to the bathroom. So, Pete and Ray went looking for a port-a-potty. They found one down by where the new town homes were being built. Pete ran down and Ray followed, but Ray got stuck in the mud. He had mud in and around his shoes.

He was yelling, "Tyler." But I thought it was just the wind. Then I heard Pete come out of the bathroom giggling and I knew that something was up. I ran over there and Pete and I helped Ray up the hill. Then he took his shoes and socks off. Then after a little while he started to say that his feet were cold. He said, "Can we run over to my house to get me a new pair of socks and shoes?"

Pete and I said, "Can't you wait?"

He said, "No." Then he asked for Pete's shoes.

Pete said, "No. You can wear Tyler's."

I said, "No way. Then my feet will get cold." I pointed to a light tan house. "Go ask them."

Ray said, "Alright. Just as long as you're right behind me."

I said, "Alright."

So, Ray went up to the tan house, knocked on the door, and asked a man for socks and shoes. He went into his house and came back with a pair of shoes. Then Ray realized he needed to clean his feet before he put those shoes on, so we knocked on the door and asked for some paper towels. When we went to Ray's house, Ray and Pete traded shoes so Ray's mom wouldn't find out about the mud.

We have missed Ray at school and hockey this year. I wish I could laugh about this story with Ray.

Denise and I eventually went to the tan house to return the socks and shoes. I held the items in my hand while Denise knocked on the door. A woman answered, and before I could say a word, she said, "How do I know you? You look familiar."

"Um. I don't know," I answered.

"Do you live around here? Where do you work? I know I know you from somewhere."

"I teach at Carver Elementary, but I don't think we've ever met."

"My daughter goes to school there. That must be it. I probably saw you there." Then she glanced down at what I was holding in my hands and said, "Hey. Those are my shoes. How did you get them?"

"Well, my son was here one day. A while back. He …"

She interrupted before I could finish. "Oh, wait, I remember. My husband told me he gave a young boy a pair of shoes." She chuckled before adding, "But I didn't know he gave him *my* shoes. I've been looking all over for them."

Failing miserably, I stammered for the least shocking way to tell her that Ray had passed away that night. Then I tipped the scale, adding that her husband was one of the last people to see my son alive. She began to cry.

When I asked the woman if her husband had told her any details of his interaction with Ray, she said, "All I know is that your son knocked on the door, told my husband his name was Ray and that he lived up on Ferndale Street. Then he asked to borrow a pair of shoes because his were wet and muddy."

"I can't believe your husband actually gave my son a pair of shoes." I shook my head.

"Well, let's be clear." She smiled. "He didn't cough up his own shoes. He gave your son a pair of *mine*."

Denise laughed and said, "Typical guy. Wouldn't think twice about that."

The woman went on to say that Ray had sent her husband back inside the house for paper towels so he could wash off his feet. Before he slipped into the clean *borrowed* shoes, Ray had said, "You wouldn't have a pair of socks, too, because my feet are cold." So her husband retrieved a clean pair of, as it turned out, his wife's socks.

I chuckled and asked what had made her husband buy into Ray's little sales pitch, adding that if some kid came to my door asking for shoes, I'd probably tell him to hit the road. Especially if he told me he lived just up the block.

"I don't know what it was, but my husband said this little boy showed up and was so charming, he couldn't say no. And for some reason, he trusted that he would return everything the next day."

I assured her that my son was a good kid and, if that night had turned out differently, Ray would have stuck to his word.

When I got home, I kept picturing Ray sitting on the man's front step, washing mud from his feet with a paper towel. Ray died on Maundy Thursday—the Christian holy day that commemorates the washing of the feet, a symbolic act of love and humility.

Maundy Thursday also commemorates communion and the Last Supper of Jesus and his Apostles. I thought about Ray's first communion and the fact that we had had what would

209

be our last supper together at Famous Dave's. Maybe it's a silly correlation, but it's one I haven't been able to shake.

Later that same night, my shoes came off in the Heutmakers' yard while Rusty tried to revive our son. My socks were soaking wet, my feet uncomfortably cold. I physically felt what my son had felt earlier that night. Maybe it's another insignificant parallel that doesn't mean a damn thing, but I believe our children are bound to us. We are tied. And so it is that I remember sitting next to my lifeless son in the hospital, wishing I had dry socks and shoes.

While for centuries the church has called the Thursday before Easter Sunday "Maundy Thursday," for me it will always be Muddy Thursday. It's the night when an adventurous twelve-year-old boy tore around with his buddies, getting dirty like young boys do. His pants, his shoes, his fingernails—all caked in mud.

Ray and his sister were summertime, barefoot kids. If time didn't allow for a shower at the end of the day, at the very least I washed their feet with a wet washcloth before my children could crawl under clean sheets. It was a contest to see whose washcloth was the dirtiest. Evidence that they had played hard that day. So in some ways, Muddy Thursday is a reminder of how Ray had lived his life—playing hard right up to the end. But that Thursday is also the night that muddied up my life, my psyche, in ways that nearly destroyed me.

Penny Wars

Dr. Milla called asking that we come in to talk about the autopsy results. Rusty and I took a seat in his office before he announced, "It was his heart." Rusty broke down the second the words left Dr. Milla's mouth, later telling me how ironic it was. Here was a kid with the biggest heart ever, the pulse of the neighborhood, and it was the organ that did him in.

"It appears Ray passed away from something called Arrhythmogenic Right Ventricular Dysplasia, or ARVD," Dr. Milla said. He explained that, in ARVD, part of the muscle cells around the right side of the heart turn to fat cells, and the fat acts as an insulator, blocking the normal electrical current of the heart. He went on to say that ARVD is a rare type of cardiomyopathy, adding that it usually affects young males, often times athletes, but is rarely seen in someone as young as Ray. I couldn't help but think how the word *rare* means absolutely nothing to the Garvey family.

When I asked if there was anything we could have done to prevent Ray's sudden death, Dr. Milla asked if Ray had ever complained of light-headedness or said that his heart felt like it was racing. Rusty and I couldn't think of a single time when Ray had expressed those concerns. Dr. Milla said that that is often the case, noting that athletes, like basketball players, can suddenly drop on the court and even with a defibrillator on the scene, they can't be saved. He assured us there wasn't anything we could have done that night. Ray's death was immediate.

There was some comfort in thinking it was quick. Perhaps our son hadn't suffered. Yet I couldn't help wonder what his final moments were like. No one saw him go down. No one knows if he cried out for help. When I shared those thoughts with Stu and Kari Ronsberg, Stu said, "Ray was tough, Darla. If there was any chance he could have survived, even if he were in pain, that kid would have crawled home."

Dr. Milla went on to say that you wouldn't have known Ray had cystic fibrosis from the autopsy because his lungs looked clear. They didn't even show signs of scarring, which is common in CF. I was both proud and extremely angry. Proud that Ray had worked so hard and was winning the CF war, and furious that we'd been blindsided by an undetected heart problem.

During our conversation with Dr. Milla, something occurred to me. "Could the feeding tube have something to do with this? Changing muscle cells to fat cells?" I asked.

Dr. Milla shook his head.

I persisted. "Think about it. We were pumping in all that formula every night. Ray was getting chubby. What if his heart couldn't handle that much fat intake? Did we do this to our son?" I cried.

Dr. Milla stated that Ray's arteries weren't blocked with fat or cholesterol like you'd expect from an unhealthy diet, and certainly not something you'd see in a child. This was an electrical problem, not a plumbing problem. Dr. Milla insisted that the feeding tube had nothing to do with Ray's death, yet I've never stopped wondering.

Rusty asked, "If we knew Ray had ARVD, could it have been treated?" Dr. Milla told us that there are medications that are effective for some people; others require a pacemaker. I couldn't imagine what a pacemaker would have done to Ray's active lifestyle, but I'd have given anything to find out.

When Martha learned that Ray had died from a heart problem, she burst into tears. She cried for a long time before stating, "I need my heart checked." I was surprised she'd made that connection at such a young age. Years later she told me that when she was a little girl, she assumed everything about her brother would happen to her. She figured she'd eventually get a feeding tube, like Ray, and was convinced she had the same heart problem.

Dr. Milla referred Martha to a pediatric cardiologist. While Martha didn't show any signs of ARVD, we discovered that she had a hole in her heart: an atrial septal defect, or ASD. With chronic bacterial infections lurking in her lungs, the otherwise simple procedure to close the hole was too dangerous to perform. Her cardiologist assured us that ASDs are common and generally pose no problem, even if left alone. Nonetheless, we have kept a watchful eye on Martha with annual testing to make sure the hole hasn't gotten any larger.

Sometime after Ray's death, Don Boxmeyer, a newspaper columnist for the St. Paul *Pioneer Press*, interviewed us for a human interest story. Don crafted a beautifully written piece about a local young boy who had died young but lived a full life. After the article came out, Ray's classmates and teachers began raising money for cystic fibrosis. Students paid a dollar to wear a hat to school, something otherwise not allowed. They also had a week-long penny war. Teams of students competed to see who could fill their jars with the most pennies. But the excitement of a penny war is to sabotage the jars of rival teams, adding coins other than pennies, which score negatively. It was a fun, competitive way to encourage donations—raising over $3,000.

We were invited to attend a sixth grade school assembly to receive the student-raised money. I asked Dr. Milla to accompany us, as we had decided to split the money between the CF Foundation for medical research and the University of Minnesota CF clinic to cover costs for families in need. Dr. Milla spoke to the students about CF and told them their donations would help find a cure. I addressed the students as well, informing them that Ray had died from an undetected heart problem but that he'd lived with CF. I thanked them for their generosity and assured them that the money they had raised would help Ray's little sister. I also expressed gratitude for their being Ray's friends and credited those special friendships for the reason Ray had come to school every day with a smile on his face.

When the assembly was over, and students made their way back to class, I heard Elvis music blaring over the intercom. Ms. Beske explained, "In honor of Ray, instead of the usual bell, we've been playing Elvis music during the three minutes between class periods."

Sometime later, Rusty and I went to Maplewood Middle School to clean out Ray's locker. It was easy to spot, his entire locker covered with heartfelt messages from his classmates, written on colorful paper. Inside we found an unorganized mess of his books and school supplies. Not surprising. I imagined him in a rush each day, tossing books in his locker, then tending to more important things—screwing around with his friends in the hallway.

We placed all of his belongings in a bag, including an envelope containing his school pictures that never made it home. They were ruined, covered in red sticky liquid from a spilled juice box that we found at the bottom of his locker. Luckily the school photographer agreed to reprint a new packet for us.

Before closing Ray's locker, Rusty reached for an item propped up in the very back. It was the didgeridoo I had helped Ray make for music class. It was a fun project we had done together, nicely replicating an aboriginal wind instrument.

As if it had been perfectly timed, Ray's music teacher suddenly appeared in the hallway. She expressed her condolences, speaking fondly of our son, as well as the didgeridoo. Before I could suggest that it would make for a nice wall piece at home, Rusty handed over the didgeridoo. He said she could use it as a model, but only if she told her future students about the boy who had made it. With tears in her eyes, she promised.

Next we went to the boys' locker room to clean out Ray's gym locker. Besides his tennis shoes and gym clothes, we discovered his calculator pushed all the way to the back of the top shelf—which would explain a lot about his math grades.

It felt so wrong to walk out of the building with the last remnants of a sixth grade boy who had once graced the hallways and classrooms with his big personality.

A few weeks later, the principal informed us that Ray's teachers had pitched in and planted a tree in the school courtyard as a tribute to our son. We were honored and decided to do the same, planting trees in Ray's friends' front yards, a lasting reminder of the Ferndale ringleader. But the most profound neighborhood landmark would come later, spearheaded by a remarkable woman we had just met.

"And now that you don't have to be perfect, you can be good."

~ John Steinbeck

Heaven or Hell

Setting up the Taj Mahal-size tent in the backyard should have been a kickoff, the beginning of family adventures to come. I had imagined all of us sprawling out on sleeping bags, discussing all the places we would explore *together*. Ironically, it was Memorial Day when Martha asked that I please set up the tent. It tore me up that Ray had died before he ever set foot inside the tent. Even so, I gave in to Martha's request.

After pounding in the last stake, I stood back and watched Martha smiling brightly. Brushing wavy brown hair from her face, she held the tent flap open for her friends. One by one they pushed their way through the opening. Pain had twisted my perception, and I did not see enthusiastic children eager to be the first ones inside the tent. Instead I saw loud hooligans shoving their way to a place they didn't belong—not without Ray. I watched as wet grass, once attached to the bottom of their bare feet, fell to the floor of the tent. Suddenly I felt ill. Dropping the hammer to the ground, I fled to the front porch.

Rusty walked past me, a shovel propped atop his broad shoulders. I knew he was absorbed in his own thoughts, pretending yard work might somehow help. He glanced at me with sad eyes and a quick nod—a nod that acknowledged his awareness that pitching that damn tent was a heartbreaking exercise. If I had paid closer attention, I might have noticed a hint of relief on his face, as well. For I was at least out of bed and dressed. But I was too busy thinking about something else.

While Ray got ready for what would be his final day of school, I had told him there were only seven more Mondays in the school year. I thought that sounded better than thirty-eight days. Ray was getting tired of the hectic routine of middle school and was looking forward to the lazy days of summer. And he was looking forward to camping in our new tent. We talked about all the places we would go. I suggested Yellowstone National Park or Mount Rushmore—every camper's rite of passage. Ray asked if we could go to Indiana to visit our friends the McIntosh family. "You and Dad can sleep in their house and Martha and I can camp out with Paul, Ryan, Matt, and Sarah. We'd all fit, too."

I smiled at his enthusiasm.

"Oh, and what about Graceland, Mom? I'd love to see where Elvis lived. They gotta have campgrounds in Memphis, right?"

Lost in those memories of my last morning with my son, I hardly noticed a woman walking up our driveway. Annoyed by the intrusion, I wanted to duck inside the house, but it was too late. As she got closer, I recognized her from Ray's visitation. She had waited in the long line of mourners that stretched around the block outside the funeral home. She had come to say goodbye to a twelve-year-old boy and to pay her respects to the parents she had never met. I had navigated through a strange fog that night, making the faces of life-long friends somehow foreign. Yet the words from a stranger have never left me. "You don't know me," she said, "but my name is Kay. I live at the end of your block. Your son was the first to welcome me to the neighborhood."

Now here Kay was a second time, taking an uninvited seat next to me on my front porch. We sat in silence for a moment before she said, "Darla, I would recognize your pain if I saw you walking down the street. I'd recognize it even if I didn't know what had happened to your family."

My eyes were red and swollen, my cheeks stained with tears. I hadn't washed my hair, and God only knows what I was wearing. When she told me she would recognize my pain, I wanted to ask, "Well, aren't you intuitive? What was your first clue, lady?" Instead I mustered up a barely audible "Really?"

"Yes," Kay said. "I recognize your pain because I lost my son, too."

My heart sank, and I felt ashamed for what I had been thinking. I waited a moment before I dared to ask what had happened. She told me that her son, Stephen, had drowned in the St. Croix River when he was ten years old.

Kay looked to be somewhere in her sixties. I wanted to ask her how she did it. What was the secret to surviving a lifetime of suffering? Instead I asked, "How long ago did your son die?"

She drifted off for a second before answering, "Nineteen sixty-eight … yesterday … an hour ago."

So that's how it is, I thought. *There is no secret. An hour is as good as it gets.* But I didn't understand. Kay walked so tall. Her eyes were full of life and joy, her voice strong and zealous. Her earrings even matched her blouse, for God's sake. Happy people had become offensive to me. Happy people who had lost a child? Well, that was absurd. Clearly Kay had to know something I did not.

Finally I asked, "How do you do this, Kay? All this time. How have you done it?"

Kay relayed a Bible story in which Jesus asked his disciples, "Have I been with you all this time and you do not recognize me or know me by name?" She told me that after her son died, when she heard that passage one Sunday in church, she asked herself, "Do I not recognize my own son? Do I not recognize my Stephen?"

I wasn't sure what she meant, so I pressed for more. "What do you believe, Kay? Do you believe in a heaven? Do you believe you will see Stephen again?"

"I don't believe God took my boy and brought him to some white fluffy cloud. That's not my vision of heaven. I had that boy. I wanted that boy. And no one took him from me." She continued, "I believe there's a cycle of life. I see Stephen when the seasons change or when the sun sets. I see him in the beauty of this world. And ... I recognized him when Ray stood on my doorstep and welcomed me to the neighborhood four years ago."

I was a little surprised that she and Ray had had a four-year relationship that I wasn't even aware of. Then something came to mind. "Did you used to give Ray and Martha Popsicles?"

"Yeah. That was me."

I remember the two of them walking home from the end of the block one summer afternoon, holding Popsicles in their hands. When I asked where they had gotten them, Ray said, "From the lady on the corner."

"Ray, you shouldn't ask her for Popsicles. You don't even know her."

"Yes, I do. She's really nice. You should meet her, Mom." Then he added, "And we don't ask for Popsicles. We just bike down there and talk to her for a few minutes, and then pretty soon she goes inside and gets us one."

There was no stopping the neighborhood charmer from engaging with everyone. On the other end of the block, an older gentleman pretty much did the same thing as Kay. Ray occasionally stopped to visit him, inevitably walking away with a piece of candy in his mouth. Everyone in the neighborhood, adults included, referred to him as the Candy Man. No one seemed to know his real name—just the one Ray had dubbed him.

Pulling me back into conversation, Kay continued, "You know, Darla. Heaven can be right here on Earth."

222

I cringed at the thought of one more person pushing their religious ideology. As Kay paused to study me, it was almost as if she knew what I was thinking, sensed my anger. She pointed to herself and carefully continued. "For *me* heaven is right here on earth. You can make your own heaven right here if you extend yourself. Extend yourself to other people or to a good cause, and you will see the beauty in this world again. For *me,* that is *my* heaven."

Extend myself? To someone else? I tried to understand, but my mind was numb. I wanted to extend myself to Ray, and it didn't seem likely that anything less would do. We sat quietly for a moment longer before Kay warned, "You know, Darla. You can make your own hell, too."

I raised an eyebrow, giving her permission to continue.

"For *me,* hell is when I'm alone and stuck with myself. When I'm aware of every miserable thought I have—every painful emotion I feel. When I'm stuck alone with myself, that, to *me,* is hell." And with that, Kay got up and left the porch. She smiled and said she'd visit again soon.

I was left to ponder Kay's interpretation of heaven and hell. Or, maybe more accurately, her perspective on life— good or bad. I had to hand it to her. It was the least offensive thing anyone had said to me on the subject of death thus far.

While nothing resembled a heaven to me, I seemed to have the hell thing locked down tight. I *was* stuck alone with my miserable thoughts—the most haunting of which were my feelings of guilt. I couldn't stop hashing over all the times I had messed up. All the times I'd lost my cool, when my punishment hadn't matched my children's crimes. I'd tried to excuse my bad behavior because I was exhausted, overworked, or crazy premenstrual moody. Sometimes, for a second or two, I'd convinced myself that those were actually valid reasons for being crabby and impatient with my children. But were they?

I was especially tortured by the memories of the time or two, or five, that I had spanked Ray. Who does that? What kind of mother spanks a child with a chronic illness? I would lie awake at night holding endless debates with myself. Was I a monster, or had I taught Ray a lesson?

Martha was troubled by her own sense of guilt. One day she came to me and asked, "Remember when me and Ray used to fight?" Before I could say anything to comfort her, she settled upon her own answer. "Well … that was just a game."

Later in life, Martha would still wrestle with the demons of guilt, troubled by the milestones Ray did not get to experience —yet she did. But in that moment, as a little girl, she quickly reasoned away the shame she felt for fighting with her brother.

It wasn't that easy for me. Every day I begged Ray for forgiveness, and every night I wrote letters to my son. And I constantly cried to Rusty—telling him how awful I felt about my shortcomings. "What if Ray didn't know how much I loved him?" I asked my husband one day.

Fed up with me, Rusty stated, "I'm not going to listen to this anymore. You and Ray had a close relationship, and you were a lot alike. Which is probably the reason you clashed once in a while."

"But he's gone, and I can't apologize. I don't get to make it better."

"That's nonsense. You *did* make it better every day that he was here."

"But what if he didn't know just how *much* I loved him?"

"Darla, that's all he knew. You two were good together, but he did get out of line once in a while. He needed discipline."

"But I am the adult and I should have been more patient."

"Look, I feel bad for the times when I was probably too hard on him, too," Rusty admitted, "but ninety-nine percent of the time, you two were laughing and goofing around together.

If you want to share a good memory, I'll listen. But I'm not going to listen to the one percent of the time when you think you weren't a good mom ... because you were."

While Rusty's words were of some comfort, they didn't quiet my thoughts. Because here's the thing about guilt. It screams a hell of a lot louder than forgiveness. Acceptance is just a whisper, something you have to be still for in order to hear above the clanging noise of failure. After Ray's death, the cringe-worthy memories of the friction in our home seemed to overshadow all the wonderful times. I suppose I could liken it to someone who receives hundreds of accolades on social media, yet they focus on the one hater who posts something negative. That logic holds up whenever I revisit our last vacation to Lutsen.

Memories of that ski trip are still so vivid today, even the drive home. I can picture Martha sleeping in the back seat when we stopped at Split Rock Lighthouse along the North Shore of Lake Superior in Two Harbors, Minnesota. There was no one else in the parking lot, so I locked the car door and left Martha sleeping while Ray and I ran as fast as we could, up to the lighthouse and back, just to say we had been there. I can still picture Ray laughing the entire time, like he was committing a serious crime leaving his sister unattended in the car for all of forty-five seconds.

Three weeks after that ski trip, Ray was gone. And, while I am left with memories of those wonderful vacation days, too often I find myself stuck on the moment when I pinned my son to the wall, insisting he take back his words about how his life sucked. I doubt Ray ever gave it a second thought, and I know Rusty is right—I made things okay while Ray was still here. But I didn't completely let go of the guilt until Cathe Carbone sort of broke the spell.

She took me to her cabin one weekend, insisting I needed a retreat. While sitting around the campfire, I told her that it had been an honor to be Ray's mom. That it was pretty special to know that I was the only one who could claim that title. *I* was Ray's mom. Then I suddenly broke down. "But I screwed up, Cathe. I wasn't good enough for him."

She listened to me drone on about how horrible I felt for all the times I had messed up, including what happened in Lutsen, before she finally snapped. "Who the hell do you think you are?"

I was confused by her anger. I mean, really, who yells at a grieving mother who's struggling with guilt? "Excuse me?"

"Seriously. Who the hell do you think you are that you could have done it perfectly? What does that say about the rest of us moms?"

I stared at her blankly.

"Come on, Darla. Every mother says and does things she regrets."

"I suppose, but my son's not here. I can't apologize. I want a do-over, Cathe. I just want to do it better."

"Well, I hate to tell you, but you couldn't do it over any better than you did, because you're not perfect."

Cathe went on to describe what she had seen in Ray, insisting he wouldn't have been who he was if I had been a total screw-up. Like Cher in the film *Moonstruck,* Cathe's "Snap out of it!" words of wisdom changed things for me. I started to accept the fact that in spite of my flaws, my son had developed into a happy, thoughtful, funny young boy. I had given Ray a *normal* life, not a Norman Rockwell life, and that was okay. Maybe it was better than okay. I don't know. What I do know for certain is this: One, I have to forgive myself for what I can't undo. Two, there's exactly a one-hundred-percent chance that I'll screw up some more. And three, as long as I try to do my best by Martha, then that's okay.

Ray Garvey Court

It was mid-October, the summer behind us now. I watched from the back of the crowded council chamber as Kay McDonough took the floor, offering her voice before the Maplewood City Council. Wiping sweaty palms on my pants legs, I shifted in a folding chair. It didn't seem likely that anyone knew who I was, yet I had a strange feeling that some city officials were looking directly at me.

A transplant from the East Coast, Kay leaned into the microphone and began her pitch in her Boston accent. "The neighborhood lost their little firecracker," she said. "We just want a way to honor the memory of a child."

Before she could continue, Mayor Robert Cardinal interrupted, raising an unexpected question. "What happens to the street sign if the family decides to move?"

Self-assured, Kay answered without the slightest pause. "It doesn't matter if the Garvey family ever moves. That's not the issue here," she argued. "We want Ray's friends to drive down Ferndale Street when they have families of their own. We want them to tell their children and their grandchildren that this was the street where they played with an exceptional boy named Ray Garvey. We want them to remember their friend with a street sign bearing his name."

The mayor, busy reviewing the written proposal, looked up over his reading glasses. He seemed caught off guard by Kay's direct response. Sometimes her candor surprised me. Before the voting process began, he addressed the city council members, summarizing the proposal. "Ray Garvey lived for most of his twelve years on South Ferndale Street. Ray Garvey had a positive impact on the lives of Maplewood residents in this neighborhood within our community. All the property owners of Ferndale Street have signed a petition requesting that Ray Garvey be remembered by placing a second street name plate at the north and south end of Ferndale Street in his honor."

I scanned the panel and tried to read the businesslike expressions of the city officials. Maybe they weren't interested in erecting an honorary street sign. Maybe they were afraid it would start a trend and the city would be inundated with similar requests.

Earlier at the house, Rusty had decided to stay back with Martha. He'd said he would get too emotional if the sign was approved, too angry if it wasn't. Kay had no doubts about the outcome. "I've got a glass of wine riding on this. It'll be your loss, Rusty."

After Kay finished addressing the city council, she took a seat next to me. I sat there thinking how the honorary street name had come to be. I hoped the explanation in the proposal letter might somehow help the city council members' decision, if any of them were wavering.

~

Linda had asked that I come to her house one day. As we sat together on her front porch, she said, "I looked up the meaning of every word I could think of in place of *street*. Like *trail, way, road, path*, etc. Nothing seemed to fit until I came to the word *court*." She handed me a piece of paper and said, "Take a look at this list and tell me if there's one single word here that doesn't describe Ray."

The list of synonyms for *court* included *allure, attract, captivate, charm, flatter, go together, keep company with, pursue, run after, seek, spark*, and *love*. Wiping away tears, I said, "No, Linda. There's not a word here that doesn't pertain to Ray."

Just then, Janny and Daryl walked over. Linda informed them about what we were discussing. "What do you guys think?" She handed them the list.

"Court is perfect," Daryl agreed. Waving his arm from one end of the block to the other, he said, "This was Ray's court."

"Ray brought everyone together, Darla. And he was a charmer." Janny weighed in. "Did you know *Ray* was Katelyn's first word?"

"You're kidding me."

"No, I'm not kidding. Katelyn learned to say 'Ray' before she even learned to say her brothers' names. Now she wakes up in the morning, looks out the window at your house, and asks, 'Where's Ray?'"

"We couldn't get our boys outside all summer," Janny continued. "I kept telling Justin and Tyler to just try to go out and do something. I thought they might feel better, but they told me it wasn't the same without Ray."

"Tyler is having a hard time," Daryl added. "He doesn't feel like he got to say goodbye to Ray. I told him, in a way, Ray said goodbye to *him.*"

"What do you mean?" I asked.

"I remember Ray on his scooter that night. He saw me putting Tyler's hockey bag in the back of our truck. He said hello, then called out to Tyler as he was getting in the cab, 'See ya, hockey boy.' Then he scooted off down the street."

~

I wanted the sign for Martha. For Tyler. For the whole neighborhood. More than anything, I wanted a spark to return to Ferndale Street.

Clasping my hands in my lap, Kay and I nervously waited for the voting to begin. Mayor Cardinal led the process, casting the first vote. "Aye," he said into a microphone. Each council member took his or her time, as if pondering the decision, suspense building. One by one we heard a string of *ayes*. I fought back tears and anxiously waited to hear from the last voter. He paused for a long time, then gradually bent down and reached for something off the floor. I couldn't see what it was from where I was sitting, but it seemed he had placed an object in his lap. He locked eyes with me and smiled. In disbelief, I watched as he slowly extended his arms high above his head. Holding a large brown street sign that read "Ray Garvey Court," he cast the last vote. "Aye."

Crying softly, I mouthed the words *thank you*.

After the city hall meeting, Kay and I had that celebratory glass of wine she had bet, then rushed home to tell Rusty and Martha the good news. Rusty thanked Kay for her persistence. Leading the campaign, she had gone to each neighbor with a clipboard, gathering signatures on the petition. Kay was one of the strongest women we'd ever met. She and her husband, Bill McDonough, had made it their mission to help other parents cope with the loss of a child. They certainly made a huge impact on our family. I told Kay once how her words about choosing to create my own heaven or hell have stayed with me. She said she was glad I had caught her on a good day when she had something clever to say. Then she laughed that wonderful, hearty laugh of hers.

Many years have passed since the "Ray Garvey Court" signs were erected. The city placed one at each end of our block, like bookends. One sign stands at the corner of Ferndale and Nimitz Street, the corner where a young boy once waited for his first bus ride to kindergarten. The other sign adorns the corner where Ray caught the middle school bus. To me the signs symbolize the beginning and end of Ray's short life on Ferndale Street. The beginning and end of a young school boy's dreams. They also remind me of the love people had for him.

Ray would have graduated from high school in 2007, his name absent from the commencement program. I missed six years of seeing his name quickly scribbled at the top of home-work assignments. Martha must have felt the loss of his name in print, as well. I used to find scraps of paper in her bedroom in the weeks following Ray's death. In her first-grade penman-ship, she wrote his name on notebook paper, folded it up and tucked it away in random places in her room. At some point, she scratched her brother's name into her window sill.

There are days when I glance up at the street signs just to see my son's name in print. Sometimes I picture him skating with the puck, "Garvey" stitched on the back of his hockey jersey. Other times I see him as a preschooler. He's bent over the kitchen table, a pencil too long for his small hand firmly gripped between his thumb and fingers. He presses the lead against the paper, too hard for it to glide smoothly. He con-centrates until he slowly shapes a legible R, then an A, and finally a Y. He has proudly spelled his name and smiles. Some-times, when I look at Ray's name on the street signs, it makes me smile too. But there are just as many days when I drive past the signs, keeping my eyes on the road. Sometimes it's best for me to look straight ahead.

When the signs had been mounted, Ray's friends were on their bikes, waiting for me to come home. As I rounded the corner in my car, the kids flagged me down, forming a circle beneath the street sign. From their bike seats, they cheered and pointed to the sign. Then they signaled for me to follow them as they rode to the other end of the block—pointing and smiling below that street sign, too. I wish I'd had a camera to capture the moment when the Ferndale Street gang came outside to acknowledge their friend. It doesn't seem possible that a simple gesture like the honorary signs could change much, but kids started coming outside more, and I started to engage in the world, too, watching the neighborhood slowly come back to life.

Scotty Too Hottie

In the years that followed, Martha continued to thrive in school, developed close friendships, and began playing youth hockey. And little by little, she also took over her brother's bedroom.

One day while cleaning what had now become Martha's room, I noticed Ray's hat was no longer hanging from the mirror above her dresser. In its place was an NHL knit beanie with the words "Minnesota Wild" stitched across the front. Later in the day, I would find Ray's old hat on the top shelf in my bedroom closet. This had become Martha's way. She clung to the things she needed at the time, comforted by their familiarity. Then slowly, as she came into her own, she made a small change here and a bigger change there.

Gradually her bedroom theme changed. At some point, Ray's Jailhouse Rock wall clock with pendulum legs came down to make room for a photo of James Shepard, the Wild's cute new player. An old phone, that instead of ringing had an Elvis figure dancing to "You Ain't Nothing but a Hound Dog," somehow made its way across the hall. In its place, on Martha's dresser, there sat a glass canister with the Wild logo stamped into it. It was filled with Red Hot Tamales. The Elvis photo calendar, a must-have for several years, no longer made her Christmas wish list. Tacked on the wall instead was the Wild's game schedule.

I straightened out the hockey pucks lined up along Martha's window sill and thought about her respectful timing. Her requests had always been put so gently: "Mom, I'd like to put these hockey pucks on my window sill. Where can I put Ray's trophies so they'll be safe?" And that would be my cue to pack away a few more things. Things like a football-shaped piggy bank, a bobble-head dog she had given Ray when he was hospitalized, his Scooby-Doo pillow, or some of his t-shirts she loved to wear but had since outgrown. These things were not discarded—just shifted over a little to make room for today. To make room for life.

While dusting off the top of Martha's desk, I bumped her mouse pad. An image of Brent Burns, a Wild defenseman, appeared on her screen—his front tooth missing. Next I tidied up the miscellaneous items sprawled across Martha's dresser, then reached to straighten out the most recent change to her room. I shifted her beanie so it was centered above her mirror. Since he was a skater and enthusiastic hockey fan himself, I knew Ray would have approved of his sister's love of professional hockey—the Wild beanie included. Especially the beanie. Ray loved wearing hats. Loved playing the part.

I thought back to the morning before Ray had caught what would be his final bus ride to school. On that day, I found him checking himself out in the mirror—trying to adjust the very hat Martha had removed from her mirror. A hat that Scotty Too Hottie, a professional WWE wrestler, was famous for wearing. Ray was a big fan of Scotty Too Hottie. After all, he was a part of a hip-hop duo named Too Cool, and Ray was all about cool.

Scotty Too Hottie's hat was a bright blue-and-yellow, ridiculous-looking thing. It was basically a top hat without the top. It looked as if someone had taken a scissors to the crown—leaving only the brim and band. Ray liked to spike up his hair to show through the opening of the hat, just the way Scotty Too Hottie wore his hair.

When Ray was ten years old, Rusty had ordered the hat from a wrestling magazine that our son had insisted he purchase while the two were at a gas station. When the box arrived, Ray tore it open only to discover that the hat was too big. It slipped right down over his eyes. But that didn't stop Ray from wearing it. He would tie a bandana around his forehead and prop the hat over it. Many times I watched him strut across the street to his friends' homes with that silly hat perched on top of his head. In time, the novelty wore off and the hat stayed somewhere in the back of his closet. So I was surprised when I found Ray checking himself out in the hallway mirror before he left for school that day.

"Hey Mom, can you see any toilet paper sticking out?" Ray spun around full circle so I could examine the hat from every angle. I laughed when I realized he had stuffed the lining of the hat with toilet paper so it would fit his head more snugly—the hat still too big for him.

"I don't see any toilet paper, but if clumps of it start to fall out, you're going to get teased on the school bus." I laughed.

He smiled at the possibilities and kissed me good-bye.

I shook those memories loose and had turned to leave Martha's bedroom when I spotted her hand-me-down backpack lying on the floor. I noticed, in permanent ink, she had written the word "Burnsy" on the outside pocket of her bag. Burnsy is the nickname for Brent Burns. Her hockey obsession was never-ending. It pleased me so much that I didn't even balk at the fact that she had defaced her brother's old backpack, the same backpack that had taunted me at one time.

On that fateful day in April, anxious to run off and hang out with his buddies, Ray had tossed his backpack on the front porch after school. I picked it up and set it in my office when I got home from work. Day after day, slumped in a corner, the barely-worn backpack begged me to unzip it. And day after day, I resisted, knowing whatever I found inside would send me to a place I wasn't prepared to go. I don't recall now, but

I'm guessing at least a month passed before I surrendered to the bag. I clutched it in my arms for a while before convincing myself to unzip it. Each item I pulled from the bag that day represented unrealized dreams. And each item stopped the clock. Time had become defined as *before Ray* and *after Ray*.

The first thing I removed from the backpack was Ray's school agenda. It was filled out with reminders of events that had either taken place or would never come to be. Ray's last entry, dated April 12, 2001, stated in bold print: "No school tomorrow. Good Friday." An earlier entry said, "Girlfriend's birthday. Get flowers." I wondered where my little sixth grade lover-boy would have gotten flowers for this mystery girlfriend of his.

I continued searching through Ray's backpack. I found homework tucked in folders that would never be completed, graded, or discussed. I felt around and pulled out an empty juice box crushed flat, along with a Ziploc baggie full of crumbs from a snack I had packed for him. My heart ached and my blood boiled at the same time. I was sad and lonely, and I was pissed off that I was sitting on the floor—sad and lonely. I crumpled both the juice box and Ziploc in one hand and flung it across the room. *I want to take care of my son. I want to pack his snack, damn it! I want to be his mom all over again.*

I sobbed for quite some time. When I recovered, I unzipped another compartment. Digging around inside the bag, my hand touched something soft. I pulled out a handful of toilet paper, and then another and another. I dug around at the bottom of his bag until I grasped what I was looking for—the Scotty Too Hottie hat. Clutching it in my hand, I brought it up to my face and nearly suffocated in Ray's scent.

Martha walked in to find me on the floor, bawling. I faintly heard her ask, "Mom ... are you okay?" She lingered in the doorway, waiting to see if I would offer her more than the distance and hysteria of late. I quickly collected myself and shared the story of Ray stuffing toilet paper in the lining of the Scotty Too Hottie hat. When I finished the story, Martha reached for the hat and asked, "Can I have it, Mom?"

"Sure. It's yours now," I said.

Ray's raspy voice had been silenced, no longer plotting out adventures with his little sister, but Martha has found solace in things that once belonged to her brother. Things like his silly Scotty Too Hottie hat. Back then, I also had an intense ache for anything that was Ray's. I often searched his room in the days after his death, hoping to find a secret journal somewhere, which was a ridiculous thought. The kid could hardly sit still long enough to do his homework, much less keep a journal. But I longed to communicate with my son. Death had abruptly ended our conversations. If I couldn't hear his voice, I at least wanted to read his thoughts. Maybe there was a letter somewhere he had forgotten to give me.

While I never did find a letter from Ray, I was reminded of the one he never got the chance to write after discovering his favorite book, *Maniac Magee* by Jerry Spinelli, tucked inside his dresser drawer. Ray was so moved by the story that when he finished the book, he asked if he could write to Jerry Spinelli. He wanted to thank him for writing such a good story, and he wanted to ask Spinelli if he was actually Maniac Magee. Eventually, I wrote the letter on Ray's behalf, thanking Jerry Spinelli for providing me with a wonderful memory of sitting on the edge of my son's bed, reading *Maniac Magee* together. To my surprise, Spinelli wrote back:

Dear Darla,
I often say no book of mine is finished until it's read.
That was never more true than with you and Ray. You
and your son have honored me.

Thank you.
Jerry Spinelli

Jerry Spinelli also sent a signed poster of his book cover. Ray would have loved the poster, as it answered his big question:

For Ray and Darla, from Maniac and me.
Jerry Spinelli

Some days, while Martha was in school, I crawled in the lower bunk—the last place where Ray had slept—and cried myself to sleep. When I woke up from one such grief-filled nap, Ray's boom box caught my attention. This was another one of those little finds that I had held onto. I knew if I hit the play button, I would discover the last CD my son had listened to. I hoarded these treasures like a prisoner of war might ration food. I had to be careful not to use up everything at once. If I went through all of Ray's stuff in one day, I feared the rest of my days would be too empty to endure. So I paced myself and savored my pieces of Ray.

Music was a huge part of Ray's life. He could hear a dance beat from ordinary objects that most people tune out. The thumping sound of an agitating washing machine transformed his normal stride through the laundry room into a dirty-underwear-tossing ceremonial dance. The tapping of his pencil against the kitchen table often turned into a heavy metal drum session—a purposeful distraction from his homework.

I made a bet with myself that day. If I turned the boom box on, Elvis Presley would belt out one of Ray's favorite songs. I stood frozen in the middle of his room for a moment, picturing all the times I had walked into Ray's bedroom to find him dancing and singing along with Elvis, his wiry body moving to the beat and his face filled with the joy only someone who truly loves music understands. And most often, I found a little girl at his side, trying to copy her brother's dance moves.

I lost my own bet when I finally pressed the play button. The Temptations—not Elvis Presley—belted out "Ain't Too Proud to Beg."

While Martha's bedroom was no longer what it had been when it was Ray's, some things remained the same. Some things screamed out to her brother, in the words of The Temptations: "I refuse to let you go."

The bunk beds were long gone, and in their place sat a computer desk. But each night Martha crawled under Ray's heavy denim quilt in his original bed with the antique iron headboard.

A single-wrapped Oreo cookie has remained in a heart-shaped porcelain box on a shelf in her closet. It was the dessert item from the kid's meal Ray had ordered at Famous Dave's the night he died. He had asked that I put it in my purse to bring home for his sister.

An old-fashioned school desk—the kind with a hole for an ink well—houses Martha's art supplies in its side drawer. The top of the desk has been scribbled on over the years. I asked Martha once if I could refinish the wood. "No! I like it the way it is," she snapped. "Ray's name is scratched in it, so don't do anything to the desk."

The growth chart in her bedroom closet is still there. Ray's ends abruptly—the last measurement of his twelve years is a reminder of an unfinished life. Martha's growth chart has surpassed Ray's—a sign of a life that continues to flourish.

Pieces of her brother have remained and have provided guidance for Martha in unexpected ways. She has held Ray close as she bravely makes her own way. That same bravery would become a vital necessity as Martha's strength would be repeatedly tested in the years ahead.

The Chemo Circle

In 1999, my mom was diagnosed with Stage 3 colon cancer. Two months prior, Ray had had surgery to have his G-tube placed. So, just as Mom was heading into surgery, her ten-year-old grandson offered up these words of encouragement: "If I can do it, Grandma, then you can do it, too."

Not long before Mom's cancer diagnosis, my father had retired after forty-two years of building more brick and stone structures than he could ever count. I'm sure being a caregiver did not rank high on the list of things he had planned for retirement, but Buzz rose to the occasion. He helped my mother through her surgery and chemo therapy, and we all celebrated when her cancer went into remission.

But then, in 2002, Buzz himself was diagnosed with non-Hodgkin's lymphoma. It had only been a year since we'd lost Ray, and now our grief was compounded by more cancer. My parents had led a pretty healthy lifestyle. They weren't smokers or heavy drinkers. So *both* of them getting cancer seemed unusually cruel.

Buzz received a clean bill of health after he completed chemotherapy. Sadly, that was short-lived. In 2003, Buzz's cancer returned, this time with a vengeance. Our anguish didn't stop there. Within days of learning that Buzz's cancer was back, Mom's oncologist discovered that her cancer had metastasized to her bones. Both of my parents received even more treatment and clung to the hope that they could, perhaps, beat cancer a second time around.

But on July 4, 2004, I found myself at my father's bedside —in the home he had built on Upper Afton Road—and it was there I would watch him die.

In the days leading up to his death, I enjoyed a cup of coffee with my father. Sitting at his kitchen table, I listened intently as he took stock of his life. First he said, "I've got more money than time. Ain't that a shame?" Then he told me that he'd had a good life. That he was lucky to have worked in a profession he loved. He'd had a long, happy marriage, and he had four nice children.

Hoping to hear the sound of the laughter he was known for, I teased Buzz. "Well, three out of four ain't bad."

"No, Darla. You were good too."

"What makes you think I was talking about me?" I smiled.

He smiled back, but I didn't hear that wonderful laugh of his, nor would I ever hear it again.

That morning at the kitchen table, he told me something else—something he had been hanging onto for over two decades. "I could have been just like you," he said. "I could have been the parent of a dead child."

"I know, Dad."

"No, you don't know. I never told you everything about that day at Lake Phalen." His voice cracked. "I thought you were dead when I found you in the water. You weren't breathing."

Why did he think this was news to me? Maybe cancer had gone to his brain.

Buzz continued, "I never told you that you stopped breathing on the way to the hospital. The driver had to pull over and help the medic bring you back to life for a second time that day."

I thought back to that moment in the ambulance when I had had the sensation that I was floating away from my father.

Buzz wiped tears from his eyes and added, "I wish you and Rusty would have had the same outcome with Ray as we did with you."

"Me too, Dad."

Buzz left this world in a most dignified manner. He was coherent right up to his last breath. In his final hours, he spoke privately to my mother, his beloved wife, and then to each of his four children. At the end, still in command, he asked that we gather in his bedroom, where he led us in the Lord's Prayer. Then he asked God not to make him beg. "Just take me home, Lord."

At one point, I took his hand and asked him if he was afraid. He kind of stared at me blankly. "If you are, Dad, remember this: You're going wherever Ray is."

He smiled and said, "Yeah, Ray. I'm going to see Ray."

Days later, at his funeral, I delivered my father's eulogy—telling everyone who was there that day what they had meant to Buzz. And, in the end, I hope I was able to convey to them what that man had meant to me.

Mom would hang on for another five years before she passed away in a nursing home. We helplessly watched the quality of her life slowly diminish as cancer took over her body. But she was still with us when life took yet another unexpected turn for the Garvey family.

~

In 2007, during a breast self-exam, I felt something different in my right breast. Not necessarily a lump, but something seemed a little off. A year prior, a mammogram screening had come back clean, so I wasn't too concerned. It was probably just an area of dense breast tissue, like my doctor had described to me in the past. I shrugged it off for a couple of months before making an appointment for a mammogram. The radiologist said that the x-ray showed a suspicious lump, or mass, or area, or whatever term it was he uttered. It was mostly the descriptor *suspicious* that got my attention. I asked if he thought it was a tumor.

"I've learned not to answer that question," he said. "But whatever it is, you should see a surgeon."

I immediately booked an appointment with a surgeon, who performed a fine-needle biopsy in her downtown St. Paul clinic. She said the fluid came out easily, which was a good sign. "I think I hit something solid, though," she said. "It's probably just a fluid cyst, but I won't know until I get the lab results back."

Next she took the specimen of fluid that she had just extracted from my breast and set the container down on the counter. I hadn't even moved off the exam table yet when she began presenting me with a series of *ifs*. "*If* this sample comes back positive, you're going to need a lumpectomy. And *if* it is cancer, you're going to want to do everything. After all, you're young," she told me. "You have a life ahead of you."

Then at some point her *ifs* turned into *whens*. "*When* you come back in, we might have to talk about treatment options. *When* you have a lumpectomy, and there's cancer, you will need radiation and possibly chemo. *When* you have chemo, you can expect ..."

I stopped her mid-sentence. "Why did you just take my *if* away?"

"Excuse me?"

"My biopsy specimen hasn't even left this room. It's still sitting over there on the counter —" I pointed. "—and already you took my *if* away."

"I don't understand."

"You started out by saying *if* I have cancer. Then you launched into treatment options as if I *do* have cancer. You took my hope away before I even changed out of this gown."

"I'm sorry. I didn't mean to scare you. I was just trying to prepare you in case the results come back positive."

"You don't understand. I *can't* have breast cancer. My twelve-year-old son died. My daughter has cystic fibrosis. My father died of non-Hodgkin's lymphoma, and my mom's colon cancer has returned." I burst into tears.

"I didn't know. I'm so sorry. I hope I have good news for you when I get the lab results."

"That should have been the *only* thing you said to me."

I left the surgeon's office, reasoning that breast cancer wasn't remotely possible. After all, I had already used up a lifetime supply of horseshit luck.

A few days later, my surgeon called. "Good news, Darla. We didn't find any cancer cells. But you're going to need surgery. You never want to leave a lump in your breast."

Let's get this thing out and move on, I thought, and immediately scheduled surgery with her. Still insistent that it was just a fluid cyst, I refused to call it a lumpectomy. But that's what it was. After surgery, I waited several days for my surgeon to call with results.

I had only taught school for one more year after Ray passed away. My principal had been supportive and encouraged me to continue teaching, even when I told her I didn't think I was ready. She reminded me that the staff at Carver Elementary were my family and they would be there to support me, so I returned to the classroom. But at the end of that school year, I was laid off due to district-wide budget cuts. The lay-off was a blessing in one regard. Rather than suck it up for twenty-seven students, I could reserve my strength for Martha when she came home from school. But with all that time alone during the day, I spiraled deeper into the dark side of grief for a number of years.

However, just a month before my lumpectomy I had started a part-time clerical job at an office in Minneapolis. It wasn't exactly the most fulfilling job, but I didn't feel mentally strong enough to work with students yet.

It was there, in my new office, where I received the call from my surgeon. And in four simple words she took my *if* away. "You have breast cancer."

I grabbed a notepad and a pen from my desk and ran out into the hallway with my cell phone. I dropped to the floor and choked back tears while my surgeon spoke in that matter-of-fact manner that surgeons are known for. "The tumor was bigger than I thought," she said. "I couldn't get it all. But the margins from what I did remove were not clean. You have lobular carcinoma. It's a rare form of breast cancer. You're going to need more surgery."

I scribbled on my notepad: *rare, lobular, surgery.*

Then she casually told me, "I'm going on vacation next week. I can squeeze you in on Thursday before I leave town."

It was Tuesday. I couldn't even wrap my head around the fact that I had cancer, much less think about surgery in two days. "So you're saying I just need to have the rest of the lump removed and I'll be okay?"

"Darla, it's not that simple. You had a large tumor hiding in your lobes," she warned. "I could take another swipe at it, but if I don't get a clean margin, I'd have to go back in again. That would leave you pretty deformed. You'd be better off having a mastectomy and clear away all of the breast tissue at once," she said.

A disturbing image flashed through my mind: her slicing up my breast tissue the way a fisherman would fillet a walleye. Breaking through my nightmarish thoughts, I heard her say, "I know an excellent plastic surgeon. He does beautiful breast reconstructive work."

"Am I in trouble here? Can't I take some time to think about this?"

"I would not wait weeks if I were you. Can I put you down for Thursday?"

"No, I'm not scheduling anything right now." At that time, I didn't know much about breast cancer, but I knew plenty about overbearing surgeons who insist on performing a mastectomy—or an irreversible Nissen—without educating or guiding the patient. In that moment, two things became crystal clear. One, I needed to find an oncologist who specialized in breast cancer, and two, I would never again lay eyes on that surgeon.

I walked back into my office to find my supervisor. She took one look at me and asked if I was okay. "No," I told her. "I just found out I have breast cancer. I need to go home."

"I'm so sorry, Darla. Are you sure you're okay to drive?"

"Driving will be the easy part. I have cancer."

On my drive home that day, every random thought running through my head was interrupted by that one absurd phrase: *I have cancer. I have cancer. I have fucking cancer. What will this do to Martha? What if I'm not here to watch her grow up? What if I die, you know, from cancer? Maybe I should call my friends and tell them. I have cancer. I had better teach Martha how to cook because, well, I have cancer. And what will this do to Rusty? Will he help Martha pick out a prom dress, or talk to her about boys? He might have to because I have cancer. I have fucking, fucking cancer.*

Still on the late shift, Rusty was sleeping when I got home. I took a seat at the edge of our bed and nudged him awake. "What are you doing home?" he asked.

"Rusty. The surgeon called. It's not good. I have cancer." I burst into tears.

He hugged me tight for a long time before he offered these words. "I think cancer is a mind game, Darla. You better get your head right."

When we told Martha about my diagnosis, she set the tone straight out of the gate. She patted me on the back and without shedding a tear, she told me, "You'll be okay, Mom. They'll remove the tumor and you won't have cancer anymore." It was a message of resilience and an amazing show of strength from my then fourteen-year-old daughter. Not only was she living with CF, but a year earlier she had been diagnosed with diabetes and was now insulin-dependent. I was absolutely terrified of cancer, but I already knew my strength to fight it would inevitably come from Martha.

Searching for answers, I saw three different oncologists. I was told I had Stage 2 lobular carcinoma, and all three oncologists described my cancer in the same way: "It's a sneaky type of breast cancer. It's hard to detect, and it likes to come back on the other side." They were all of the same opinion that I needed to be aggressive in my treatment. Their recommendations were that I have a bi-lateral mastectomy, followed by chemo and radiation therapy. The trifecta. I went back and forth between believing this treatment plan was the only thing that would save my life and believing that none of it was necessary. Either way—just like my parents—cancer might get me in the end.

Ultimately, I chose to receive my care from a team of doctors at the Mayo Clinic in Rochester, Minnesota. After much discussion about my prognosis, I reluctantly agreed to the trifecta plan. But the realization that this meant losing a big part of my femininity would become one of the most intimate and emotional moments in my life. I would have avoided a bi-lateral mastectomy like the plague, but I was only given an 85% chance of surviving past the five-year mark with surgery, chemo and then radiation. Without the trifecta, my chances of survival would be significantly less. I wanted as many years as possible to watch my daughter grow up—so I chose the plan with the best survival rate over my vanity.

Rusty didn't initially agree with my decision. He thought a *double* mastectomy was extreme considering only *one* breast had a confirmed diagnosis of cancer. "You should not start removing body parts out of fear," he reasoned.

"But that's just it, Rusty. Cancer *equals* fear. In fact, that's all cancer really is. Fear." Then I reminded him that my type of cancer likes to come back on the other side. "I am not coming back to the Mayo in a couple of years to do this all over again," I argued. "I am not dying over a boob."

I may have sounded sure of myself in that moment, but here's the thing about cancer—surviving it is a total crapshoot. No matter the course of treatment, it can return. And if it does, it's not good. My oncologist had already informed me of that fact. "If the cancer comes back," she told me, "we treat it. But the treatment almost always fails."

I had made up my mind that if my cancer were to metastasize, I would refuse further treatment. I had already seen the hope—and the taking away of hope—that a second round of cancer treatment had done to my parents.

On the day of my dreaded surgery, Rusty and I sat in a small room at the hospital, waiting for someone to take me into the operating room. Occasionally we broke through our nervous silence with unexpected laughter. Suddenly a woman wheeled a bed just outside the doorway and said, "We're ready for you now."

Her voice was so cold and so void of emotion that I immediately thought of the film *Dead Man Walking*. Rusty must have had the same thought—that I was being led to my execution. "I'm sorry, Darla," he half-smiled. "Looks like the governor didn't call."

After surgery, we were told the cancer had not spread to my lymph nodes, but they had discovered ductile carcinoma cells in *both* breasts. With that revelation, I stopped questioning my cancer treatment decisions, including my decision to opt out of radiation therapy. The size of my tumor was just a hair smaller than the cut-off guidelines for radiation. I took that *hair* and ran with it, deciding I didn't want radiation anywhere near my heart and lungs. I also decided I wanted my curves back and elected to have reconstructive breast surgery with implants —reclaiming my femininity.

Once I had healed from my surgeries, I began chemo-therapy. And I hated every second of it. Every time I started to feel better, I had to go back in for another round. It was like a scheduled appointment to get sick. I felt the side effects of chemo from head to toe. No one had told me that losing my hair would be painful. True, it was emotional, but I mean physically painful. When chemo *forced* the hair out of my head, it left my scalp raw and tender. Chemo drugs made my mouth taste like metal, as if I were sucking on a nickel. My skin be-came dry and itchy. I walked with a slight wobble, as each treat-ment weakened my legs. I developed neuropathy—a stabbing, prickly pain in my hands and feet. And chemo zapped my energy.

So, with all the drug side effects, chemo appointments were met with dread. But the first round of chemo was met with fear. Fear of the unknown. To complicate matters, Rusty was away in Florida at a national K9 trial. When he offered to skip the trial and stay back with me, I pretended it didn't matter if he left town. "If chemo makes me sick, I'm sure I can manage vomiting without you holding back my hair. Besides," I re-minded him, "Martha will be here with me."

On my first day of chemo, I took a seat with a group of cancer patients. We sat in a large circle, our recliner chairs facing one another, each of us tethered to an IV pole. Eye contact seemed to be discouraged, yet I studied each and every one of them, regardless. Most of the patients were women. Many of them were bald, an indication of how far along they were in their treatment. Soon enough, I would be just like them. Completely bald.

Every patient appeared to be much older than me, which sort of pissed me off. At forty-seven, I didn't belong there. And yet, maybe it was exactly where I belonged. That day in the chemo circle, while the cancer-killing poison dripped into my veins, I asked myself, *Who am I to squander the life I was given, no matter the challenges? Who am I to not fully appreciate the same world my son so whole-heartedly embraced—the same world my teenage daughter is courageously navigating?*

I sat there thinking back to the one and only time I had sought out counseling from our minister. I took a seat in his office at King of Kings Lutheran Church and asked him to explain to me why a child dies. To my surprise, he admitted, "I don't know."

I stared at him blankly and thought, *Do you mean to tell me this guy of all people doesn't have any biblical wisdom to bestow upon me? Hell, everyone else seems to.*

"I don't know why a twelve-year-old boy dies," he continued on. "I don't know why an entire school bus full of children die in a crash, any more than I understand why an eighty-year-old woman dies. What I do know is this: whether you live to be twelve or eighty, your time here on earth is but a small grain of sand compared to an eternity in paradise." Then he did something I didn't expect. He shifted responsibility onto me and not God. "Darla, how are *you* going to spend your limited time here?"

"I don't know." I stood, then started for the door.

He stopped me. "I know you're in pain, Darla. But whether you like it or not, you're still here. How are *you* going to live your life?"

On that day, I did not have an answer to his question, but I'm pretty sure fighting breast cancer was not on my list. Yet there I was, sitting in the damned chemo circle, thinking the long, miserable life I had been so certain was mine might actually be a short life. After all, that 85% chance of survival I had been given was only to live beyond the five-year mark. Funny how that works. When the clock starts ticking down, you realize you want more time.

While my breast cancer diagnosis was absolutely devastating, in truth, it was not entirely surprising. A couple of years out from losing Ray, I remember telling Rusty, "I think this is the kind of thing that makes people sick."

"What are you talking about?"

"Grief. I don't think the body can handle it. There's nowhere to put it, or release it." I repeated, "I'm pretty sure you can get sick from this. Grief festers, and eventually it attacks the body."

In doubt, Rusty shook his head.

"Think about it, Rusty. People die of heart attacks from a stressful job. But grief is bigger than a lousy job. I think it can take you down … mentally … and physically."

Sadly, my theory would prove to be all too accurate. After Ray passed away, there were still moments of joy in my life, especially when I was with Martha. Yet too often I found myself alone, swimming in the murkiest depths of grief and allowing it to fester. I had let my broken heart become all that I was. And then—I got sick.

A couple of years after my recovery, Rusty, too, got sick. He was diagnosed with prostate cancer. My husband was presented with a number of treatment options, each one more dreadful than the other. He opted to have surgery to remove his prostate, which promised him the best outcome.

Maybe it was genetic, perhaps it was environmental, or it might have been just more horseshit luck, but I think it's just as likely that grief played a role in stirring up both my and Rusty's cancer cells. It could even have played a role in my parents' cancers.

So, if there's any advice I can give a parent who has lost a child, it is this: Grieve like hell. It's necessary. But do not get stuck in the depths of it for too long, because it can fester. It can take you down. Find something meaningful to do. Search for peace wherever you can, and fight to live the life you were given—no matter its challenges.

I know I'm not the only mom who has suffered the loss of a child. Nor am I the only woman to hear the earth-shattering words "You have breast cancer." So I am not unique. Millions of courageous women have been dealt the same hand that I was dealt. It was never even my intention to share my cancer story. It was a personal experience that I desperately wanted to keep private. But I think it's worth noting that sometimes the challenges we face, even the ones that drop us to our knees, turn out to be the unexpected things we need to change our perspective on life. I am fortunate that I was able to connect the dots during my cancer treatment and begin to live my life more fully—before it was too late.

"Although the world is full of suffering, it is also full of the overcoming of it."

~ Helen Keller

Mount Heavenly

Every winter my parents took us out west to ski in the Rocky Mountains. Earning a modest living, I imagine Buzz squirreled away a little money all year long to save up for those ski trips, which were responsible for some of my best childhood memories. I needed to see the mountains again, this time with Rusty and Martha. This time Mount Heavenly in the Sierra Nevada mountain range.

At nearly every turn while in Lake Tahoe, I seemed to find signs that spoke to me. Just the name "Mount Heavenly" alone symbolized a peaceful place to embrace after much turbulence in our lives.

We stayed on the north side of Lake Tahoe at the Cal-Neva Hotel and Casino, a historic lodge once owned by Frank Sinatra. It is appropriately named as it spans two state lines—California and Nevada. A bold stripe is painted on the floor at the center of the hotel lounge. Cal-Neva guests can straddle the state borderline and literally stand in two places at one time. That simple act reminded me of earlier days when I had straddled a borderline of my own—a twisted line that separated a place I wanted to leave and the exact same place I needed to stay. It took a long time to accept that it was okay to move forward with my daughter and, at the same time, honor the past with my son.

After months of cancer treatment, I felt relatively healthy. And after a long hospital stay for a lung infection, Martha's breathing had significantly improved. While Rusty spent our first vacation day in the Cal-Neva casino, Martha and I skied at Heavenly Resort. Midday we took a lunch break in the chalet, where I spotted another one of those *signs*. A Mark Twain quote stenciled on the wall, a quote that might just as well have been written for Martha. "To obtain the air angels breathe, you must go to Tahoe."

It took the better part of the day before Martha was ready to take on more challenging ski runs from the top of Mount Heavenly. She was new to snowboarding that year, so we spent the morning on the easier green runs on the lower half of the mountain. I suggested she take a snowboard lesson, but she refused, insisting that she could figure it out on her own. Soon enough she did, and we found ourselves at the top of Mount Heavenly at an elevation of ten thousand feet. Boarding the plane in Minneapolis, just five weeks after my last round of chemo, I had questioned my stamina. But reaching the mountain's ridge with my daughter that day, I had never felt stronger.

Scooting off the chairlift, we descended down the platform. Slipping my hands through the straps on my ski poles, I shoved off. Martha was at my side.

"Which is the easiest way down, Mom?"

Stunned by the view, I was unable to answer. The sapphire-blue waters of Lake Tahoe glistened from one side of the mountain. On the other side, golden yellow and brown hues of dry earth formed a boundary between desert and mountain. All the while, we stood amongst snow-capped pines. Twirling around full circle on my skis, I took in this amazing wonderland.

"Mom, are you ready?"

"Hang on a second. I can't believe how gorgeous this is. Look at the lake—the desert. I've never seen anything like it."

"Oh my God. Are you going to cry?"

"Well … I didn't know if we would see the mountains this year."

Unwilling to go there with me, Martha rolled her eyes. "The next thing you know, you're going to try and tell me you're my hero." With one boot strapped into her bindings, she pushed off with her free foot, gaining speed on her snowboard.

Skiing up behind her, I shouted, "Not every woman would tie a bandana over her wig and just go for it. Nothing stops me. I *am* your hero!" I teased.

"Not if you have to tell me you are."

She had a point.

The muscles in my legs burned, but in a good way, as I sucked in the mountain air. I was not in top shape by any sense of the word, but I didn't care. I convinced myself that this old gal could still fly. I even managed to tackle a few moguls along the way.

I videotaped Martha snowboarding that perfect spring day in the mountains—her smile and thumbs-up sign an image to cherish. At one point I asked that she take the camera down a ways and videotape me. She looked at me in total disgust. "Are you kidding me? What adult asks a kid to videotape them?"

"Do you think only children are film worthy?" I shoved the backpack that held the video camera into her arms and added, "When I'm older, I might want to see that I used to be a decent skier." But, truth be told, I asked Martha to film me because a recurrence of cancer lurked in the back of my mind. I wanted her to remember her mom on one of our happiest days together—just in case.

Martha took the camera and rode down the hill a ways. Propping herself up against a tree, she got the camera ready, then gave me a hand signal to begin skiing.

Weeks after returning home, I finally watched the footage that Martha had shot. The sky was clear blue, and I was only wearing a light jacket and wind pants, a reminder of how lucky we were to experience spring skiing at its best. Snow sprayed up and glistened in the sun with each turn I carved. Even in that damn wig, in that moment I did not look like a cancer patient, but rather a healthy, happy skier—a woman who had finally come to the realization that the sun also rises for her.

I laughed at my daughter's commentary as she filmed her mom coming down the slope. "It's a nice, sunny spring day. We're in Lake Tahoe on Mount Heavenly." Then in the most sarcastic, drawn-out voice ever, she added, "And … here comes … my hero."

The final few seconds of footage were a close-up of me laughing into the camera, stating, "I *am* your hero!"

Ejecting the tape, I thought about the chairlift ride to the top of Mount Heavenly that day, when Martha had questioned my strength. "You okay, Mom?"

"I feel fine. But you have to promise me something."

"What's that?"

"If my wig shifts or starts to blow off when I ski, promise you'll tell me."

"Yeah … I probably won't." She chuckled, with a devious twinkle in her eye.

"I figured as much, you little jerk." This was the same girl who had once planted dog food in my wig while I slept on the couch after a chemo treatment. I awoke to our little beagle jumping on my head to get at the food—and Martha cracking up as she watched from across the room.

Through the years, Martha's humor is a constant, providing levity when we least expect it. It certainly showed up after Rusty and I had battled cancer. One day at the dinner table, out of the blue, Martha asked, "So … how many body parts are you two missing now? Just need to know where to draw the line on what I can say."

Martha's *line* has always been skewed, but in the best way possible, and there is nothing more profound than the love we have for our strong, courageous, smart-ass daughter.

Steamboat Springs

During Martha's junior year of high school, we took a ski trip to Steamboat Springs, Colorado. On a gondola ride up the mountain, Martha asked a couple of young guys riding with us if there was a college nearby. It turned out they were both college students attending Colorado Mountain College (CMC) in Steamboat Springs. I chuckled to myself, thinking Colorado Mountain College sounded like a made-up name for a school. But the guys on the gondola raved about CMC and encouraged Martha to check it out.

We scheduled a campus tour and discovered that CMC was a beautiful campus nestled up in the hills overlooking the Yampa River, Howelsen Hill Ski Jump, and the quaint little town of Steamboat. The campus was small and easy to navigate, and the dorm rooms were exceptionally clean with amazing mountain views. Even though Steamboat Springs was halfway across the country, I thought, just maybe, it might be a wonderful opportunity for Martha.

At that time the only two campuses Martha had visited were polar opposites: a conservative Christian college in Minnesota and a school with a laid-back hippie feel in Colorado.

I remembered that as soon as we got in the car after the Christian college tour, Martha had said, "I need a beer and a cigarette." I busted out laughing. Then she added, "Well, this secluded campus is on an island of its own—away from normal people. It's the kind of place that would make me rebel."

On our drive home, however, she did ask one serious question. "Are you religious, Mom?"

"If being religious means going to church, then no, I'm not religious. Maybe spiritual. Or just lazy." I laughed. "I guess I don't believe in organized religion, but I believe there's something spiritual about life. Does that make any sense to you?"

"Yeah, that makes sense."

"Listen, if you feel the need to be close to God," I assured her, "I believe you can find that anywhere. You can find the peace you're looking for by listening to music, looking at the stars, or ... hiking in the mountains in Colorado."

~

In August of 2012, we loaded up our truck and made the trek out to Steamboat Springs to move Martha into Hill Residence Hall at Colorado Mountain College on Bob Adams Drive. My cousin, Kim Bodin, and her husband Rick live in Steamboat Springs, but just during the ski season. While Martha didn't know a single soul in town, there was some comfort in knowing that Kim and Rick would be in Steamboat Springs during her second semester of college.

We stayed at Kim and Rick's condo for a few days leading up to new student orientation. This gave Martha time to adjust to the idea that she was about to embark on the biggest adventure of her life. Other than shopping for dorm room accessories and unpacking boxes, the three of us kicked around town like we were on vacation, pretending the impending goodbye wasn't just days away. Martha hung close to us and skipped most of the campus social activities, claiming she had all year to get to know people, but she wouldn't see us for a long time. She also lost her appetite, something unheard of for her.

Soon enough, new student orientation was in full swing. While Martha was discovering the ins and outs at CMC, Rusty and I attended a parent meeting where we learned what to expect each month during the school year. August was homesick month. In September, friendships would be made and students would ease into the rigors of college. Many would also ease into the rigors of partying. The dean assured parents that CMC had a strict no-tolerance policy when it came to drugs and alcohol. He wasn't joking. Martha told us, in the months ahead, how the student population was shrinking—kids expelled for getting caught with alcohol and weed on campus.

October was the month students experienced an increase in anxiety—even depression—over grades and exams and God knows what else. November, we were warned, was the month when CMC saw an uptick of unwanted sexual advances on campus. I leaned into Rusty, sitting next to me, and whispered, "Make note of that. November is sexual assault month."

That year, CMC's student population had an 80:20 boy-to-girl ratio, and that made me nervous. Especially since Martha had requested a single dorm room. She wanted privacy to do her treatments and the extra space to store her medical equipment. Truth be told, Martha didn't want to be known as the girl with cystic fibrosis, at least not straight out of the gate.

As we organized Martha's dorm room, it began to take on some personality, and a little enthusiasm seeped in through her obvious nervousness. Martha hung a framed collage of her friends back home and a picture of Ray. It was the carpet head photo in a sunflower-shaped frame. On her window sill she placed a wonderful picture of her Grandpa Buzz, a shot of him ski jumping in mid-air. Tina and Morgan, Martha's closest college friends, still laugh at all the times the wind blew through her dorm window and Buzz's picture fell off the ledge. Inevitably, someone would yell, "Oh, no. There goes your grandpa again."

The photos were a homey touch, but also a reminder of how much Martha had lost before she even got to college. She was just ten years old when Buzz passed away. That same year, Boone died—the only dog Martha had had since she was born. Then, at fifteen, she lost her grandma. So Martha has always looked a little lonesome to me. We wished so badly that she had more than just *us*. That her brother and grandparents could see her off to college, too.

On our final day in Colorado, we had our last meal together at Sweet Peas Café on the Yampa River. Rusty said his goodbyes outside of the café. He hugged his daughter, told her he'd miss her, and assured her that she would do fine in college. Then we drove up the steep hill on 12th Street to Bob Adams Drive. I walked Martha to her dorm room to have a final moment with her while Rusty waited in the truck. We sat across from one another on twin beds. I wanted to impart words of wisdom that she would always remember, a thoughtful, eloquent message I envisioned she'd proudly repeat to her friends over the years. *My mom gave me the best advice when I went off to college. She told me ...*

Instead, I cried. I just sat across from my daughter, bawling, unable to muster up a single word for the longest time. Martha cried as well, and we both admitted we felt sick to our stomachs. Eventually, I found the words to tell her something halfway constructive. That I had done everything I could for her, but now it was time for her to take care of herself. I made her promise that she would do her best. "Don't skip your treatments. Have fun, but pace yourself. Rest and eat well. Stay safe. Make friends. More specifically, find smart, caring friends —not idiots. Keep your door locked ... especially in November. Try your best in school. Call us if you need anything."

She promised she would do all of the above; then I told her I loved her and hugged her goodbye. I cried all the way to the truck, wanting nothing more than to turn around and spend just a few more minutes with my daughter, but I thought that would make it harder on both of us. When I hopped in the truck, I noticed Rusty had tears streaming down his face, but he said he was just sweating. "From your eyes?" I asked. As we pulled out of the school parking lot, I asked Rusty if we were doing the right thing—leaving Martha in a different state. Saying goodbye had been worse than I had imagined.

"She'll be fine. If she decides she can't make it on her own, she can come home. It's not a prison sentence." He added, "Remember, she wanted this."

Rusty was right. Martha wanted this. During her senior year of high school, she had gotten really sick. After fighting an infection with oral antibiotics at home and not improving, she'd called her CF doctor and said she needed to be admitted. A self-scheduled hospitalization.

The night before she went into the hospital, she had mustered up the strength to finish an English paper during a vest treatment. I emailed her teachers asking that they gather up her assignments for me to pick up—an all-too-familiar routine. Then I asked Martha what she wanted me to pack in her bag. Feeling like crap and crabby as hell, she said, "I don't care, Mom. Just throw in the usual." I hated that she even had *the usual* hospital bag.

In that moment, I could not help but question Martha's decision to attend Colorado Mountain College. How could we let her go? I'd spent eighteen years being her mom, her chef, her tutor, her respiratory therapist. I had taken her to all of her doctor appointments, refilled her prescriptions, and tried to make her daily life as easy as I could. The very idea of giving up control in a few short months was killing me.

"Martha, can I talk to you?"

"What?" she snapped at yet another interruption to her homework.

"Look at everything that's going on right now."

She glanced away from the computer just long enough to throw a dagger.

"Seriously, look around. You're trying to finish up an assignment in the final hour. I'm packing and emailing your teachers to make sure you don't fall through the cracks."

"I know. I know. What's your point?"

"My point is, do you think you can do everything on your own this fall? If you get sick in college, will you be able to manage without me and your dad?"

She stopped typing and said, "I know I don't have an easy future, but I will have CF and diabetes whether I'm in Minnesota or Colorado. If I get sick out there, I'll seek medical attention." Then she added, "Mom, you have to let me go and at least try. You can't take care of me forever."

Later that night, I relayed her words to Rusty. He got choked up and said, "Then we have to let her go. If she fails, she fails on her own terms, not because we didn't give her the chance to discover what she's made of."

Rusty and I talked about that conversation on our drive back to Minnesota, trying to convince ourselves that we were supporting Martha and everything was going to be okay. But then my phone rang. It was Martha, and she was crying.

"What's wrong?"

"I think I made a mistake, Mom. I don't think I belong here. Where are you?"

"We're in Nebraska." Maybe she thought we'd turn around and rescue her if we were closer. "Tell me what's going on."

"Everyone's at some party up in the mountains. They're probably all getting high. I'm the only one in the dorm who didn't go. I don't think these are my people, Mom."

"Listen, I'm sure you're not the only one who stayed back."

"Yes I am."

"You don't know that. When we hang up, promise me something."

"What?"

"Promise that you'll leave your room and go to the student center. Find the kids who didn't go to the Rocky Mountain high party and talk to them. They'll be your people. You aren't going to make any friends if you stay in your room."

Still crying, she repeated, "I think I made a mistake. I don't want to be here."

I handed the phone to Rusty, too upset to continue the conversation. I dug in my purse for a tissue while he talked to Martha.

After listening to her for a minute, he said, "You're going to be fine. It's your first day. Trust me. Every kid there is feeling the same way as you are right now."

There was a pause, then he said, "No, we're not turning around."

My stomach did a flip, picturing Martha alone in her room, pleading for us to come back for her.

"Winter break will be here before you know it," Rusty said. "We'll fly you home then, and if you decide you don't want to go back, you don't have to. But please, just give this a chance."

He handed the phone back to me. I told Martha that she was stronger than she knew and once she made friends, she wouldn't feel the way she was feeling.

We called or texted each other every day, and by the end of the week, she sounded happy, like herself. She told me all about her classes, her instructors, and her new friends—Maddie, Morgan, Tina, Colin, and Ivan.

During Thanksgiving break, I decided to fly out to see Martha. We drove down to Denver and took in a Bruce Springsteen concert as well. By the end of my visit, Martha was coughing more than usual and had a fever. I wondered if she should come home with me, but she insisted she'd be fine and would be home at Christmastime. But she wasn't fine. She came home two weeks before winter break, completing her final projects electronically from her hospital bed. She recovered and returned to CMC after Christmas and finished out the year strong.

After her freshman year, Martha switched her major from mass media and marketing to recreation, park & leisure services. CMC doesn't offer that field of study, so she made the difficult decision to transfer to Minnesota State University in Mankato. Her Colorado outdoor adventures were definitely responsible for this new direction. Not only for the sheer enjoyment she got from being outdoors, but she often stated that she felt closest to her brother when she was surrounded by nature. I guess life was spiritual for her, too.

After one year at Mankato State, Martha moved back to Steamboat Springs to complete a summer internship program at BookTrails. The owners of Off the Beaten Path bookstore had founded the camp, which combines reading with outdoor adventures for school-age children. Martha was hired as a teacher for their summer camp, called Reading on the Ranches. Often times she worked out of a beautifully renovated barn on Fletcher's Ranch. Periodically, she sent pictures of her and her campers reading in the barn, kayaking down the Colorado River, or hiking at Hahn's Peak. Her most common message was that she was living her dream—which was to never work in an office cubicle.

Kim and Rick, who basically became a second set of parents to Martha, let her live at their condo that summer. She once asked, "Is it bad that that was the best summer I ever had ... and I lived *alone*?"

Moving a thousand miles away from home was a brave decision for an eighteen-year-old girl living with cystic fibrosis and CF-related diabetes, but Martha didn't become brave over-night. Her independence might have been fostered by her trek out to Colorado, but she had been slowly carving a strong path to independence throughout her adolescence.

A Ray of Hope for Martha

Janeane Garofalo, one of my favorite comedians, once said, "Taking into account the public's regrettable lack of taste, it is incumbent upon you not to fit in." I have tried to instill that same philosophy in my daughter, but I am not nearly as eloquent as Garofalo.

Our hope was that Martha would stay true to herself when she entered middle school, and then high school—but teenage angst is real. They are judged for what they wear, looked up to if they can play it cool, looked down upon if they can't mask their inner nerd, and are even critiqued on the model of their cell phone.

One day, in middle school, Martha came home complaining about some of her classmates. "How did kids get so mean over the summer?" she wanted to know. "Last year, the exact same kids were nice." I reminded her of what our neighbor Kay McDonough once told us. When her children complained about what someone else said or did, she warned them, "Don't let the bastards get you down."

It didn't hurt that Martha was a tomboy and an athlete with a mind of her own. Her personality and interests did not depend on hair and make-up. She hadn't needed a whole lot of coaching from her parents, but at some point, I felt compelled to deliver a remarkably detailed sex education lesson, which went something like this: "Martha, let me tell you a little something about boys. Boys who like girls, really like girls. I mean, they really, *really* like girls. So they don't need to see your bra straps or your underwear peeking out above low-cut jeans because, trust me, they already like girls ... even in a sweatshirt."

Years later, she told me she remembered our "little talk" and said I could just as well have shortened it to, "Boys are horny. Don't egg them on."

Thankfully, Martha did not easily succumb to peer pressure. She never tried to be someone she was not. But, like any young teen, she searched for belonging. Even though Rusty and I had stepped away from organized religion, Martha gravitated toward youth group activities at church. I asked her about it once. She said, "With all the crap going on at school, I just wanted to be around nice people."

As parents, we never get a full picture of what our kids go through each day at school. Many teenagers, like Martha, keep their experiences to themselves. It would be years before we learned that she was teased for having a low voice. So she avoided talking to certain people. She was teased for being Justin Rick's girlfriend, so, she stopped sitting next to him on the school bus. Worst of all, she became known as the sister of that dead boy. She even got teased when cystic fibrosis kept her out sick from school for long stretches of time. Insensitive teens would blurt out, "Oh, you're back. We thought maybe you died, too."

Luckily, Martha surrounded herself with wonderful friends who more than made up for those kids who were less than wonderful. But missing out on school, plus social events with her friends, and feeling misunderstood about her illness, weighed heavily on her. I often wondered how different life might have been for Martha if Ray had been there to pave the way. That boy didn't take any crap from anybody, and he was super protective of Martha. He got in a few physical altercations when kids were rough on her, playing in the neighborhood. I'm sure he would have taken care of any issues she might have had in school—and he would have championed his sister when she got sick.

From sixth grade to the writing of this book, Martha Garvey has been hospitalized for lung infections annually, sometimes twice in one year. Her first couple of hospitalization stays were anywhere from three to five weeks long, with a course of IV antibiotics administered through a PICC line. But as she got older, the hospitalizations grew shorter, her IV care more often administered at home. We wanted to keep Martha out of germ-infested hospitals, so we learned to do her IV treatments. But there is a really good reason why I'm not a nurse. Just creating a sterile field to change her dressing, or flush out the IV line, made me nervous. I can't count how many times I heard Martha say, "Oh my God, Mom. You're the worst nurse ever." It was hard to argue with her while fumbling around with a syringe, two fingers stuck in one hole of a surgical glove. So, as it turned out, the most knowledgeable health care professional has been Martha herself. She paid close attention to everything her doctors, nurses, and parents did, all too often correcting their decisions.

At thirteen, Martha was diagnosed with diabetes. Not Type 1 or Type 2 diabetes, but something called CF Related Diabetes, or CFRD—adding yet another acronym to her list of illnesses: CF, ASD (atrial septal defect), and now CFRD. A significant number of the cystic fibrosis population end up with CFRD, as thick, sticky mucus creates scarring and eventually blocks the pancreas from releasing insulin.

Martha took charge of her health at an early age. She was only in middle school and about to be admitted to the hospital for the third time in her life. That was when Martha let her doctor know who was really calling the shots. It was a Friday morning. She was in his office, being seen for a pulmonary acerbation. Dr. Warren Regelmann told her that yet another hospital stay for IV antibiotics was necessary. When Martha asked when she had to be admitted, Dr. Regelmann looked confused by the question, clarifying that he was getting a bed ready for her now. Martha looked him straight in the eye and said, "I'm the captain of my hockey team. We have an out-of-town tournament this weekend. My team needs me, so … I'll see you Monday."

Remarkably, Martha has shown a great deal of empathy for others in spite of her own health issues. When she was fifteen, she was hospitalized just before the holidays. She talked about how lucky she was to get discharged before Christmas. Then it dawned on her that other children weren't as lucky and they had to spend that Christmas in the hospital. She vowed to do something special for the young patients the following Christmas. Even though she had to do another stint in the hospital just before the holidays, she made good on her promise. She got her driver's license that year and applied for a job at a concession stand in a hockey arena—still sporting a PICC line during the interview. She got hired and then went shopping with her first paycheck. Rather than splurge on herself, she came home with several shopping bags full of stuffed animals, fuzzy socks, cozy fleece blankets, and Christmas candy. She put together numerous gift bags, telling us she was going to do a Christmas gift drop-off at the U of M Medical Center—to the children's floor, where she herself had been hospitalized just a few weeks prior.

Rusty worked that Christmas Eve, but I accompanied Martha to the hospital. The look of joy on all of the young patients' faces, as well as their parents', was heartwarming. In fact, it was the most meaningful Christmas we'd had in a long time—and has since become a family tradition. It's grown into a huge gift drive, as Martha has asked friends and family to donate items. This past year she hosted a Christmas party and collected over 250 gifts, spreading holiday cheer to *four* hospitals in the Twin Cities.

Our hope was that we wouldn't mess things up too terribly for Martha. That we'd give her a happy childhood in spite of our loss. That she would develop into a strong, independent woman who would learn to manage her life even with all of its challenges. She hasn't let us down. More importantly, she hasn't let herself down. She appreciates life when she feels well, and fights like hell when she doesn't. Her humor certainly plays a role in how she deals with her illness. It's quite remarkable, actually. When friends visit her in the hospital, they always enter the room with a sad look on their faces, seeing their pal in a hospital bed, tethered to an IV pole. They come to cheer her up, but inevitably, they're the ones who end up laughing. She has a knack for that—turning a bad situation into a humorous one. So I guess it shouldn't have surprised us when she started doing stand-up comedy. Making her friends and family laugh is one thing. Entertaining strangers on stage is quite another. But one day she called and said, "Hey Mom, I did stand-up last night."

"Stand-up what?" I asked. My first thought was stand-up paddle boarding.

"I performed at an open-mic night at this little bar in town." At the time, she was still living and working in Mankato, about an hour and a half away from us. Most days we had no idea what she was up to. Certainly, we were unaware of any aspirations to be a comedian.

"You've got to be kidding me."

"No, I'm serious."

"What kind of jokes did you tell?"

"I didn't tell any jokes."

"How is that possible?"

"I just told a couple funny stories. The promoter asked how long I've been doing comedy. He didn't believe me when I told him I've never even held a mic in my hand before. He said I was phenomenal. *Phenomenal,* Mom. He even invited me back."

"I'm shocked. I can't believe you had the nerve to get up on stage."

"Me either, but it was so much fun. I loved it."

"What were your stories about, can I ask?"

"One of them was about having diabetes."

"You made diabetes funny?"

"I guess so, because everyone was laughing."

Peter McGraw, a psychologist and director of the University of Colorado at Boulder's Humor Research Lab, once said, "Humor is something people inherently enjoy. But there also needs to be something wrong, unsettling, and threatening in some way. We call those violations." McGraw further explained how comedians spin the truth into something they can live with.

I was initially surprised that Martha had gotten up on stage and told her personal stories to a crowd of strangers, hoping they would laugh at her *violations*. But I understand now why she does it, and what it does for her. Cystic fibrosis is her truth. Comedy is how she copes with that truth. And humor is as much a part of her make-up as is fighting.

Martha is a blog writer for the Cystic Fibrosis Lifestyle Foundation, where people living with CF can give each other advice, and/or inspire one another through their personal experiences. The following is an excerpt from her CFLF blog. While Martha may never fit in, she does stand out, and *this* is who we hoped and imagined our daughter would become.

What Drives Me to Fight?

Cystic fibrosis is a relentless disease. Every day is a fight. Every day I enter the ring with my opponent. It's the exact same opponent who knocked me out the day before. I know my opponent well—we've been facing each other for years. We go toe to toe, sometimes for several rounds. Once in a while I think I might have the upper hand, but my opponent is sneaky and tends to come out of nowhere. I know I'm in trouble. I go down. The whistle blows. It's another knockout.

New spectators are worried for me, but those familiar with the sport know what comes next. It's time to seek medical attention. After weeks of treatment, I start training again. Like it or not, it's time to go back into the ring. There's another fight. My opponent never quits, and neither do I.

Cystic fibrosis is a hard fight but it's also the most meaningful fight. I think it's important to know why I'm fighting and who I'm fighting for.

I know CF is different for everyone, so I can only speak for myself when it comes to what inspires me to fight this disease. My friends and family will be the first to roll their eyes when I explain what a huge Rocky Balboa fan I am. I grew up watching the Rocky movies and I don't think I'll ever outgrow them. Quoting Rocky quickly became my weird hidden talent as a kid. I even tried to become Sylvester Stallone's pen pal when I was eleven years old.

In *Rocky IV* there's a line in a song by Survivor that states that in the warrior's code, there is no surrender. And how a body might cry stop, but the spirit cries never. I can't think of a message that better describes the resiliency of people with cystic fibrosis. There are many times my body and mind are not on the same page, but these are the reasons why my spirit cries never.

First and foremost are my parents. They have sacrificed so much for the sake of my brother, Ray, and me. My dad worked his butt off as a police officer to ensure that we had good health care coverage. My mom put her teaching career on hold to take care of us at home until we were old enough to attend school. She majored in elementary education, but like many CF parents, she also earned an honorary nursing degree. Taking care of two rambunctious children with cystic fibrosis was no small feat. Before the vest came along, my mom did our respiratory treatments by hand. She sterilized and prepared our neb cups every day. She made sure we took all our medication no matter how much we hated it. My mom made home cooked meals to ensure we had the high caloric diet we needed. She brought us to the University of Minnesota CF clinic every three months for a full day's worth of appointments. She learned how to administer tube feedings, IV antibiotics, and insulin pumps. When we were too sick to go to school, my mom was our tutor.

Both my mom and dad encouraged us to participate in sports, school activities, church events, and neighborhood gatherings. They never held us back. They had this wonderful balance of caring for Ray and me without babying us. I can never thank them enough. They are the reason why I continue to take great care of myself. I cannot think of a bigger slap in the face than slacking off after all their hard work.

My biggest inspiration, still, is my brother, Ray. He passed away in April of 2001 from a non-CF related issue. He and I were very close, despite our five-year age gap. We were the biggest trouble makers, together, and our number one goal in life was to have fun. Ray's death was sudden, unexpected, and life changing. I know I have a different perspective on things because of losing him. I don't take people or moments for granted. Life has greater meaning because I know it's not a given.

Ray was robbed of so many life experiences, and he didn't get to benefit from new CF drugs that are improving the quality of my life. His ended. I get to keep going. So, out of respect for Ray, I plan on experiencing life with a smile, because that's how he would have done it.

I think Rocky Balboa said it best when he described the world as a mean and nasty place that isn't all sunshine and rainbows. If you're not tough, he warned, life can drop you to your knees—but only if you let it. Rocky said that nothing will hit as hard as life and cautioned that it's not how hard you get hit. It's about taking the hit and still moving forward.

There are days when CF nearly drops me to my knees. Days when I'm bitter, overwhelmed, and fear that I'll lose my drive. But then I dig deep and fight to regain my fire. Cystic fibrosis is my reality. It's part of my life. A life worth fighting for.

"To live in the hearts we leave behind is not to die."

~ Thomas Campbell

Graceland

Throughout Ray and Martha's childhood, we often talked about a CF cure. We were hopeful that day would come in our children's lifetime. Frustrated with his daily care, however, Ray had his doubts, often stating, "They're never going to cure this stupid thing, are they, Mom?" I encouraged him to be patient, assuring him good things were coming down the pipeline. He usually responded with, "When?" And I usually responded with, "Someday soon." It's not the absolute, concrete answer a young boy wants to hear, or one that he could necessarily hold on to, but there was hope, and that was all I could give him.

Ray had plans for the airway clearance machine if and when medical research led to a cure. Sometimes he said he was going to push the machine off a cliff and watch it break into a million pieces. Other times he said he wanted to throw it into a fire and watch it go up in flames. And sometimes he insisted he'd take an axe to it himself. One way or another, the machine was going to be destroyed—a celebration of freedom from vest treatments.

After Ray passed away, our insurance company called to say we needed to return the airway clearance machine. The request came so quickly, and I remember thinking, "Wow. You people don't waste any time." They said they were sending a special padded box for us to package it in. Before Rusty placed it in the box, he held the machine in one hand and gave it a good punch with his other. "This is for you, Ray," he said.

Some nights before Ray and Martha drifted off to sleep, they discussed how they would celebrate a CF cure. I told them when that day came, we would take them anywhere they wanted to go. Anywhere in the world! The two of them came up with many ideas over the years. Ray said we should go to Evansville, Indiana, to see the McIntosh family again. As much as we love our friends, I laughed and told Ray to think bigger than Indiana. Often times, Martha suggested Disney World. I told her to aim higher too. But to a young girl, Disney World is as big as it gets. After all, it has the word *world* right in it. No matter where we thought a dream of a cure would lead us, Graceland always made the list.

After graduating college, Martha was hired as the program coordinator for LEEP (Leisure Education for Exceptional People), a nonprofit organization that offers recreation programs that enhance the quality of life for people with disabilities, including vacations.

On one such individualized vacation, she took her favorite participant, an older gentleman named Ernie, on a trip to Memphis. Ironically, Ernie was an Elvis fan, even dressing as Elvis on Halloween. One day, just before her trip with Ernie, Martha called and asked if I would email a photo of Ray in his Elvis Halloween costume. Occasionally she will frame a photo of her brother, or the two of them together, to display in her apartment, or she posts it on Facebook. So it wasn't an unusual request, and I didn't bother to ask what she was going to do with the picture.

When she came home from Memphis, Martha texted some of her vacation photos—images of her and Ernie at various landmarks. Ernie looked so happy, which was no surprise to me. Martha goes out of her way to make everything special for her participants. But the next several photos were a complete shock. As it turned out, Martha had laminated a stack of baseball-card-size photos of Ray in his Elvis costume and took them with her on their Graceland tour. I was stunned to see that she had scattered her brother's image in random places throughout Elvis's home. She'd left a photo of Ray sitting on an end table in the Jungle Room. She'd propped another against a glass case that held Elvis's jumpsuit in the Trophy Room. And yet another outside, resting on Elvis's headstone. The one next to Elvis's white jumpsuit is my favorite. Ray's Halloween costume is a perfect replica. He looks like he could be Elvis's son.

Smiling at the images of the young boy who had longed to go to Graceland, I called to thank Martha. I also asked how long she thought the pictures would stay there before the Graceland staff scooped them up and threw them away.

"Don't worry, Mom. They won't find them all—at least not right away."

"What do you mean?"

"They're not all out in plain sight. I planted them all over the place."

"Seriously? How many photos did you hide?"

"Dozens. Ray even made it on the *Lisa Marie* airplane."

Before ending our conversation, I choked back tears and said, "Looks like your brother made it to Graceland after all."

Our daughter continues to use humor to deal with her illness and has never let go of the hope that one day there will be a cure, but there are plenty of days when we hear despair in her voice and days when she's slow to smile. One day, while coughing up mucus into a wastebasket during a vest treatment, she asked, "Why did I get hit so hard?" Then she added, in her sarcastic way, "I get it. I get it. Life is precious. I don't need all this to see that."

Her CF care is complicated. There are frequent hospitalizations requiring a slew of IV antibiotics when she has an acerbation—sometimes with adverse side effects. Often times, blood clots form around the PICC line and require blood thinner shots, or worse, the PICC line has to be pulled, which prevents her from getting a full course of antibiotics. Her blood sugar goes crazy out of control from infections, her liver function changes, her gallbladder can develop sludge, and the list of complications and side effects goes on. It's a lot to handle and still keep up a good attitude, but she's one tough young lady.

However, everyone has a breaking point. Not so long ago, with tears in her eyes, she told me that she wished she could have just one day without CF. One day when she could experience life without vest treatments. A day when she could see what it feels like to breathe easy. It broke my heart. Not just because she longs to feel healthy, but because she only asked for *one* day. It brought to mind an old adage: People who have their health wish for a thousand things. People who don't have their health only wish for one thing.

While there isn't a cure for cystic fibrosis yet, there has been an exciting breakthrough in medical advancements. In October of 2019, the U.S. Food and Drug Administration approved Trikafta, a triple combination therapy drug that helps transport chloride ions which are needed for the production of thin, freely flowing mucus. Quite the opposite of the thick, sticky mucus that has been wreaking havoc on Martha's body. She has been waiting for this her whole life—a drug treatment that targets the cause of cystic fibrosis, not just its symptoms.

Martha was fearful that her health insurance would deny her prescription for Trikafta, as the annual cost exceeds $300,000. But in December of 2019, she received news that her health insurance had approved Trikafta. Within a short period of time after taking the drug, Martha saw dramatic improvement in lung function and started gaining weight. She woke up well-rested and had energy to get through the day—her sleep no longer interrupted by steady fits of coughing throughout the night. In fact, we rarely hear her cough or witness her bringing up sputum any longer. This is something I still haven't gotten used to. For twenty-seven years Martha has lived with a constant cough. Whenever she walked through the front door, we could hear her coughing before we ever heard her say hello.

Even with this promising new drug, Martha's CF care has not changed. She still does two vest treatments a day, takes enzymes before every meal, and relies on an insulin pump to manage CF-related diabetes. However, there has been a remarkable change in her mindset. Over the years, I can't count how many times I have heard her say, "I do all this crap and I *still* get sick." That soul-crushing sense of defeat has now been replaced with one of hope. The reward for being compliant in her respiratory care isn't a few short months between hospital stays. It's the ability to take a deep breath without the pain of a mucus plug blocking her airways, and the routine need for IV antibiotics to treat a lung infection no longer looms over her head.

Martha recently told us that if Trikafta slows the progression of her disease, and her lung function remains stable, she will have a bright future. Until now, the words *bright* and *future* have rarely been uttered in the same sentence.

Trikafta isn't a CF cure, but it's the most promising thing that has come out of decades of medical research, and I believe there is a cure coming. And when it does, one way or another, the airway clearance machine will be destroyed, and we will go anywhere in the whole world.

Christmas Eve at Applebee's

In 2017, still recovering from the flu, Martha felt pretty crummy leading up to the holidays. So much so that she didn't even shop for gifts to bring to patients in the children's hospital. We didn't plan a ski trip or anything particularly special, either, knowing it was unlikely Martha would be up for it. Our only plan was to eat tacos and have a margarita at LaCucaracha, our favorite Mexican restaurant in St. Paul. Tacos are oddly this Scandinavian family's traditional Christmas dinner. I make them every year and fondly refer to them as Nativity Tacos. So LaCucaracha made sense.

After dinner, the plan was to meet Rusty, who was providing security at The House of Hope Church on Summit Avenue. It had been a long time since we'd gone to church on Christmas, but with Martha not feeling 100%, we thought it would be a low-key way for the three of us to be together.

I had called ahead to make sure LaCucaracha was open, but when we arrived, we found a note tacked to their door stating they had closed early for the night. Feliz-not-so-much-Navidad.

Martha and I drove down Grand Avenue looking for a second option. Nothing was open. We drove down West 7th Street. Again, there wasn't a restaurant in sight with its lights on. We kept driving, getting further and further away from The House of Hope—eventually too far away to make it back in time for the church service.

With plans unraveling by the second, I grew more anxious and angry with myself for not having a plan B. Nearly in tears, I kept driving, searching for anywhere to eat. I apologized for the debacle, but Martha assured me that it didn't matter. "It's okay, Mom. I don't even care. Let's just go home."

"I can't even make nativity tacos at home. I didn't get to the grocery store, and they're all closed now, too." Then I swore —on Christmas Eve—because I'm so incredibly nice. "Goddamn it, LaCucaracha! You said you'd be open."

Martha started to laugh and said, "You know what that makes you, don't you?"

This is going to sound awful to anyone outside our family, but it's one of our twisted inside jokes. Each year, Martha dubs whoever becomes crabby or stressed out over the holidays the "Christmas Bitch." However, it's never been much of a competition. The title is always awarded to me. Overwhelmed with shopping, gift wrapping, cooking and cleaning, I might say something snippy, and inevitably, Martha will proclaim, "And there we have it. Mom's the Christmas Bitch once again."

Grumbling about our failed plans, in an attempt to lighten the mood, Martha awarded me her special holiday moniker. Then she used her cell phone to search for open restaurants in our area. The closest option was Applebee's. I pulled into their parking lot, threw the car into park, and complained, "This is so pathetic! Who goes to Applebee's on Christmas Eve?"

Turns out a lot of people do. The place was packed. So we walked in and took a seat with all the other misfits and immediately ordered two margaritas. Our waitress asked to see Martha's ID. She studied it for a second and said, "Hmm. Garvey." Then she turned to me and said, "You're Ray's mom."

"Yes, I am. How did you know Ray?"

"I went to Maplewood Middle School with Ray. I remember you came to our school after he died. Can I ask what happened? We all heard it was from his illness, but there were other stories going around, too. We were just kids and never really understood how he died."

I briefly explained what had happened to Ray, then asked, "What's your name?"

"I'm Ashley Downs." With a beautiful smile, she added, "I just loved your son. Ray was in my language arts class. He was so much fun."

"Ms. Beske's class?"

"Yeah, you have a good memory."

"Well, she was pretty special."

"Want to hear a funny story about Ray?"

Martha and I were all ears.

"Ms. Beske assigned jobs for us, and Ray always seemed to get the recycling job. Ms. Beske let him pick another student to help. I was happy when he chose me, because he'd stuff me in the recycling bin and wheel me up and down the hallways."

"That sounds like Ray." Martha smiled.

"We had so much fun that he just started *telling* Ms. Beske that I was his partner. That made me feel special."

Ashley left to grab our drinks. Wiping my eyes dry with a napkin, I said, "I guess it was meant to be, Martha. To end up here tonight. Who knew?"

When Ashley came back with our drinks, I asked what she was doing working on Christmas Eve. She said it was hard, explaining that she has two young children and they were at her grandparents' house with the rest of her family. "It's killing me to be here," Ashley said. "I can't watch them open their gifts."

I told her about our night and how bummed out we were, aimlessly driving around trying to find a place to eat. Then Martha pointed to me and laughed. "Yeah, this one here was getting all worked up about it."

"No offense, Ashley, but this is the last place I wanted to be tonight. But maybe we were supposed to come here. You made our night pretty special ... just to hear Ray's name."

288

"I think you're right. You guys were definitely supposed to be here tonight, and seated in my section."

A little later, Ashley brought out our food and told us she had called her mom when she was back in the kitchen to ask if she remembered Ray Garvey. Her mom had said, "Sure. I remember Ray. Why?"

"I'm waiting on his mom and his little sister."

Ashley's mom had reminded her that she gets to join her family when she gets off work. The Garveys don't get to spend the holiday with Ray. And with that, Ashley wasn't feeling sorry for herself any longer.

The three of us talked about Ray throughout our dinner, Ashley stopping back to our table often. Somehow Michelle McDonald's name came up. Ashley, as it turned out, was good friends with Michelle. So I told her how much Ray had liked Michelle and how Rusty had teased that he was aiming too high. She immediately corrected me. "No way! He wasn't aiming too high. Michelle thought the world of Ray. All the girls liked him. He was so cute." Later she texted Michelle to tell her we were seated in her section.

Before we left, we thanked Ashley for giving us the best Christmas gift ever. Ashley hugged us goodbye, saying we had made her Christmas more special, too. Then she told us to stop back anytime if we wanted to hear another story about Ray. She said she had plenty more to share.

Snap Shots

Sometimes I wonder if Rusty and Martha are the only others who still think about Ray. But then something happens, like meeting Ashley at Applebee's. When we least expect it, and need it the most, someone shares a memory of Ray, assuring us that we are not alone.

For example, about the time Ray should have been off to college, in trade school, or living in a van down by the river, I brought my car in to get fixed. Out of the blue, our mechanic, Roger Anderson, said, "Just so you know. Your boy made it to college."

"What are you talking about?" I asked.

Roger's daughter, Jordan, had a big crush on Ray when they were in grade school. Now Jordan was in her first year of college at St. Cloud State. Roger told me that she'd brought a picture of Ray and hung it in her dorm room. It was a sweet image, and I thought that was the end of the story, but Roger continued. "Jordan went to a party in another kid's dorm room. Turns out he was one of Ray's friends, Brandon Juarez. He had the exact same picture of Ray hanging up in his room."

"You've got to be kidding me."

For a second, like it was yesterday, I could see Ray and Brandon jumping on our trampoline in the backyard, Martha right in the mix with the boys. It made me smile, thinking even in his passing, Ray had brought his friends together.

"There's more, "Roger continued. "Brandon and Jordan went to some other kid's dorm room one night, and he had a picture of Ray hanging on his wall, too. So you see, Ray went to college with his buddies. He isn't forgotten, Darla."

A couple of years ago, with the holidays fast approaching, I took time out to join my girlfriends for a drink at Obb's, a neighborhood watering hole in St. Paul. December tends to be a difficult month for me. With Christmas and Ray's birthday, I often find myself holding my breath, just waiting for all of it to pass. Sometimes it helps to be with friends. That night Martha was out Christmas shopping and ran into the Ronsberg family. She texted to see where I was. A short time later, she walked in with Seth, Sidnee, Stu, and Kari. We gathered around a large table and spent the evening talking about Ray and all the old neighborhood adventures—and misadventures.

At one point, I looked across the table at Seth. There sat the little boy from Ferndale Street, now a big, strong man and accomplished hockey player, with tears streaming down his face. I reached over and took his hand in mine, while he assured us that he's never stopped thinking of Ray as his closest friend. He said he still has Ray's baseball cap in his bedroom.

That night at Obb's was one of those unexpected gifts, when our hearts were filled with laughter and joy, sharing stories about our little Ray of sunshine.

On a walk around our neighborhood park, I recently ran into Amy Richards. She told me that a few days prior, her whole family had sat around the dinner table talking about Ray. Her girls are grown women now, yet Amy said they still talk about how special Ray was. McKenna, her oldest, said, "Ray *owned* the park." McKenna went on to describe how Ray had left his mark on every part of the park. Like the steep hill he'd called Dead Man's Hill and dared everyone to sled down in the winter. A secret wooded area along one pathway was known to everyone as Ray's fort. The bike jumps he built, the ice rink where he organized pick-up games of hockey, the playground where he invented silly games—all of it was Ray's.

Over the years the neighborhood gang—and Martha's ever-growing circle of friends—have been a support to her. If they knew Ray, they talked about him. If they didn't, they asked about him.

Justin Rick became part of our family, almost like a step-brother to Martha. He even went to our family reunions at my grandparents' farm in Atwater, Minnesota. And on any given day, we kidnapped Justin from the neighborhood. When I took Martha bowling, or to a movie, or simply to the Dairy Queen for ice cream, Justin often found himself in the back seat of our car—whether he liked it or not. Judging by his and Martha's laughter, I'm going to say he enjoyed our outings.

On the tenth anniversary of Ray's death, Martha reached out to the old neighborhood gang on Facebook. She asked if they would share a story about Ray. The following is a snapshot, so to speak, of their memories of Ray.

Stu Ronsberg:

> It was early spring, the neighborhood was starting to come out of hibernation (the kids on the street were between two years of age and eight years of age). The families had been waving to each other through car windows for the last four months of winter, so no one had really seen each other up close. Janny Rick had a baby and no one in the neighborhood even knew.
>
> One day, the doorbell rang and there stood Ray. I barely got the door open and Ray was already into his third sentence. "Where is Seth? Are you going to be able to come out and play, too? You should see my dog." Etc.
>
> I looked at Ray and said, "Ray, your Mom's teeth are in your mouth."

He said, "I know. Do you like them?"

Ray lost his 'practice' teeth that winter and came out of the house looking more like a little man than a little boy.

I miss Ray ringing the doorbell, and I miss the neighborhood.

Kevin Carver:

Lots of memories of the junk yard, playing WWF wrestling on the trampoline. If I remember right, Ray was always Dwayne "The Rock" Johnson. I'll never forget when Ray tricked us into eating dog food and Tyler puked up pink stuff from his bubble gum. Haha.

Audra Richards:

I'll never forget when we were in the white truck and Ray got to lay in the back and he was spitting sunflower seeds up at us. Or when we thought he was a BMX biker and he convinced Martha and me that it was a great idea to lay down next to the jump to see if he could clear us. Or when we walked down to get 50 cent pops at Carver Auto Body for our Carbone's pizza. Or the squirrel incident when he poked the dead squirrel with a stick but once he poked it, the squirrel was still alive.

Patrick Bagan:

When I was in first grade, I can remember getting pushed around at the playground by some older kids.

Ray stepped in almost immediately and backed them off real quick. I thought he was the coolest kid!

Jessie Heutmaker:

One day, we were waiting for the bus in the middle of the winter. Ray came walking down the street in a t-shirt, no jacket. A few minutes later, his mom drove down the street with his jacket. He, of course, refused to take the jacket. So his mom threw it out the window into the snow. The bus arrived a few minutes later and the bus driver had to wait for Ray to climb up the giant pile of snow to grab his jacket. I specifically remember sitting on the bus watching him out the window, digging through the snow. Everyone was laughing but the bus driver was not too happy with him. And I cannot count how many times he pretended to eat worms off Laura's driveway after it rained.

Pam Holm:

• Darla's whistle, and how Ray would leave running, even if he didn't want to, no matter how much fun we were having. I swear he could even hear her whistle from inside our house.
• He LOVED all of my friends and they all became his girlfriends, whether they knew it or not.
• Ray eating crayons in our basement. I don't remember what his reasoning was. Maybe something about tasting the colors, but he did love the fact that we thought he was crazy. I'm pretty sure that's why he continued to do it.

- Ray always had the best flashlight for flashlight tag and you guys had the best porch to hide on.
- Watching Ray pull on Boone's tail and sit on him in the front yard. All ... the ... time.

Justin Rick:

Greatest memories that will never be lost were with Ray. From taking up the whole street playing hockey to the backyard football games!! He was the master of ding dong ditch and flashlight tag! Everyone will remember the junk yard house because of Ray. The smile, the laughter, the personality he had, was one of a kind. The memories he gave all of us will bring joy, laugher, and stories that will live on forever!!

At just the right time, Linda Holm shared a journal entry with us. We cannot thank her enough for simply loving our son, her feelings about Ray so beautifully expressed.

As a neighbor, it seems almost poetic to me that Ray would "suddenly" be taken from us on a crisp night in April running through the neighborhood to find Martha at Brooke's. This was a dark time of the night when flashlight tag would have been great, but, ahhh it was a little too soon to let the summer games begin. This night in April was much too soon for Ray to die— and much too sudden.

I know I was not alone when my heart broke that night and the feeling that this was simply not right, not fair, was extremely overwhelming.

We could have never prepared for such cruelty, such an abrupt ending of life for our fun-loving neighborhood charmer. The pain is real, it is deep, and the questions and memories keep replaying themselves in my mind.

Thank God for a kid like Ray! His smiling, mischievous, innocent face will live on in my mind forever and—I pray the pain will ease as I remember his acts of silliness and that funny little accent that he spoke with when the occasion was just right.

Ray left his impression on everyone he met. Just about anyone who visited our house met Ray. Ray's days had purpose. And Ray certainly had good timing in virtually everything he said and did. Ray reminded us to: Have fun, don't sweat the small stuff, smile, laugh, be fair, be considerate, lie a little, brag a little, dream a little, laugh at yourself, be confident, take a risk, don't hold back, try something new, set goals, get off your butt, be kind, honor your family and friends, dare to be different, be creative, think less and do more, and so much more…

Boise, Idaho Says Hello

Even my former third graders, all grown up now, remember Ray and his little sister. When Martha was in high school and new to Facebook, she received several friend requests from my former students. By then most were in college. One day she asked, "Do you know this girl?"

"Sure I do. She's a former student of mine."

"How about this guy?"

"He was a student, too. Why are you asking?"

"Because they're on Facebook. A bunch of your old students are asking that I say hi to you."

"Oh, that's so nice. Tell them hello back."

"I don't get it, though. Most of them post stuff like, 'Tell your mom I still remember my state.' "

"You've got to be kidding me." I laughed.

"What does that mean? This girl wrote, 'Tell your mom Boise, Idaho says hello.' "

"Oh my God. That's hilarious."

I went on to tell Martha how I had assigned my students a capital city and state and they had to stand up and recite it when I took attendance. I utilized their assigned state in a number of ways throughout the year. *East coast states, line up at the door for lunch.* Or, *partner up with someone whose state borders yours.* Or, *if the Oregon Trail runs through your state, you'll present your project first.*

By the end of the year, my students were geography experts. But the best part about that year was the special friendship my students developed with a frequent sixth grade visitor. Several times a week, rather than go straight home, Ray hopped off the bus at a stop close to Carver Elementary. He checked in with Mrs. Priebe, the school secretary, to get a visitor's badge before coming to my classroom for the last half hour of the day. When he walked in, my students nearly jumped out of their seats, shouting, "Ray's here!"

Ray had one rule to follow if he didn't stop in at Carver. He had to call my classroom and let me know that he had gotten home safely. Whenever he called, my student of the day answered, "Mrs. Garvey's room. Student speaking." The kids knew if the phone rang at 3:00, it meant having a conversation with Ray, making the job of student helper a coveted one. Ray enjoyed talking to my students, too. There was always laughter —and sometimes the whispering of secrets—when my students talked to Ray on the phone.

When Ray passed away, my third graders were devastated. Not only did they lose their friend and role model, they also lost their teacher. Two Garveys no longer walking through the door of their classroom. But I was proud of my students. They were brave and kind, providing comfort to Martha when they saw her in the hallways. Often times they sent cards and drawings home with Martha, wherein they shared memories of Ray and expressed their grief—as best as nine-year-olds could. They also pleaded for me to come back to school. I reached out to my young, grieving students, sending letters back with my daughter.

Ultimately, I went back and taught for the last two weeks of that school year. My students needed to see me, and I needed to say goodbye and let them know what they had meant to me and my family. Those final school days were filled with laughter, parting hugs, and plenty of tears. The Carver third grade class of 2000-2001 will always hold a special place in my heart.

Sunflowers

Sunflowers became symbolic after I heard a quote by actress Helen Mirren. She might just as well have been describing how Ray had lived his life. "I don't think there's anything on this planet that more trumpets life than the sunflower. For that's because of the reason behind its name. Not because it looks like the sun, but because it follows the sun. During the course of the day, the head tracks the journey of the sun across the sky. A satellite dish for sunshine. Wherever light is, no matter how weak, these flowers will find it. And that's such an admirable thing. And such a lesson in life."

I began to take notice of sunflowers after Ray died. It seemed like they showed up everywhere, lifting my spirits. After all, they're bright and cheery. I once read that sunflowers symbolize adoration. They provide energy in the form of nourishment and vibrancy, stunning qualities that mirror the sun. Sunflowers are also known for being "happy" flowers.

The first time I planted sunflowers in our garden, I was surprised how they start out so thin and frail, drooping over in the dirt like flimsy weeds. They look hopeless, as if they'll only amount to an ordinary daisy, at best. But over time, they stand tall and sturdy on their own, no support of a stake required. They're quick to show their unique beauty to the world. Ironically, their brilliant yellow petals are also known as "rays."

In his early years, it was expected that Ray would fail to thrive. But like the sunflower, he sprouted and flourished, standing confident on his own, the light within him impossible to ignore.

Friends and family are privy to how I feel about sunflowers, bouquets of them a frequent gift, often displayed on my kitchen table. But the most remarkable display of the flower mysteriously appeared on the day of Martha's high school graduation party.

My friend Shelly Saulka was helping me prep for the party when she suddenly gave me a once-over and asked, "Have you even showered yet?" I was so worried about the party details, I had forgotten about myself. Still scrambling to blow my hair dry and slap on some makeup, I panicked when the doorbell rang. I was so relieved to see that it was only Justin Rick and not a whole group of early arrivals.

With a strange expression on his face, Justin said, "Darla, you have to come with me."

"I can't right now, Justin. I'm getting ready for the party."

"It's important."

"Can you quickly tell me what this is about?"

"No. You have to come over and see for yourself!"

Barefoot, I followed Justin across the street, mascara on only one eye.

Janny stood in her front yard, tears streaming down her cheeks.

"What's going on?" I asked.

"Look. Over there." Justin pointed to the Ronsbergs' old house, next door to his. There, against the brick, stood a tall, giant sunflower. "It was not there yesterday," Justin insisted.

"How can that be? They don't shoot up overnight. You probably just didn't notice it." But then it occurred to me that I didn't remember seeing the sunflower either, and I *always* notice sunflowers. How could I have missed this one when it was right across the street, facing my kitchen window? Especially given its size.

"Darla," Janny said, "trust me. It wasn't there until today. The neighbors have been gone all week. Justin's been taking care of their lawn."

"Yeah, I've been mowing the grass, and I even pulled some weeds right there." He pointed directly to the sunflower. "I'm telling you, Darla, this thing wasn't here yesterday. I swear."

"Maybe the flower just hadn't opened up until today."

"Even if the flower hadn't bloomed, the stem is like five feet tall. I would have seen it."

"Darla, Ray's here today," Janny said. "He's here for Martha." Then she hugged me, all three of us now in tears.

I ran home and put mascara on my other eye. First things first. Then I told Rusty and Martha about the sunflower. When the Ronsberg family arrived, we told them about the sunflower, too. Stu said it was appropriate that it had grown outside their old house. "Definitely something Ray would do," Seth agreed. Then we all laughed, deciding that Ray had chosen the perfect place for the flower—growing in fertile ground where Seth had frequently relieved himself when he was a little boy.

I often wonder if the dead can really send a sign. Could it be Ray calling out to his sister, recognizing her milestone with a sunflower? Or do we just take something and turn it into a sign to make ourselves feel better? I don't know how it works, but the timing of that particular sunflower was not lost on any of us.

At some point Martha took a picture of the flower and posted it on Facebook, explaining how it had mysteriously shown up. Some of Ray's old friends drove over to see the bright-yellow sunflower for themselves.

Over the years, I used to watch my son and think, "Don't shine so brightly, buddy, or you'll fade out too fast." But I had it all wrong. While Ray's stay here was brief, he never faded out. Like the sunflower, wherever light was, Ray found it. And that bright, happy glow of his seems to be what people remember most.

"There are some things you learn best in calm, and some in storm."

~ Willa Cather
American Novelist

Epilogue (2020)

In March of 2020, I spent a carefree week in Steamboat Springs, skiing with Kim and Rick Bodin. My cousin Holly Rome, her husband Greg, and their two teenage sons were also vacationing there. With live music and spectacular sunset views, the après-ski scene at Thunderhead Lodge, a chalet located at the top of Mount Werner, added allure after fun-filled days skiing with my family. I was in my happy place. But by week's end we learned that Covid-19 had hit the small town of Steamboat Springs. Two visitors tested positive and were hospitalized at Yampa Valley Medical Center. The ski resort immediately shut down, and I flew home the following day. Martha had plans to snowboard in Steamboat with her friend Tina a week later, but quickly cancelled her flight.

The three of us were now sheltered in place in Minnesota as the spread of a deadly virus devastated the world. Our hearts ached for the growing number of people who were losing their lives to Covid-19. Worse yet, they were dying alone—their loved ones unable to be at their bedside. Things were quickly unraveling and we were concerned, to say the least. We couldn't imagine what Covid-19 would mean for Martha. Anytime she has contracted the flu, she has landed in the hospital with a lung infection. One year she contracted H1N1, which lead to pneumonia and an eight-week hospital stay. If people *without* underlying conditions were being placed on ventilators, many losing their lives, what would Covid-19 look like for someone with a serious lung disease like cystic fibrosis?

If we had one thing on our side, it was preparedness. Of course, we have never experienced the fear and uncertainty of a global pandemic, but as a CF family who has been fighting a life-threatening disease for over three decades, we were probably better prepared than most. The CDC protocols and Minnesota Governor Walz's executive orders to shelter in place were not a shocking lifestyle change, or an expectation beyond our comprehension. Now the same restrictions and expectations were being placed on the rest of society. Many people struggled to accept the changes that Covid-19 brought to their lives, but to us, making sacrifices to stay healthy has always been a critical necessity, not an option. So we were prepared.

We knew a little something about the isolation and disappointment of cancelling events that many people were experiencing during quarantine. Cystic fibrosis can be a lonely disease when pulmonary acerbations pull CF patients out of normal activities, whether isolated at home or in the hospital. Cystic fibrosis is the epitome of a life interrupted, and the disappointment of missing out is a familiar trend. Over the years, due to illness, we missed birthday parties, graduations, weddings, or holiday gatherings, to name just a few.

We understood the challenges imposed on families when schools shut down. I have done my fair share of homeschooling, so I know that distance learning for a child is frustrating both academically and socially. It's something our family has had to deal with throughout Martha's education. As a college instructor at Minnesota Independence College & Community (MICC), Martha was now on the other side and had to get creative to teach her classes virtually. As businesses were shutting down and the unemployment rate was skyrocketing, Martha felt very fortunate that she was able to work remotely from home and not lose her income or health insurance.

CF families are no strangers to social distancing. People with cystic fibrosis have been taught from day one to stay six feet apart from one another, as bacterial cross contamination between CF patients can be very dangerous. Additionally, avoiding exposure to *anyone* with cold or flu symptoms has been a common practice in our family. After all, a common cold for a healthy person can mean a hospitalization for someone with cystic fibrosis. So in our opinion, social distancing was a small ask to help stop the spread of Covid-19.

Wearing a mask is not a novel concept to CF families, either. We've been wearing masks for years—in the hospital, at the CF clinic, and when we travel by plane. And frequent and thorough hand washing is a daily habit we give little thought to.

We were grateful that so many people were adhering to Covid-19 protocols and mandates, doing their best to keep themselves and others safe. Yet, at the same time we were disappointed that just as many refused to stay home, mask up, or social distance. As the number of positive cases and the death toll rose, so did our fear and frustration. Health privileged people seemed to justify their irresponsible behavior by saying that they didn't have the same worry as someone with an underlying condition. My reaction to that was always the same. *If you worried more, maybe we could worry less.* Those feelings only deepened when Covid-19 claimed the life of my smart, talented, wonderful Aunt Darleen Hovey.

Our hearts went out to the selfless health care workers who were putting their lives on the line to care for Covid-19 patients. We know from Martha's friends who are in health care, as well as our long-standing relationships with doctors, nurses, and respiratory therapists, that they have a tough job on a good day. We empathized with the stress Covid-19 was putting on them.

Throughout 2020, we practiced patience and held on to hope. Something we have clung on to for over thirty years—waiting and hoping for medical advancements to help combat, or cure, cystic fibrosis. Now we were waiting and hoping that scientists would find a Covid vaccine.

Trying to maintain a positive attitude is as much of a coping skill as having hope. People with CF really only have two options to choose from when deciding how they live their lives: wallow and give up, or fight like hell and appreciate every moment they are given. Make no mistake, the latter of the two options does not come easily. It takes a lot of strength to keep a positive attitude when you have a life-threatening disease. Somehow Martha has managed to *mostly* look at the bright side of life. She kept up that wonderful spirit in 2020, largely due to the health benefits of Trikafta, the CF drug she has been taking for over a year now. The pandemic was the first time she was quarantined, but healthy. She took advantage of the time and the improved energy she now has, and found safe ways to enjoy herself. She took long daily hikes with her dog, Charlie. She started a side hustle and began training and walking other people's dogs, too. She purchased a movie projector and large screen and invited a *trusted* friend or two over for backyard movie nights. They wore masks and were seated in lawn chairs that were spaced out well beyond six feet apart. Martha and I like to kayak, and that summer she also purchased a stand-up paddle board. We spent a lot of summer days on any one of the many lakes in Minnesota. It was a perfect way to relax and momentarily set our Covid-19 fears aside.

Even though she was coping quite well, an additional health risk weighed heavy on her and the CF community. Depression and anxiety are already very real for people with CF. During the pandemic, mental health was a concern for many. So, Martha created an Instagram account solely for the purpose of reaching out to the CF community. Within a few weeks @saltygirlsunnyworld had over 1,400 CF followers from all over the world. They shared their ups and downs and formed a strong connection that was very powerful. Martha commented once that she didn't realize just how much she needed that support.

When the vaccine rolled out, and we learned that cystic fibrosis was not on a priority list to receive the vaccine, even though it is a lung disease, Martha was devastated. She argued that people with CF were told to stay home, stock up on food and necessities, and hunker down because they were at high risk of not surviving if they contracted Covid-19. Yet, suddenly they were not high risk enough when it came to the vaccine. Martha was especially upset that, at least in Minnesota, smokers and vapers made the priority list for the vaccine, while cystic fibrosis wasn't even on the list. She couldn't understand how someone who voluntarily breathes in cigarette smoke every day and *damages* their lungs would be a higher priority for the vaccine than someone with cystic fibrosis who breathes in nebulized medication every day to *help* their lungs.

CF is considered an orphan disease because it does not affect enough people to garner attention, even during a pandemic. Martha grew tired of not being seen. Not being heard. So she became an advocate and called on the support of her Instagram followers to put pressure on the Minnesota Department of Health. Not long after, smokers and vapers were removed from the priority list and cystic fibrosis patients were added. Mission accomplished!

During the pandemic Martha continued to use her voice as a blog writer for the Cystic Fibrosis Lifestyle Foundation (CFLF). Brian Callanan, the founder of CFLF, was diagnosed with CF at birth. Brian learned the value of exercise, recreation and positive mindset for his health and created an organization that would benefit others. CFLF awards Recreation Grants to CF patients. Martha is a four-time recipient of the CFLF grant and has applied it to snowboard season passes. One of her blogs, titled *Putting Life on Pause for Covid-19*, caught the attention of Brian, Julie Winn, Communications Coordinator for the CFLF, and board member Tiffany McDaniel. They chose Martha to be their winter STROLO Star. The CFLF community highlights CF "stars" who are examples of what living STROLO (STROnger and LOnger) means. In a virtual interview, they discussed what Martha was doing to stay healthy and positive during the pandemic. The interview can be viewed at: https://www.cflf.org/blog/strolo-star-martha-garvey

At one point in the interview, Martha speaks about how she used her time wisely during the pandemic, which included starting a business with her mom. We named our company Sunny Rays in honor of Ray's sunny disposition. For years we have had this idea to invent a product that would help solve a common problem for respiratory therapists and CF patients. Quarantined for over a year, we finally had the time to make our business dreams a reality and developed the first of its kind customized storage holder for nebulizer cups and medication vials.

Martha has and always will be our inspiration. Her resiliency and ability to find the silver lining during one of the darkest times in our history has been a remarkable thing to witness.

Acknowledgments

To Martha, for making me laugh and for being the most amazing, strong, caring daughter we could ever ask for. And no, I decided not to name this book *Bing, Bing, Bing, Bong,* by Darla Garvey. But thanks for the suggestion.

To Rusty, for standing by me through the good, the bad and the ugly. Thank you for putting up with me for over three decades and for encouraging me to tell our son's story.

To my wonderful parents, Buzz and Merilyn Johnson. I miss you both so much.

To Don Boxmeyer, for being the first to call me a writer.

To my fellow Eastsider and friend Steve Thayer, *New York Times* bestselling author of *The Wheat Field.* Thank you for being my mentor and for providing first round editing. Thank you for pushing me to dig deeper and to write with more intensity. Your critical eye made this story stronger, and we're still talking.

To my editor, Jennifer Adkins, for not only polishing up my manuscript, but for asking important questions that readers might want answers to. Thank you for bringing more clarity to my story.

To Julie Kramer, Minnesota Book Award–winning author of *Stalking Susan.* Thank you for your invaluable editorial feedback. I'm forever grateful for your encouragement and support.

To my amazing writing group and instructors at the Loft Literary Center who helped hone my writing skills: Mary Jean Port, Mary Carroll Moore, Sue McCauley, Lindsay Nielsen,

Jeana Fox, Elizabeth Folie, Elissa Maunter, Atrid Slungaard, Laura Ehramjian, Ruth Sloven, and Helen West.

To Cathe Carbone, the gold medalist. Thank you for loving Ray the way that you did. I can still see the two of you together and it makes me smile. And to Sue Anderson, the bronze medalist. Rest in peace, my dear friend.

To my life-long friends who patiently waited for me to *come back*. Thank you for staying in my life for the long haul. A special thank you to the Fettes: Lori Lemke, Lori Swanson, Donna Ryan, Mary Pat Mahowald, and Janene Slagle. To Karyn (Chuck) Tayne and Anita Hager, thank you for giving me a shoulder to cry on when I needed it and providing laughter to make it all seem better.

To Kay and Bill McDonough, for teaching my family how to move forward after our loss. Thank you for showing us what strength and love look like.

To Ray's fabulous teachers: Barb Beske, Harv French, LouAnn Henderson, Patti Life, Dick Press, Paul Vogel, and Jackie Robinson. Thank you for sharing your memories of Ray and for having such a positive influence on him.

A special, heartfelt thank you to all of Ray's neighborhood friends, classmates, and teammates. Thank you for being Ray's friend and for making him so happy. You meant the world to Ray, and you mean the world to us. Thank you to those who stayed in Martha's life and helped her to carry on without her brother.

To those who went before me—who lost a child of their own. I knew you were hurting, I just didn't know how badly … until I walked in your shoes.

Kay and Bill McDonough: *Stephen McDonough*

Irvin and Martha Hovey: *Kermit Hovey*

Glen and Marsha Hovey: *Jim Hovey*

Norma Buer: *Jaquelin Buer*

Pete and Eve Denisson: *Kip Denisson*

Gary and Jean Ales: *Kevin Ales*

Daryl and Janny Rick: *Adam and Aaron Rick*